SCHOOL SC/

Blowing the Whistle on the Corruption
of Our Education System

Pat Thomson

First published in Great Britain in 2020 by

Policy Press, an imprint of
Bristol University Press
University of Bristol
1-9 Old Park Hill
Bristol
BS2 8BB
UK
t: +44 (0)117 954 5940
e: bup-info@bristol.ac.uk

Details of international sales and distribution partners are available at
policy.bristoluniversitypress.co.uk

© Bristol University Press 2020

British Library Cataloguing in Publication Data
A catalogue record for this book is available from the British Library

ISBN 978-1-4473-3855-0 paperback
ISBN 978-1-4473-3857-4 ePub
ISBN 978-1-4473-3856-7 ePdf

Cover design: blu inc, Bristol
Front cover credit: Adobe Stock/Thomas Bethge

This book is dedicated to the education journalists who persist in investigation, despite spin, secrecy and the undermining rhetoric of 'false news'. Without you, we would know a great deal less.

Contents

List of tables and boxes

Table

Boxes

Glossary

Key terms related to the English school system

academy   A school directly funded by the English state which is legally constituted as a self-governing, non-profit charitable trust.

free school   A type of academy set up by community members who have to submit a proposal and business plan to the government. They may be set up via a local authority competition.

GCSE   General Certificate of Secondary Education, generally completed by students by the age of 16. The level below A Level.

maintained schools   Schools funded by the English state and run by a local authority.

Multi-Academy Trust (MAT)   A legally constituted body which has overarching responsibility for a group of academies. There is a shared funding agreement but each academy has individual financial agreements with the government.

orphan school   A school which is no longer part of an MAT but where no new sponsor can be found.

rebrokerage   The process of transferring an academy to another sponsor.

trustees   People appointed by trust members to run an academy trust who are also company directors.

Major organisations featured in the book

Education Skills Funding Agency (ESFA)	Provides formula funding to schools, and monitors and handles complaints. It is an executive agency established by the Department for Education.
National Audit Office (NAO)	Scrutinises public spending on behalf of Parliament but also holds Parliament to account.
Ofsted	The inspection agency for schools.

Acknowledgements

This book was a long time in the making and writing, and there are several people to thank. This is by way of a small inventory of people who made the book a reality.

My employer. I was supported in writing this book by the University of Nottingham. The annual research allocation in my workload made possible the necessary data-generation, analysis and writing phases. I also received a small internal grant to pay for some much-needed research assistance in processing some of the media clips I have amassed. Thanks to Professors Howard Stevenson and Simon McGrath for their ongoing support.

Research help. The independent journalist Warwick Mansell talked with me early in the writing and provided helpful perspectives on the practices of investigative journalism. While I have not cited his subscription-only news service *Education Uncovered*, his work informed my approach. Dr Liam Maloy went through the nearly 2,000 'pins' I had accumulated. Without his thoughtful sifting and sorting, this manuscript would not have happened. And as I pondered once again whether there really was anything new to say about the current situation in England, it was highly reassuring to read in a signing off email, and cited here with permission, Liam's personal responses to the material: 'I have now finished going through the near-2000 pins. It's been very enlightening! I'm angry at hearing about the rogue and criminal practices that are taking place, and the way that they seem endemic in a largely-deregulated and nepotistic system.' Thank you Liam, this was important for me to hear. It wasn't just me then.

Readers. Particular thanks to my colleague Paul Heywood, Professor in Politics at the University of Nottingham, a key international figure in corruption research. Without ever seeing what I was writing, he continued to reassure me that writing about corruption in the school system was a sensible undertaking. He did finally read a draft manuscript and was again supportive and helpful. My long-term research partner Professor Chris Hall listened patiently to me complain about lack of progress on the book, read it when it was done and responded with kind words, as usual. Thanks also to the anonymous readers who provided pointers for revision.

My publisher. Policy Press allowed me several extensions of deadline, a significant gift from a small independent publisher. I was particularly keen to have this book as part of their list, and I thank them for their continued patience and faith that I would eventually get the manuscript together. Our continued dialogue about the elusive title ought to be the subject of an instructive academic writing blog post.

Family. My partner Randy not only put up with daily disappearances to the office-loft and my unreasonable exasperation when he 'interrupted', but also cooked delicious meals and attended to domestic matters. Charlie, our surly and eccentric elderly poodle, needed to be put outside at regular intervals; she ensured that I did not end up with completely overwhelming back and neck troubles from too much screen work. RIP Charlie.

Friends. I wish I could have included all of the stories you told me about the various goings on in the networks you are associated with. Thank you for your conversations; we all know that what is written in this book is not a complete picture.

A little of the material in Chapters 3 and 9 has appeared before but has been reworked here.[1]

Preface

This book was written and made ready for publication before COVID-19 changed our world. Or perhaps didn't.

When schools in England locked down on 23 March 2020, the government knew it had to do something for students whose families were economically struggling. These students are officially categorised as Free School Meals (FSM) – schools provide dinners free of charge to the 1.3 million children[1] whose families have difficulty affording food and shelter. For many of these children, school dinner is their major meal of the day, perhaps supplemented by cereal and toast at their school's Breakfast Club. FSM children and their families may be among the half million who regularly also rely on food parcels[2]: 8–10 per cent of UK families are food insecure, with 2.8 per cent severely food insecure. Food-poor families usually depend on some form of state income support or tax relief, but many also have someone in the household in precarious, often part-time, work.[3]

In recent years, policy conversations about school food have centred on whether meals are healthy or not, how and where they should be prepared, and whether sufficient money is allocated for them. But schools serving the poorest communities have always known that school dinners were vital in alleviating the impact of poverty, even if hunger and malnutrition had dropped out of the conversation. Schools also knew when lockdown was announced that they needed to act to ensure that their FSM children continued to be fed. Senior leaders in schools serving economically struggling communities understood that the school dinner was a high priority which needed quick and decisive action. Many schools organised food parcels, changing their catering systems almost overnight. Then, it took all bodies available to ensure that school dinners were distributed, via cars, bikes and feet.

Media coverage was quick to follow:

The hero teacher walking over five miles a day to deliver free school meals to the kids who need it most

Grimsby Telegraph, 27 March 2020

Cheltenham headteacher delivers packed lunches to free school meals children by bike

Gloucestershire Live, 27 March 2020

Headteacher delivers food to kids on free school meals

The London Economic, 3 April 2020

From delivering food to being a football buddy: how COVID-19 has changed my life as a teacher

Global Citizen, 3 April 2020

Some schools organised vouchers for families to use at local supermarkets, figuring that this way they could help local business stay afloat as well as provide much-needed food support for families.

A week after lockdown the government launched its own voucher scheme, weekly shopping vouchers worth £15 for every eligible child. The vouchers were to be provided to families through their schools. Schools would have the choice of ordering vouchers which could be sent direct to families by email as a code to be scanned at a supermarket checkout, or they could arrange for bulk delivery of codes to be sent on to families or to be posted as an e-card if the families were not online.[4] Schools that were already providing their own vouchers had a choice to continue with their own scheme, with no guarantee that they would be refunded, or switch to the centralised government system. The contract for providing the vouchers was given to French-owned Edenred, a company which had previously unsuccessfully sued the government over propriety and transparency of the procurement process.[5] This new pandemic contract, worth up to £234 million, did not go out to tender as it was awarded under the emergency powers introduced to manage COVID-19.

The scheme has however not been without hiccups, and its critics. Again media headlines tell the story:

UK's poorest families suffering as free school meal vouchers delayed

The Guardian, 9 April 2020

DfE urges schools to stop checking swamped free meal voucher website, as system labelled 'farcical'

Schools Week, 14 April 2020

Headteachers urge government to fix UK free school meals website

Financial Times, 21 April 2020

How the government's free school meals voucher is leaving children without food

Schools Week, 24 April 2020

Coronavirus: free school meals scheme branded 'disaster' as parents struggle to get vouchers

Sky News, 26 April 2020

Coronavirus: families still waiting for free school meal vouchers

BBC News, 30 April 2020

Headteacher puts £5,000 on his credit card to get free meal vouchers to kids in lockdown

The Daily Mirror, 6 May 2020

Coronavirus: 'humiliation' as school meal vouchers fail at till

BBC News, 7 May 2020

The free school meals voucher scheme still isn't working properly, 7 weeks after schools closed due to Coronavirus

Buzzfeed, 7 May 2020

Coronavirus: education leaders criticise 'failed' free school meals voucher scheme for children during lockdown

The Independent, 19 May 2020

Community group steps in as parents impacted by Coronavirus face delays for free school meals

On The Wight, 19 May 2020

The Guardian reported that the three-month school meals contract was given to a 'woefully underprepared' Edenred, whose 150 UK staff were experienced in handling childcare vouchers. But by mid-May, Edenred claimed to have distributed over £92 million in supermarket vouchers delivered through 17,000 schools.[6]

On the ground the story is somewhat different, with tales of ongoing problems. The chief executive of a multi-academy trust (MAT) with over thirty schools told me that the first vouchers were issued for posh supermarkets which didn't even exist in the suburbs that his schools served. He reported a conversation with a civil servant who talked about the vouchers allowing people to get 'meal deals', as if these were on offer in the cut-price supermarkets and corner shops near the trust's schools. He talked of teachers and administrative staff logging on to the Edenred voucher website throughout the night to try to make sure families had enough food. He mentioned a distressed parent who had been loudly told to put her shopping back when her voucher failed at the till, and another parent whose waiting time on the voucher helpline had cost her £20, a sum she could not afford. School staff picked up the pieces, consoled parents and made sure that no one went hungry. The trust simply paid for food when vouchers failed. The CEO was, he said, apoplectic at the dismissive attitude of various officials he had spoken to and their lack of understanding of the real poverty that existed in his schools and the sheer numbers of students who were FSM.

However, trial by school meals voucher was not all that schools have had to contend with. At the same time, there was also the provision of laptops. In recognition of the digital deficit in poor communities and the potential for further educational disadvantage, the government initially announced laptop provision for all disadvantaged students. This was rapidly amended to disadvantaged Year 10s and other young people with a social worker. The laptop scheme also worked primarily through schools. Schools were to apply to the DfE's supplier, Computacenter, based in England. Like food vouchers, the laptop scheme has run into problems.[7] While the government promised delivery of laptops in May or June,[8] schools reported much longer delays, as well as shortfalls in the numbers they needed.[9] *Schools Week* reported that some academy trusts had been given an initial allocation of less than a fifth of what they need, and that the scheme would start to deliver at the end of the month.[10] The same MAT CEO who was plagued by FSM voucher difficulties told me that he needed 903 to cover all eligible Year 10s, but had been told he would only get half of this number – in September. The MAT schools had of course been teaching online since 23 March. Fortunately he had been able to solicit a donation of 500 laptops and internet access from a local, but multi-national company,[11] and the school had footed the bill for the rest.

The dinner voucher debacles did not stop there. Charities, opposition politicians, schools, and health and welfare workers worried about the severe hardship endured during the pandemic by the families at the very bottom of the economic barrel. A concerted national campaign was launched to extend the food voucher scheme beyond the school term and into summer. The government refused. School dinners were only provided during term time; summer provision would be a precedent-setting shift in policy. But there were high-profile supporters for a summer food voucher scheme – the young Mancunian footballer Marcus Rashford spoke eloquently on national media about his experiences of growing up hungry and poor. In the face of mounting concerns, the government made a U-turn.[12] They would, they said, provide vouchers over summer as a one-off measure. But this backdown accomplished more than ensuring the poorest children were fed. The government was forced to recognise widespread poverty and the ways in which the pandemic had exacerbated long-term social and economic inequities. Their capitulation also showed a weakness in populist politics – the Johnson government might benefit from manipulating public approval but they could also lose the public overnight.

In addition to managing the food and technology delays and inefficiencies, schools were teaching online and catering for key workers' children. And then came the debates about how and when to open to more children and what to teach when all of the children and young people came back.[13] Teachers' unions, headteachers' associations, medical associations alike were concerned about government enthusiasm for an early June start.[14] Some local authorities refused to follow government direction to open schools and asserted their own authority to decide.[15] Where was the scientific advice that said that children would not be infected or would not carry the virus home?[16] How were cramped classrooms and corridors to be made safe? How many children could be taught at any one time given social distancing rules? During increasingly acrimonious media exchanges,[17] teachers were variously praised, chided and derided for being lazy, and labelled selfish and uncaring about children's lack of schooling.[18]

The pattern that emerged in education – dithering by government, dubious decisions, systems slow to start and the burden borne by front-line staff and those they served – was echoed elsewhere, most notably in the public health system. Ventilators were ordered and unordered.[19] UK manufacturers able to produce the much-needed equipment tried in vain to register on a government website.[20] Unusable tests were purchased.[21] Masks that didn't meet quality standards arrived from Turkey.[22] There wasn't enough Personal Protective Equipment (PPE) in hospitals let alone for care homes, dentists and GPs.[23] An army of volunteers made masks and scrubs while schools and universities 3D-printed face shields. Diagnostic tests finally arrived but the military had to be called in[24] to help the outsourced company manage the demand.[25] Centralised laboratories and the testing website[26] were initially overwhelmed while smaller university and private labs stood by.[27] Amid concerns over the knowledge base for government decision-making,[28] independent scientists provided their own advice to government,[29] finally persuading decision-makers of the utility of face masks for the general population.[30] The COVID-19 app began trials amid concerns about its data security.[31] Serco, contracted to begin tracing infections, inadvertently released the personal data of new staff.[32] And so it went on amid what became the highest death rate in Europe[33] and then, for a time, the world.

Just as a ferocious sandstorm can suddenly reveal the skeletal remains of a long-ago stranded ship, the health crisis has laid bare the real workings of the UK nation state. The lack of a 'national interest and public good' approach from government is plain to see. While Australia, whose national government shares a political agenda with the UK, established bipartisan and national-state bodies to manage the crisis,[34] the UK government sought no united bipartisan fora with its political opposition. There was dissent from Wales and Scotland.

The pandemic also showed key disfunctions in the mechanics of governing:

- serious problems in procurement practice, raising questions about transparency of decision-making and due diligence in choosing suppliers with the capacity to provide what was required to the right quality standards;
- significant issues in the supply chain – researchers investigating privatisation in the NHS reported four tiers of contractors with a further wonky linkage of up to 11 chains of provision, with multiple opportunities for profiteering and/or inefficiency at every level;[35]
- inept decision-making – schools were bombarded with constantly changing information;[36]
- inadequacies in organisational feedback processes – central decision-making was often out of touch with local needs and knowledge, and there were few effective mechanisms in place to ensure seamless two-way information and communication;
- serious data breaches and transfers of public data to private companies;[37]
- defensive political rhetoric, heavily reliant on a theatrical use of statistics,[38, 39] that ultimately produced widespread lack of trust in government decision-making,[40] with some of the traditionally right-wing print media loud in their disapproval.

Such procurement and supply problems always waste time and money centrally. At the time of writing, we have yet to see a post-pandemic analysis which probes corruption in the awarding of contracts,[41] how much money was involved and whether this amounted to a significant step-up in the transfer of public funds to private companies.

However, the pandemic has made clear how significant this wastage is at the local level. Huge numbers of school and hospital staff have worked long hours to try to make ineffective systems work. It is no stretch to say that both the health and education systems functioned as well as they did because of the commitment of grassroots staff to their jobs and to the well-being of the publics they serve. It is also clear that the inefficiency and ineffectiveness of government administration were not produced by the pandemic but were already built into the system. Inefficiency and ineffectiveness during lockdown were a direct result of the ways in which the civil service and public provision had already been restructured to contract out and privatise large parts of public provisions, such as health, transport and education.

The governance and administrative philosophy that underpins this highly modernised governing structure and its associated problems of fraud, lack of transparency, cronyism and spin, are the subject of this book. Written pre-pandemic, the book traces the realisation of a political imaginary which benefits only a few, while the majority bears the burden of its workings. The book exposes corruption, as well as what I call corrupted practices, state functions that do not work in the public interest. The argument made in the book is more relevant than ever to a world living with a COVID-19 aftermath.

The book does offer some proposals for structural change. It also calls for a re-moralisation of government and a reorganisation of civil services in order to wisely use public resources in the interests of all of the UK's publics. This call is now even more urgent as the UK, like most other nation states, faces a less economically and socially secure future. There is every reason to think now about how we might do things differently, how government might forge a new contract with the public to rebuild the nation, ensuring jobs, homes, transport, health and education services for everyone regardless of who they are or where they are. The debate about how best to organise a nation in the best interests of all of its peoples is long overdue, but now more pressing than ever.

June 2020

A book about corruption in schools

Children falling off the grid in the tens of thousands amid surge in pupils leaving mainstream education
The Independent, 5 February 2019

Disgraced superhead cannot appeal over £1.4 million in unlawful bonuses
Times Educational Supplement, 18 February 2019

Banned; Head who gave contract to his mother's firm
Times Educational Supplement, 8 March 2019

Trusts fail to make use of £500k DfE takeover funding
Schools Week, 19 March 2016

Academy boss 'ordered schools to cheat on SATS test'
BBC Panorama, 25 March 2019

These are a handful of the 2019 headlines about schooling from English media. Three are very clearly about what is generally understood as corruption: nepotism and cheating. The other two – early school leaving and waste – are not obviously so. The connection between explicit corruption and other 'bad behaviour' in the school system is at the heart of this book.

Why this book?

There are many contradictory media stories about schooling in England. We hear about lack of funds and of funds unused, misspent and misappropriated. We read of test results good, bad and fraudulent. And we read of outstanding schools, failing schools and schools that fail too many children. How are we to make sense of these stories? What kind of school system produces such a bewildering array of reports? How are we to judge what is true? What is causing the problems we read about? And if we are concerned about the state of schooling, what can be done? This book goes behind the headlines and the individual stories to piece together a more coherent narrative.

I started to notice headlines about corrupt practices in schooling some years ago. Then I started to collect them. I have been systematically compiling and filing media reports about what I initially called 'bad behaviour' for the last six years. Those listed at the start of the chapter are representative of the collection. They are not isolated examples. When I first read over my collection of some 3,800 items, it became clear that there were patterns to the events reported. There was something both structural and cultural going on. I wondered whether examining the patterns would shed light on what is, and isn't, happening in education.

It is fair to say that when I first imagined writing this book I was alternatively bewildered, despairing and angry about the contemporary school system in England. With some of the finest teaching and learning anywhere, and committed staff and governors dedicated to doing the best for students, how could so many bad things happen? These bad things mattered. A lot. Fraud, gaming, waste, greed and bullying do serious harm to staff, students and the school community where they occur. But an ongoing stream of negative headlines adds up to more than the individual instances reported – they tarnish the education profession and the institution of schooling. Public trust is hard won and easily lost. Was the English school system now damaged goods, I asked myself?

The discipline of researching means taking such a question where it leads, not making rapid assumptions. I had to set anger aside in order to produce this book. But this did not mean leaving my values out of the work. The book is embedded in a professional lifetime as headteacher, civil servant and academic committed to the goal of a socially just education system and world. As Morwenna Griffiths[1] puts it, there is no 'sitting on the fence' in relation to schooling; this book is, in an axiological sense, partial. It is situated in traditions of writing for and about justice, equity and equality. And this means that I have had to critically assess my own assumptions throughout the research and writing.

The book is about schools and the hand they have been dealt by a certain kind of public policy agenda, that which we might call neoliberalist (Chapter 2). There are now many education books which address this suite of policy changes in education and I do not offer a comprehensive history here. Readers interested in a chronology of educational policy history should start with Stephen Ball's elegant account in *The Education Debate*.[2] My focus is a slice through this history. I am particularly concerned with the notion of 'public' in the term public policy. I am thus also interested in the 'private' – the business sector – and how the public and private rub up against each other. In particular I am interested in the consequences of the interconnections and negotiations between the public and private, and who benefits.

I have shied away from simple solutions to highly complex problems which require public discussion. I do not have a definitive answer to the problems that I detail. Instead, I offer potential lines of argument and arenas for action. I hope that this approach will inform debates about what might be done, now, to intervene in a school system which is bruised from decades of political pet policies and projects. To that end, I have taken an interdisciplinary approach, bringing into the educational discussion scholarship from political theory and public administration and organisational studies. My hope is that these disciplines provide language and ideas which support discussion and practical actions.

The book centres on the organisational infrastructure dedicated to producing and measuring efficiency and effectiveness. Its argument is a form of parsing: separating out the component parts of the organisational syntax and analysing their functions and actions. Parsing produces a heuristic which opens up specific categories for intervention as well as topics for discussion.

The primary contention of the book is that if economistic logics of calculation and competition are the basis for the organisation of public sector efficiency and effectiveness then, contra the rhetoric, particular and 'bad' inefficiencies, ineffectiveness and inequities can result. I argue that if policy agendas are not framed by a commitment to the public good, and structured and regulated accordingly, then there are unintended consequences – from skewing of effort through to the kinds of corrupt behaviours seen in headlines.

I concentrate on England where policy makers have, for some 40 years, been dismantling the welfare state and creating new forms of governing practice (Chapter 2). England arguably offers an almost fully materialised case of economistic logics at work in schooling. This is in contrast to the other three nations in the United Kingdom where schooling remains much more a state provision. I draw in some examples from the United States, Australia and Sweden, to show that similar political and organisational processes are in play in other locales.

The organisation of services intended to support the public is part of a wider social ecology in which inequalities are deep and divisive. In the UK, the divide between the most privileged members of society and the rest of us has widened; those at the bottom of society are finding everyday life more and more of a struggle. The sixth report from the Conservative government's own Social Mobility Commission[3] reported that social mobility had stagnated. It said that under the Coalition and Conservative governments:

- the middle class is being supported while the most disadvantaged are not;
- developmental gaps open up between disadvantaged and affluent children;
- gaps between affluent students and others are prevalent at all stages in the education system;
- the better off are still 80 per cent more likely to make it into professional jobs than those from working-class backgrounds;
- those with the fewest skills are the least likely to get training.

But the common interpretation that social mobility is static is contested. Bukodi and Goldthorpe[4] argue that a better way of understanding contemporary Britain is that downward mobility is rising and upward mobility is falling. They contend that inequalities in mobility remain extreme for the poorest and least well educated. The solution is not, however, simply educational. Bukodi and Goldthorpe are not the only ones to suggest that education alone cannot break the connection between inequalities of social situation and social and economic opportunities. Nevertheless, education can be expected to distribute benefits and qualifications more equitably, without which young people cannot take up any opportunities that are on offer.

How well does schooling do this redistributive work? How much can it accomplish in its current form?

This book provides additional evidence to show that an apparent political commitment to equal opportunity masks a policy regime which, in best Orwellian fashion, produces the very antithesis of what it claims to promote. I document the ways in which systemic and systematic changes in the cultures and structures of schools, and the education bureaucracy, have led to an ongoing series of 'unpublic' practices which produce and reproduce a highly uneven socioeconomic playing field.

I draw on three sources of information. The first source is official government documents. Governments regularly produce, in the name of transparency, a range of documents related to public policy and the basic operations of school systems. In England, there are often questions in Parliament and official responses recorded in Hansard. There are also regular parliamentary inquiries, and reports from arms-length government bodies and commissions including Ofsted, the agency charged with the responsibility for inspecting the 'quality' of schooling. I use all of these documents. The second source is scholarly research, and reports produced by various 'think tanks' whose research is sometimes commissioned by government or funded by trusts with particular political interests. The third and major source of information is from various print and social media, a source which can be seen as biased and/or focused on the immediate event. However, media are often the first, and sometimes the only, source of information available on some topics. I bring these three sources together – triangulate them, as it is often called in research methods texts – in order to produce an inevitably particular picture.

It is important to state at the outset that this book is not intended as a criticism of the vast majority of civil servants and professionals who act ethically and work long and hard to ensure that schools, hospitals, transport and other public services work in the public interest. This is certainly the case. My critical analysis of policy and administrative apparatus is not intended as a slur. However, the efforts of individuals cannot be conflated with the structures and cultures of the civil service and schooling. My hope is that focusing on structures and cultures of the school system will unlock some potential avenues for policy change which will make it easier for those committed to social justice and the public good to do their good work.

Put very simply, the problems that I analyse in the book can be understood as corruption – as the headlines at the start of the chapter signal – but also as corrupted practices.

Corruption is a loaded term. We know that corruption is bad. And to use the term in relation to education may seem particularly inflammatory. However, the association of corruption and education is not without precedent. The Organisation for Economic Co-operation and Development (OECD) says that corruption can 'restrict equitable access to and undermine the quality' of public services such as education, and thus 'contribute to a vicious cycle of economic and social inequalities'.[5] Furthermore,

> the ethical cost of corruption is higher in education than for any other public service. … the younger generation can develop cynicism and discouragement that translates into lack of trust in the government and, consequently, a lack of civic and political participation. Both of these outcomes undermine the basic principles of democracy.[6]

Corruption in education, according to the OECD, erodes the implicit social contract between governments and citizens.

Corruption in education can occur, the OECD says, as a result of policy decisions, management decisions and service delivery decisions, including, 'capital investment; budget allocations; specific allowances and fellowships; school location; school construction; teacher recruitment; promotion and training; the purchase and distribution of equipment, textbooks, materials and food; school and university enrolment; examinations and diplomas; accreditation of programmes and institutions; and private-school licensing'.[7] Most of these decision points feature in this book.

The contention of the book is that the education-corruption problem in England, and in other locations with similar policy regimes, does not arise from the actions of a few 'bad apples'. Rather, it is the education system itself that produces some corruption, but also corrupted practices which are much more widespread and serious, as the OECD suggests. Because the term corrupted practice is relatively unfamiliar, it is imperative to outline at the start the understandings of corruption and corrupted practices that underpin the research I undertook. These are referred to throughout the book.

Corruption and corrupted practices

There is a long line of thinking about a corrupted state and corrupted practices. The very idea of corruption is complex: it is a term which is moral, social, legal and administrative. The Latin word *corruptio* is translated into English as both corruption and a state of decay. This latter meaning can be seen in religious discourse, where corruption is taken to be a fall from grace, as in the story of Adam and Eve in the Christian faith. Corruption also came to refer to a state caused by being curious, heretic or polluted, simply being human.[8] Humans were always in deficit compared to the divine. The term corruption was also applied to religious institutions; throughout its long life the Catholic Church, like its close cousin, the European monarchy, was often accused of nepotism, cronyism and the fiscal exploitation of subjects and followers.

But the understanding of corruption developed in and about the pre-modern state was not only about individuals and institutions, it was also systemic. Machiavelli,[9] for instance, argued that political corruption was not about abuse of office or extortion, but the systemic decay that occurred when civic virtues were eroded. More radical political thought, such as Marxism and its precursors, extended the civic decay interpretation of corruption further to encompass class exploitation, oppression and enslavement.

Definitions of corruption have changed over time. According to historian of corruption Mark Knights,[10] corruption has long included a focus on money, but what counts as 'unfair riches and legitimate profit' has shifted, sometimes radically. Knights offers usury – making money from interest on loans – as an example of changed social attitudes. Usury was banned in Britain in the 1400s, but legitimated and subject to a state-controlled interest rate in the 16th and 17th centuries. Today's banks rely heavily on loan-based profits, or interest as it is now called. Self-interest, another of Knight's examples, was condemned in the 16th and 17th centuries but seen in a more positive light by liberal economics pioneer Adam Smith.[11] Self-interest today is variously seen as greed, the engine of progress and a means of deterring corruption. Knights also nominates monopolies, luxury and the stock market as other touchstones where changing attitudes to the morals of money can be seen.

There is no agreement on the scope of behaviours which are called corruption. There are also various typologies. Common and generally agreed types of corruption include bribery, financial kickbacks, trading in influence, nepotism, cronyism, fraud and embezzlement, money laundering, cheating and falsification. Corrupted practices overlap these and include practices such as wilful waste, lack of transparency, selective use of information, secrecy, bullying and the deceptive manipulation of rules. The distinction between the corruption and corrupted practice is muddy but will be teased out further throughout the book. Von Alemann[12] notes that there are five types of corrupted practice now referred to in common parlance – social decline, deviant behaviour, the logic of exchange, a system of measurable perceptions and shadow politics. He proposes that a common concern in each of these arenas is trust and its loss. Trust and politics are of particular concern in this book.

Trust in, and expectations of, those holding public office have shifted over time. Corrupt financial practices have long been tangled up in both political processes and procurement. In Victorian times it was often difficult to untangle the interests and actions of local business leaders from the interests of the city and its citizens. While on the one hand this led to cronyism and nepotism, on the other the conjunction of business and governing often made it easier for citizens – they knew who to go to to get things to happen.[13] However, moves to eliminate sales of office-holding, and to make public office salaried rather than dependent on fees and sales for services rendered (Chapter 3), has cleaned up the most obvious manifestations of such 'old boys' clubs'. Paradoxically, the due processes of today's local and national governments can seem obscure and out of reach (Chapter 7).

Knights suggests that moral attitudes to public officers can be traced back through contemporary case law on public misconduct. He nominates a foundational prosecution of a public official in 1783 which established office as a matter of entrusted power. The principles underpinning trust which stem from this decision are, according to Knights, 'that trustees work for the good of the entrustors not themselves; that they should not profit from being trustees; that the trustee has a duty of care; and that trustees have discretion but can be held to account when that discretion is abused.'[14]

The term trustee is embedded in charity legal frameworks in England today, with exactly the same expectations as the case Knights quotes. Academy trusts in England (Chapter 2) are thus genealogically connected to this case law, and their trustees can be similarly understood as working for entrustors and thus expected to be trustworthy. Embedding trust in institutions, Knights argues, led to the development of society-wide accountability and transparency measures, including a free press, an independent judiciary and the separation of non-partisan administrative functions from political powers (Chapter 3).

Despite apparently neutral representations and statistics, corruption does not have a 'pure' meaning, but is highly political as well as variable in time and place. Transparency International (TI), the global non-government organisation which researches corruption and advocates for legal and administrative reforms, defines corruption as 'the abuse of entrusted power for private gain'.[15] While private is often taken to mean an individual, it can also mean an entity or organisation such as a company or political party. But the TI definition is open to local interpretation, as what counts as 'gain' varies from country to country as well as changing over time.

Modern global anti-corruption organisations such as TI usually tell a story about improvement – a linear progression from corrupt historical regimes to transparent well-governed democratic states. League tables of the least to most corrupt nations present mature capitalist nation states such as Switzerland, the US and UK at the top and countries, mostly in the Global South, at the bottom. The kind of state that is implicitly advocated through such tables is generally post-Westphalian, protective of its own sovereignty, but prepared to intervene in other 'less well-developed' states for humanitarian or political reasons. These tables support the notion that 'advanced', predominantly Western, nation states are virtuous and non-corrupt.[16] But these visual representations fail to show the ways in which both aid and business from the virtuous top of the corruption league table are often heavily implicated at the bottom, in the apparently highly corrupted nations.

The very idea of one nation state being less corrupt than others is challenged by research on the secretive interlocking practices of global finance and philanthropy.[17] Recent TI reports[18] show that the UK is heavily implicated in facilitating money laundering on a giant scale: the National Crime Authority calculate some £100 billion in illicit funds impacts on the UK national economy each year.[19] TI warns cultural and educational institutions to take greater care in handling donations; a recommendation in tune with the slow trickle of media reports about money laundering via independent schools and universities.[20] TI offers three areas in which anti-corruption work must improve: transparency, ethics and engagement, and oversight and enforcement. All three areas are of primary concern in this book.

Legal scholar Rose-Ackerman addresses the value basis of all definitions of corruption. As values vary it is important, she says, to separate behaviour that is corrupt from the value. She suggests that corruption happens when 'an official charged with a public responsibility operates in his or her own interest in a way that undermines the program's aims'.[21] Even if the programme's values are 'abhorrent and immoral', a public official that carries them out without personal reward is not corrupt. Bad apples are not the same as bad policies and systems. A bad apple can work in a good system and vice versa. This insight is important for this book: as I have already suggested, the majority of education professionals do work ethically within what I will argue is a corrupted system.

Rose-Ackerman also distinguishes violating the rules of the game through unethical actions from corrupt action. Maladministration and questionable self-serving practices such as lack of even-handedness, objectivity, neutrality and transparency are not corrupt in Rose-Ackerman's terms; rather they are unethical. These are what I call, harking back to earlier holistic definitions of corruption, bad behaviour or corrupted practices.

Rose-Ackerman argues that it is important to look for the root causes of corrupt, unethical or immoral behaviour. If, she says, 'in practice, the administration of a public programme is arbitrary or unfair, it is likely that the laws themselves are discriminatory or their administration is faulty, meaning that the programs themselves may need to be modified or eliminated'.[22] In order to reduce the potential for corruption, the state needs, she concludes, to improve efficiency, legitimacy and fairness.[23] While Rose-Ackerman's attention is not primarily on Western governments, the focus on systems and the practices she recommends – efficiency, legitimacy and fairness – thread their way through this book.

But how much is a state able to improve its legitimacy? A TI survey[24] showed that the people in the UK regarded political parties and the UK Parliament as increasingly corrupt, untrustworthy and lacking the will to fight corruption. At the same time, very few people knew how to report corruption if they encountered it. An accompanying study of UK anti-corruption systemic strengths and weaknesses[25] found that the UK had strong political legal, economic and cultural foundations with a strong judiciary, independent investigative media and independent ombudsperson network. Its weakest anti-corruption pillar was the legislature and political parties. The actions of political parties and their policy regimes are at the very heart of this book, which evidences some of their weaknesses.

The TI report also raised doubts over the capacities of various sectors to self-regulate, and identified cuts to public expenditure as a key risk to anti-corruption practices. The discourse of austerity was singled out as particularly problematic: 'The overarching public sector mantra of "do more with less" may well also create perverse incentives to manipulate figures and performance management statistics: a phenomenon that was recorded in the previous UK study, and also found in recent research on the NHS [National Health Service] and UK prison service.'[26] Significantly, the study did not investigate the school sector, which has suffered under austerity politics. But many of TI's concerns appear in schooling, as this book will show.

Michael Johnston argues that the 'strong institutions' associated with advanced democracies, 'together with long-liberalised politics and economics influence the form that corruption takes and enable them to withstand its effects.'[27] Johnston says that a technocratic approach to anti-corruption reform offers a better disguise for private interests and their use of legal corruption via taxation and company law and their use of political clout and influence.[28] At stake in 'influence market' nation states, such as the US, Sweden, Australia and the UK, are 'the details of policy' and the potential for influence and gain at multiple devolved public–private access points. Johnston argues that such points must be made visible. This is a task to which this book hopes to contribute.

Johnston proposes that 'fully understanding that turn of events may well bring back a number of classical ideas about corruption – notably that of corruption as a collective state of being, rather than as a discrete category of individuals and actions – back into focus.'[29] This is the perspective taken in this book: that there are corrupted practices as well as corruption manifest in the English school system. Here, corrupted practices are taken to be organisational structures, rules, relations, tools and routines which are arguably not in the public interest – they waste public resources and work against the ideal of a fairer and more equal society.

The book does not stop at the problem of corruption and corrupt practices. It does address solutions and the potential for reform. But possibilities for change are hard to isolate. Not only are many of the sites of corrupted practice enmeshed in larger global networks and flows of data and practice,[30] but the state itself is compromised. The modern state is, as Knights[31] explains, a source of corrupted practices as well as the means of stopping them. As he puts it, this creates a paradoxical situation in which 'the state has an interest in subordinating its officers to its control; but … it has an interest in resisting its own power being subjected to control or made accountable to others, whether they claim a higher legal or popular authority'.[32] This paradox also features in the book, which argues that technical fixes will not be sufficient to tackle practices which are profligate and fundamentally unjust (Chapters 8 and 9).

Bo Rothstein[33] agrees, suggesting that what is at issue in modern capitalist democracies is not legal and administrative measures designed to change incentives for corrupt actors, or regulatory framings, but rather policies that address the social contract between government and citizens. Tackling issues such as universal benefits – health, education and so on – is more likely to create a climate in which public officials act in the public interest. Writing with Varraich, Rothstein[34] makes the case for an anti-corruption state where overall well-being and human rights are respected and promoted. Rothstein and Varraich claim there is considerable potential in thinking about corruption, well-being and human rights together. A focus on ethics, morals and values, they say, may have a significant role in redesigning the governing practices of the contemporary nation state.

Paul Heywood agrees that the notion of anti-corruption and a universalist approach to prevention is insufficient to produce change. He proposes a move to 'integrity': 'Drawing on moral and political philosophy, we can identify the core characteristics of personal integrity as: wholeness (thinking beyond just the personal); action that is consistent with principles (doing the right things); morality (doing things for the right reasons) and process (doing things the right way).'[35]

Heywood supports moves towards transparency, citizen engagement and a commitment to justice. He cautions against impartiality, arguing that neutrality is sometimes problematic, particularly in relation to marginalised populations and minority interests. His delineation of political integrity frames questions that can be asked of policies, administrative guidelines and laws:

- What kind of justice is intended and produced?
- How open is the practice? Who is involved, when and how?
- How transparent is it? Who knows what about what, and when, and how do they know it?
- In whose interests does this practice work?

These are questions that guided the analysis undertaken in this book.

Heywood also warns against seeing the nation state as the site for all interventions. He points to the importance of supranational bodies – in education we can think, for instance, of the OECD, the European Union and the World Bank – and subnational bodies. He suggests it is crucial to examine actual practices and outcomes, not simply what is intended and written in guidelines. This kind of examination will inevitably, he suggests, involve some degree of mess and ambiguity. This is certainly my experience in doing the research for this book. I wrestled with bringing some clarity to the ambiguities I encountered in my analysis of schooling in England but, as explained earlier, have resisted any easy conclusions.

Rothstein and Varraich[36] offer a model for thinking through ambiguities in their examination of clientelist practices. They see clientelism as: patronage (where the object of exchange is a vertical move to assure allegiance and loyalty); patrimonialism (the horizontal exchange of resources and favours including cronyism, the blurring of public and private in procurement and partial and arbitrary application of rules); and state capture and political particularism (private interests dictate to or unfairly influence governing actors). They argue that these are corrupted practices related to corruption, but not the same as corruption. In this book I similarly use both a narrower definition of corruption but also refer to corrupted practices – bad behaviours

– in the wider school system. At issue in both corruption and bad behaviours are selfishness, opportunism, greed, profligacy, waste and the institutional and political use of class power.[37]

Reading the book

Corruption can easily be understood as the work of a few deficit people, the rotten apples in the barrel. This was not what I learnt from the work of corruption scholars who argue for the need to investigate both corruption and corrupted practices. They point to questions of organisation – policies, structures and cultures. It was therefore important that the question of organisation was at the heart of this book. The book details practices which are evidence of a corrupted, or morally ailing, state. I chose to focus on efficiency and effectiveness as a lens on the kinds of structures and cultures that sanction corrupted practices, as well as producing the conditions for individual corrupt acts to occur. This is not the only way in which these problems can be understood. However, it is a line of inquiry which has not yet been fully explored in education policy studies, and I wanted to see what areas for intervention and action this focus might open up.

The chapters follow a stylistic convention. Media headlines introduce each chapter to give a flavour of contemporary events. These are generally followed by a brief discussion of a principle or key text, selected to give a taste of the historical development of ideas pertinent to the coming discussion. The use of a single text is not intended to suggest that this is the only literature that matters, but rather that there is an archaeology of knowledge[38] influencing current lines of thinking. The historical can still be seen at work in the present.

The next two chapters of the book establish some key historical and contemporary context. Chapter 2 begins by showing how a local authority-based national school system was designed as a solution for an education muddle – arguably a corrupted practice. It signposts postwar tensions pulling in two directions, making the unified system more equitable and making it more businesslike. It charts the ways in which neoliberalist policy imaginaries have underpinned educational reform, and asks whether this has created a new educational muddle. Chapter 3 explores the public sector and the ideas and organisational changes that have made this new school system possible. It shows long-term historical concerns about corruption and corrupted practice which morphed neatly into the new organisational arrangements, as well as the new alignments, technical solutions and democratic deficits that have been created.

Following this history come two chapters which focus on efficiency. Efficiency is understood as the reduction of waste, not simply cost-cutting. Chapter 4 examines the costs of the new educational muddle, including academy start-up costs, costs of academy conversion and the use of private finance initiatives (PFIs). Chapter 5 explores the murky territory of businesslike practices, including high salaries for senior school leaders, financial reporting and mismanagement, fraud and procurement malpractice and market failures.

The next two chapters consider effectiveness and the impact of effectiveness measures. Chapter 6 investigates the nature of effectiveness measures and the counterproductive skewing effect of teaching to the test. It argues that political anxieties about effectiveness are manifest in policy churn. Chapter 7 canvasses some of the poisonous effects of effectiveness: lack of transparency, gaming the system, exclusions and off-rolling and toxic management.

The final two chapters raise questions about ethics and the public good and consider some strategies for further reform. Chapter 8 examines the usual areas for reform: codes of ethics, changes to regulatory practices and structural changes. Chapter 9 examines changes to value systems in looking at the move to the use of public value frameworks, public 'goods' and public 'good'. The book concludes that each of these arenas constitutes potential arenas for action, but that without a moral basis and a renewed attention to integrity, technical changes to the school system will not go far enough.

A final caveat. This book is inevitably already out of date. Information about incidences of corruption and corrupt practices is regularly reported so more and different information about bad behaviour is always entering the public arena.

Additionally, because government has to date continually tinkered with its approach, some administrative details may also have changed. However, the patterns that the book addresses are much more likely to hold: they will take longer to shift. And they need public discussion, as I argue in the book's conclusion. I hope that the analysis in this book contributes to public debate about substantial policy change. Schools, and the people who work in them, can only benefit from an open conversation about how education can become fairer and of benefit to all children and young people.

A scandalous schooling muddle

Skills Minister admits students remain without courses more than a year after training providers collapse

Times Educational Supplement, February 2018

Academy plans pose 'significant risk' to government finances

The Guardian, 20 April 2016

Prepare for lower-than-predicted budgets, councils warn

Times Educational Supplement, 19 October 2017

Thousands of pupils set to miss out on first-choice primary school

The Guardian, 16 April 2019

Headteachers: school planning remains fragmented and unclear

BBC News, 15 January 2016

This chapter examines changes in the organisation of state schooling. I begin by examining key ideas germane to the formation of a national education system using the writings of Sidney Webb. The narrative then shifts to the post-welfare state and structural changes integral to economist calculative logics. The chapter argues that combinations of New Public Management (NPM), calculation and competition have led to an academised school system that, as headteachers have recently reported to media, is once again a muddle, 'fragmented and unclear'. I do not offer a comprehensive chronology, but select events most relevant to concerns about corruption and corrupted practices. A timeline of these key events can be seen in Box 2.1 on pages 24–25.

Sidney Webb and the education muddle

Sidney Webb's work, together with that of his life partner Beatrice, laid the foundations for the 20th-century welfare state. It is worth spending a little time with Webb's educational thinking, as it establishes themes that underpinned the organisation of schooling in the 20th century.

At the end of the 19th century Webb saw the schooling problem as one of inequity and inefficiency combined. His Fabian Society pamphlet in 1901, *The Education Muddle*, begins with Webb nailing his efficiency concerns clearly to the mast. He wrote: 'Our educational machinery in England has got into a notable mess. Some places have two or three public authorities spending rates and taxes on different sorts of schools, while others have none at all.'[1]

Webb saw the fundamental and 'fixable' education problem as oversupply of schools, duplication of effort and no supply at all. The resulting waste and gaps were a grave concern because, if different children were offered very different types of schooling, they would have very different life chances. Inefficiency produced inequity. Webb regarded disorganisation and the fragmented school system – the muddle – as the culprit. There were too many partisan providers, each with their own sources of funding and their own modes of operation and curriculum. There was conflict between providers which prevented self-managed coordination. Politicians were unprepared to tackle the results of 'drift', successive ad hoc decisions which had produced a very complex and conflictual system. Policy makers preferred to tinker at the edges, adding to the layers of quick and partial fixes.

Webb's solution was a single national school system with one central administration. He wanted to cater for pre-existing religious schools, as well as manage growth, including all local authorities and faith schools. Unifying disparate sectors would, he reasoned, provide a sound basis for coordinated planning, provision and regulation. He envisaged a central administration with 'powers of inspection, criticism, and audit of all education of every kind and grade, which is maintained or aided out of monies provided by Parliament, or from endowments or trust funds derived from persons deceased'.[2] Webb advocated regulation and audit via inspection, a practice then common in mainland Europe as well as in the US, as the primary means of collecting information about the quality of schooling. Inspectors were also to challenge schools to improve.

Webb believed that was it was important to 'bring the schools into intimate connection with the everyday life of the country'. His national school system retained its links with local contexts. Webb saw that national government had an urgent responsibility 'to combine all the scattered and over-lapping authorities; and to link together the municipal life of our local authorities with the intellectual life of the schools by the concentration of all local services under one local body'. National coordination would 'secure so far as official machinery is concerned a sound and efficient educational system',[3] but the formation of one education system was only a first step. Webb saw 'the still more important and more difficult problems of what to teach and how to educate' as matters 'for separate consideration'.[4]

Webb's 'muddle' pamphlet was highly influential, and the subsequent 1902 and 1903 Education Acts followed many of his recommendations.[5] London was the only city omitted from this legislation. Webb went on to tackle this anomaly using the same centralisation-to-create-efficiency argument as before. *London Education*, a small book Webb wrote in 1904, began with an analysis of fragmentation and disorganisation and the resulting waste of effort and money that ensued:

> Looked at as a mere matter of civic administration,
> London's educational service is, at this moment,

plainly inferior in efficiency to its police or its fire brigade, its lunatic asylums, or even its water supply. The educational provision is scrappy and disjointed; its fragments are ill-adjusted and uncoordinated ... there are great gaps in some directions and redundancies and duplications in others. It is therefore not surprising that in spite of an expenditure every year of four millions of public money, and a large but unknown amount of private money, London education falls far short of decent efficiency at many points.[6]

Webb's use of the term 'decency' is significant here. Webb takes efficiency not as a neutral process but one with a moral basis, the public value of 'decency'. The *Cambridge English Dictionary* defines decency as behaviour that is good, moral and acceptable in society. In using the term decency then, Webb makes wastefulness normatively unacceptable – in other words, morally wrong. (This sense of efficiency is in tune with contemporary ecological concerns and with a broader notion of the public good, as I will argue later.)

The consequence of indecent inefficiency was, according to Webb, inconsistency in the provision of 'high-level' common schooling for all children.[7] Equitable schooling could only be provided, Webb argued, through a centralised and coordinated system with clear expectations and regulatory powers. Webb envisaged an efficient, unified London education authority that would: oversee credentialling of student matriculation from secondary school; take responsibility for the maintenance of school buildings and enlarging or establishing new schools; ensure that teachers were well qualified and paid and vacancies were filled; and deal with school attendance. Work to achieve this goal should begin, he wrote, with a complete and systematic description of the system; this should be seen as the beginning of regularly collected and maintained statistical data designed to show educational quality and equity.[8] Webb saw measurement, like efficiency, as integral to social justice.

Webb understood local control of schools as less important than overall efficiency and effectiveness. The random geography of locally run and locally owned schools[9] was to be jettisoned. Webb did not appear to be overly concerned about the loss of grassroots ownership and democratic decision making that went along with his vision of unification. Staying in touch with the local context did not mean new forms of local democratic control – but not everyone agreed.

Threads of Webb's thinking can still be seen in the school system today, for instance in (1) the importance of equitable provision for all children regardless of who they are and where they are, although this is variously understood and defined, and (2) inspection as a three-way regulatory process, working upwards to government to provide information, working laterally to ensure universality of provision and working down into the schools to provide feedback. Webb's understanding of the need for a unified system has, however, changed dramatically, as this chapter explains. And the question of how communities might have control over their schools without reproducing a patchy national system remains an issue in current educational policy debates.

The first decade of the 20th century saw Webb and his colleagues legislate for and create an education system whose structure remained largely the same for close to one hundred years. The state funded schools and set national policy guidelines. Schools, both religious and secular, were the responsibility of local authorities, accountable to communities through education committees of elected members. Local authorities were often able to add local priorities and policy interpretations to the national government agenda. They were also responsible for planning new schools as well as ensuring that all schools were adequately staffed, equipped and maintained. Their work was evaluated by inspection, through Her Majesty's Inspectorate (HMI), whose job was both to audit and support schools.

Box 2.1: Timeline of key events

From muddle to a unified local authority based school system:
- Webb's education muddle pamphlet appears in 1901.
- Education Acts to form one unified school system with His Majesty's Inspectorate (HMI) are passed in 1902–3.
- Webb's London education book appears in 1904.
- Fourteen becomes the school leaving age in 1918.

Postwar welfare state strains:
- The school leaving age rises to 15 in 1944.
- The 11+ exam sorts children into secondary moderns and grammar schools.
- Concerns about technical, early childhood and science education.
- The school system is highly centralised.
- Comprehensivisation occurs during the 1960s.
- The school-based curriculum is developed during the 1960s–70s.
- There are criticisms from both left and right. The new sociology of education raises concerns about equity and there are also worries about 'progressivism'.

Post-welfare policy settlement; choice, competition and contracts:
- Thatcher is elected in 1979.
- Ideas of 'choice' and 'competition' are espoused.
- The 1988 Education Act is passed, covering school self-management by grant maintained or local authority governing bodies.
- Students sit the General Certificate of Secondary Education (GCSE) for the first time in 1988.
- The National Curriculum is introduced in the late 1980s.
- Local authorities are broken up.
- Statutory assessment and key stage tests are introduced in 1991–95.
- HMI becomes Ofsted in 1992.

The third way adds concerns about social justice and social inclusion:
- New Labour is elected in 1997.
- Centralised initiatives such as the Literacy Hour and the National College for School Leadership are begun and an innovation focus follows.
- The first academies are launched in 2000, together with targeted interventions.

- Academies grow into chains, subject to tighter controls.
- The London and Manchester Challenges take place during the 2000s.
- Key local authorities and school functions are privatised.
- Back office functions are contracted out.

The Coalition government and the return of the education muddle:
- Voluntary converters accelerate the pace of academisation.
- The number of Multi-Academy Trusts (MATs) increases.
- Free Schools, City Technology Colleges and Studio Schools are added to the mix.

The Conservative government: tightening up?
- Mandated collaborations occur and the majority of secondary schools are now academies.
- The Regional Schools Commissioners (RSC) is established.
- A gradual tightening of rules around academy operations occurs.
- Trustee boards centralise functions and erode the influence of local school governors.
- New grammar schools and many more free schools are mooted.

Strains in the unified school system

Postwar Great Britain. A state rebuilding. A welfare state with its commitment to the universal provision of public services, including schooling, delivered by and through a tiered system of government – elected government supported by national civil services and elected local authorities similarly supported by local authority services.

The philosophy of the welfare state constituted a very particular social contract between the government and its citizens.[10] The welfare state saw the balance between individual responsibility and the state shift further towards a more collective, social(ist) understanding of state powers and responsibilities. The welfare state government would support the economic and social well-being of all British citizens providing they were loyal, well behaved and paid their taxes. Government would eliminate want, ignorance, disease, squalor and idleness.[11] Given the nation-building challenges of re-establishing social and economic life in the aftermath of war, this was a popular policy settlement. But differences between the political parties about the degrees to which the government ought to provide for citizens remained, and these were to become potent in the last three decades of the 20th century.

The welfare state, according to its political advocates, would ensure that all British citizens, regardless of their location or social position, would receive free healthcare and education as well as affordable transport. Low-cost housing would be provided for those without the means to become homeowners. All citizens were to have an equal opportunity to advance socially. Schooling had a particular role to play in nation rebuilding, and was rhetorically tied to social cohesion, economic stability and social mobility.

Postwar British policy makers were concerned about the quality of technical education, and prioritised early childhood education and science education in both primary and secondary schools.[12] The school leaving age in England, set at 14 in 1918, rose to 15 in 1944; the same year saw the 11+ examination sort children into two types of schools: 'academic' grammars and vocationally oriented secondary moderns. Each age change was politically justified through references to the needs of the national economy.

Universalist welfare thinking led to concerns about the inequitable effects of this two-tier system; government policy shifted away from grammar and secondary moderns to comprehensive schools. By the mid-1960s the national school system was largely made up of comprehensive schools, with a few selective grammar schools in operation in some localities. However, the question of technical and vocational education and economic concerns did not disappear, but eased into ongoing debates about curriculum and qualifications as well as with perceived 'fit' with students' interests and prior attainment.

But this unified school system came to be seen as imbued with problems, not of fragmentation and inefficiency, but primarily of inequity and ineffectiveness. The decision in the 1960s and 1970s to move away from centrally prescribed textbooks to school-based curriculum was designed to provide more relevant learning for students.[13] While at its best this is just what it did, across the country extreme variations in both the substance and quality of schooling could also be seen. All sides of politics expressed concern about lack of equity in schooling outcomes. Educational sociologists produced telling evidence of the ongoing classed, raced and gendered nature of schooling outcomes and children's life chances.[14] Critics derided the progressive pedagogies that were apparently to blame.[15] Progressive educators argued that their practices were far from the norm, and the practices of sorting and selecting, a curriculum distanced from students' lives and alienating methods were to blame.[16] Others argued that more choice and diversity was needed, not less. There was little agreement on the nature of the educational problem and its causes, and even less on a policy solution.[17]

The postwar economy was also under duress. The UK joined the European Economic Community in the early 1970s, a move designed in part to reinforce the ideal of a united and peaceful Europe, but also to create a larger economic region. Nevertheless, the 1970s saw burgeoning inflation, increased global competition for core manufacturing industries, mining and agriculture, new labour-saving technologies and escalating demands from a highly unionised labour force. Public service staff, such as teachers, social workers and nurses, were very politically active, focused not only on wages but also on discriminatory working conditions. The welfare state, with its postwar nation-building policy settlement, was beginning to break apart.

Ideas for change pulled in two different directions. Education is a prime example of differences in policy possibilities – one group focused on changing both schooling and society to become more equitable, and another on making schooling more businesslike. These two lines of thinking can be seen in critiques of local authorities. On the one hand, local authorities were seen as sometimes politically partial, self-serving, rigid and ineffective. Local parents wishing to make complaints or effect change in their children's school sometimes found local authority due process to be impersonal and inadequate compared to the sympathetic hearing they got in their children's school where they were known.[18] Local authorities needed to be more democratic. On the other hand, centralised procurement, despite economies of scale, was often seen as both inefficient and ineffective.[19] Any headteacher who has had to requisition stationery and textbooks or wait in line for a plumber or painter to be dispatched (as I once was) can understand the frustration with these aspects of centralised micro-management. Perhaps school autonomy, then the case for curriculum, might extend to school administration, headteachers wondered.

Enter neoliberalist thinking

Contemporary UK policy agendas are often described as neoliberal. The term is applied to other locations too, such as the US and Australia, and to various international organisations such as the OECD, the International Monetary Fund and the World Bank.[20] Neoliberalism is generally understood as a particular form of free market economic thinking in which *Homo economicus* acts in their material self-interest, the individual is seen as more important than the collective and economics is separable from and superior to politics because it does not allow any particular self-interest to dominate. The market is said to provide a space in which competing self-interests, understood as being of equal status and importance, are negotiated and settled. While the outcome is inevitably inequitable – there will be winners and losers – competition is seen as both fair and meritocratic.[21] The demos is replaced by market forces.[22]

As a philosophy, neoliberalism is universalist (predicated on the desirability of a single world market) and meliorist (humans are seen as capable of making progress via self-improvement and remaking). Neoliberalism has both 'positive assumptions (i.e. the market is more efficient than other institutions) and normative assumptions (i.e. the market should replace other institutions because it is both more efficient and liberating)'.[23] The state's task is largely to ensure that competition and open economic exchange can flourish. Neoliberalist political regimes are generally understood as characterised by the promotion of a global economy through national deregulation of trade, money and prices, reductions in the size and influence of national government, the promotion of public–private modes of governing and a move to 'core and periphery', 'flexible' labour markets.[24]

The notion of neoliberalism is contentious. However, this book is not the place to debate this broader question. Rather, the word neoliberalist is used and taken to mean practices in which politics are dominated by economics, where tropes of effectiveness and efficiency are dominant and the interests of the globalised affluent are served.[25]

There are four key points about neoliberalist states which are important in this book (and evidenced in Chapters 4–7).

The calculative tools of economism become paramount

First, if every aspect of society is to be seen primarily through an economic lens then people, jobs, goods, services and things can all be allocated a value and measured, compared and evaluated. William Davies[26] argues that it is this shift to economism rather than markets and competition which is key to understanding the de- and re-construction of the welfare state. Market-based principles and techniques of evaluation become, Davies says, state-endorsed norms. Choice, possessive individualism, effectiveness and efficiency become the criteria du jour, and their economistic practices underpin and legitimate public and private life.

The neoliberalist state is both an object of economic rationalisation as well as an agent

Second, while neoliberalising states promote and foster international and intranational markets they must attend to their own internal operations. State monopolies must be undone. A market must be created for state-provided services such as schools, hospitals, utilities, housing and transport, in order to ensure contestability, efficiency and effectiveness. Such competitive practices are initially created through quasi-markets[27] and initiatives which bring other providers into former state 'monopolies'. Evaluative measurements are used to pit one service against another, rather like supermarkets in the same chain competing against each other for sales targets. The term privatisation[28] is often used to denote the state opening up its activities to the private sector, a practice which is often sold to voters as cost-cutting and efficient.

This form of economist and calculating statecraft is sometimes called the competition state, to denote the difference from the welfare state it supersedes. A new form of governing practice emerges in which the state funds and purchases services which are competitively provided (see Chapters 3 and 4). An alternative name is the contract state,[29] to denote prevailing organisational techniques and preoccupations.

The neoliberalist state reduces public fora in which policies can be seen and debated

Third, new forms of governing (explained further in Chapter 3) are created, mobilising networks of public and private interests, often brought together in quangos at arm's length from government itself. These new institutions are generally not open to public consultation or scrutiny let alone public involvement in decision making. Almost paradoxically, the discourse of 'public'-ness proliferates, as the language of public policy is pervaded with concepts such as public value, public accountability, public scrutiny, public engagement and public empowerment.[30] However, fora where public policy can be debated are generally temporary, corralled and limited in scope.

The notion of public good is recast and contested

Fourth, an economistic view sees politics as inevitably 'contaminated' by particular and partial interests[31] and dominated by arbitrary notions such as public good, common interest and justice.[32] Economics is neutral[33] and thus not only more democratic, but also better suited to executive expert authority than politically motivated centralised agenda setting and planning.[34] The notion of meritorious competition as a basis for the production of equity replaces the principles of non-rivalrousness and non-excludability essential to welfare state traditions of public good (see Chapter 9). A new social contract, in which 'responsibilities to civil society, for the collective well-being of its citizens' create a change in relations and responsibilities of each of 'the state, the market, communities and families',[35] is formed. What counts as public and good is ambiguous, uncertain and often paradoxical, as this book will show.

Within the British government, these economic rationalities and technologies changed not only what was on offer to whom and where, but also how these were – and are – accessed.[36] Calculative technologies provide an apparently objective basis for decision making; contingent and contextual 'social' matters are ruled out.[37]

But these neoliberalist changes were not achieved overnight.

A post-welfare policy settlement

The formation of the Thatcher government in 1979 saw a policy agenda designed to make the state more businesslike and globally competitive. The private sector was to become a 'shareholder' in governing, and former 'monopolistic' public services would be opened to competition.[38] The rhetoric of modernisation and a small civil service, co-located with an imaginary of efficiency and effectiveness, legitimated actions designed to stimulate a lagging business sector.[39] The financial industry was deregulated, as were product markets, and income tax was reduced, particularly for higher income brackets. State assets were to be sold and the power of trade unions dramatically reduced.

Thatcher's initial monetarist strategy – higher interest rates, reduced spending and higher taxation via increased VAT and the Poll Tax – led to a strong currency but high unemployment and a dramatic fall in already strained core industries. The ultimately unsuccessful miners' strike of 1984 was a turning point in industrial relations, and trade unions were politically weakened through new legislation that made it more difficult to take industrial action. Structural unemployment caused by the decline in manufacturing became an everyday reality in formerly productive Midlands and northern regions. There was a marked rise in inequality.[40] But as monetarism proved less than successful in curbing inflation, it was quietly abandoned in favour of a supply side economic agenda. This new focus addressed the 'need' to privatise and marketise public services.[41]

Education was a key area for policy intervention. In the school sector, the Conservative political agenda was directed first towards the creation of a quasi-market, making the provision of schooling and associated school services contestable. The introduction of parent choice of schools and devolved funding allowed schools to develop their own offer and brand.[42] The Thatcher government initiated a series of legislative moves, which culminated in 1988 with: schools formally given responsibility for their budgets and staffing; school governing bodies mandated; a national curriculum and national assessment scheme instituted; and schools divided between those that were locally managed or grant maintained and those that were separate from the local authority and funded directly by the government.[43] (This final move paved the way for academisation.)

Consolidating the organisational infrastructure necessary for managing systemic effectiveness took time, and the combined actions and Acts of both Conservatives and New Labour governments. Large-city local authorities and their often politically troublesome education committees were particularly targeted by the Conservatives. The Inner London Education Authority was broken up into smaller jurisdictions, as were other authorities such as Manchester, Birmingham, Nottingham and Leicester. This effectively reduced the capacity of local authorities to mediate national policy, to deviate from designated 'key service deliverables'. The first students sat for the new GCSE in 1988, but although the national curriculum was in place in the late 1980s, it was not until the Education Act of 1992 that the inspectorate was transformed into Ofsted, the monitoring and audit organisation dedicated to evaluating effectiveness. Statutory assessments – key stage tests which could be benchmarked, subject to target setting for improvement and compared via league tables – were introduced between 1991 and 1995.[44]

When the Blair government was elected in 1997, this policy agenda was largely continued, although very substantial funding was set aside for social justice initiatives (for example, early intervention programmes and area-based initiatives to address poverty). Labour's commitment to equity in schooling was integral to a wider agenda to reduce the levels of inequality generated through Thatcherite policies. The 'third way'[45] espoused by New Labour maintained a supply side focus on markets and public–private partnerships. However, their concern about the growing gap between rich and poor saw a renewed focus on public investment, and small but significant adjustments to taxation and income support. Investment in public services such as education and health were understood to not only further stimulate the private sector but also address key social policy goals of effectiveness, which was once again strongly harnessed to notions of equity. Equity was understood as the gap between the lowest and highest scores on tests, exams and inspections.[46]

New Labour's initial policies featured some contentious centralised curriculum initiatives such as the Literacy Hour in primary schools, designed to 'lift' the performance of schools and students 'at the bottom'. The National College for School Leadership developed a mandatory accreditation system for school leaders: this too was intended to reduce variation in the system and to ensure that systemic effectiveness requirements were understood and implemented.[47] The uniformity push was followed by a loosening up via a series of initiatives – creativity, outdoor education and health education, for instance – designed to stimulate local innovation but also seen as important to 'closing the gap'.[48]

The very worst school buildings were replaced and linked to a new intervention for those schools that stubbornly remained at the bottom of the league tables – academies. While most schools were encouraged to adopt specialisations, recalcitrant improvers were to be closed, and reopened as sponsored academies. This new type of state-funded school, initiated in 2000, was to engage philanthropists with business acumen in designing more effective and efficient legally autonomous schools in some of the most deprived areas of the country (see Chapter 4). Becky Francis[49] sees two stages in the growth of academies under New Labour. The first stage, from 2002 to 2007, saw a 'small bespoke intervention' designed to 'replenish struggling schools'. The next stage, which lasted until the end of the New Labour government in 2010, saw gradual growth in academy numbers, but a shift to academy chains with 'more rigorous funding agreements' which would 'effectively direct groups of schools, deliver professionalism and value for money, and to share expertise between the schools within them'.

The meddlesome middle tier continued to be a target for central government. Local authorities were urged to focus on core business, statutory services and support for schools requiring Ofsted-mandated improvement. School support services – catering, cleaning, maintenance, building, accounts, specialist support services, additional complementary places in further education, supply teachers, insurance and pensions and even examinations and tests – were to be made subject to procurement processes and thus privatised. Any public discussion of education policy was to occur centrally, and in schools, not through a more open local government.

An academised school system

The Coalition and then Conservative governments not only continued but accelerated the academy agenda. As Secretary of State for Education, Michael Gove promoted academisation for all schools and set the civil service to work to make it happen. The number of mandatory academies from failed schools was rapidly overtaken by 'converter' schools that 'chose', often under some duress, to become academies.[50] As more and more sponsors acquired multiple academies, MATs were legislated for. The Coalition government also introduced free schools – new schools started by parents or community organisations (there are more details about this initiative in Chapter 4). Becky Francis[51] evocatively describes the years from 2010 to 2013 under the Coalition as 'A hundred flowers' and 'The Wild West'.

Francis[52] suggests that the next period of Conservative government was one of 'Mandated Collaboration'. Academy growth continued apace. In December 2016, there were 2,083 secondary, 59 special and 3,557 primary academies. A further 799 primary, 175 secondary, 60 special and 28 alternative provision academies were in the pipeline. As of January 2018, academies and free schools made up 72 per cent of secondary schools and 27 per cent of primaries.[53] The majority of secondary schools and a rapidly increasing minority of primary schools are now independent of their local authorities, a significant development since the first 272 'converter' academies opened in 2010–11.

About three quarters of secondary school students now receive their education in academies. But this is highly dependent on where you live. Academies are now spread variously around the country and have various population mixes. The National Audit Office (NAO) sets the scale of academisation across the country as 6 per cent of all schools in Lancashire and 93 per cent in Bromley.[54]

The vast majority of academies are in stand-alone trusts or in small groups of up to ten schools. The large-scale MAT is, however, on the increase. In December 2016, there were five trusts which had over 40 schools each, four with 31–40 and 12 with 21–30.[55] There were, however, only 433 free schools open or scheduled to open.[56]

A telling sign of policy shift – from the initial New Labour emphasis on academies as a discrete and small targeted social justice initiative to a new school system – is the Conservative government's definition of academies and free schools. It is their contractualised status that matters.

> Academies and free schools are state-funded, non-fee-paying schools in England, independent of LAs. They operate in accordance with their funding agreements with the secretary of state, and are independent of local authorities. Maintained schools, on the other hand, have varying degrees of council involvement. Free schools are new state schools, whereas many academies are converter schools that were previously maintained by local authorities. Free schools operate in law as academies.[57]

An important point to note is the line of authority. Academisation moved school accountability directly to the secretary of state. Academies and free schools are primarily regulated through three mechanisms: (1) the Education Funding Agency, an executive agency of the DfE; (2) the activities of Ofsted, the inspectorate; and (3) the DfE, which appoints Regional Schools Commissioners who oversee academy expansion, conversion and compulsory brokerage and rebrokerage. The first two bodies are arm's-length civil services, not accountable to a central civil service executive but answerable to the secretary of state (see Chapter 3).

However, the middle tier is a muddle. Less powerful local authorities now have variable responsibilities in relation to the mix of schools in their areas. They have a statutory duty to ensure that all students have a place, although they no longer control the number of places available. They arrange transport for pupils where necessary and ensure that students with special needs and those excluded from school are still able to access schooling. (More information about various details of academies, MATs and free schools will be provided in forthcoming chapters, particularly in relation to costs, financial practices and transparency of decision making.) Most parents apply for a maintained or academy school place via their local authority. This local arbitration is designed to ensure that selection is fair and that academies are unable to select students on the basis of their attainment (but see Chapter 4). Academies are also required to 'cooperate' with local authorities about the education of children with special education needs.[58] However, there is widespread suspicion that such cooperation does not always occur (see Chapter 4). Local authorities also run schools.

Political promises made about the wholescale academisation agenda are subject to debate. Take the question of school choice, a fundamental premise of neoliberalist policy reform. Not only are there concerns about whether there is actual choice for everyone (see Chapter 6), but choice between schools is often more about reputation and league tables than actual pedagogical and curricular differences. The cultural restorationist[59] and neo-Conservative[60] agenda for change has also produced a remarkable consistency of 'good school brand'. Uniforms, strong discipline and pedagogies which favour direct instruction and 'knowledge' are increasingly the norm.[61] And choice, where it exists, may not be equitable. Because converter schools (those with good inspection ratings) typically enrol a smaller proportion of disadvantaged pupils than sponsored academies,[62] there is potential for skewing through choice making, leaving those schools forced to become academies at the bottom of local choice hierarchies (discussed further in later chapters).

What's more, school autonomy – the capacity of a school to decide its own fate, thus assuring more effectiveness and efficiency[63] – the very raison d'être of the 1988 reforms – is also under duress. Many heads now report less autonomy under MAT 'ownership' than they experienced under local authorities.[64] The DfE explains that MAT control offers more effective 'support' than any local authority can now muster.

It is worth examining the rationale for the substitution of MATs for local authorities. A DfE release designed to dispel 'myths' about academies[65] says:

> Empowering the frontline and moving control away from managers and bureaucrats and directly to the frontline is an effective way of improving performance – holding them to account for the results they achieve, and to much stricter standards of financial propriety than we ever have with local-authority schools. That is exactly what a system where every school is an academy does – providing weaker schools with the expert support they need to improve and giving the best schools the ability, freedom from meddling, money and power to innovate, build on their success and spread their reach further.
>
> Whereas one-size-fits-all approaches dictated from County Hall gives an impression of local control, in fact, it's academy head teachers and governing bodies that hold direct relationships with the parents they serve and have the power to be much more responsive to their communities. If a parent tries to lobby County Hall for change, they'd have to persuade them to change things for the whole local authority; if the academy is approached, it's their responsibility to make a change at the school the parent cares about.

Here we see a rhetoric that has held sway for over 30 years (see Chapter 3). Professional autonomy is conflated with structural devolution of budgets. Accountability to parents is conflated with accountability to MAT trustees. Control by MATs is always about support and freedom. Local authorities by implication are universally inefficient, financially lax, interfering, tiresomely bureaucratic, remote, unresponsive and irresponsible. That they are democratically elected and open to public scrutiny is not mentioned at all.

In reality, the advent of MATs *has* made academies more open to surveillance and day-to-day regulation than they were under the local authority system.[66] Final budgetary control no longer resides with an individual self-managing academy but with the central MAT board of trustees. MATs vary considerably in how much autonomy they allow schools and teachers to exercise over day-to-day procedures, curriculum, pedagogy and assessment. Anecdotes suggest that MAT teachers often have little capacity to exercise the kind of professional autonomy that mainstream school improvement scholars advocate,[67] and is the rhetoric and rationale of policy advocates. There is also a steady stream of media reports which raise doubts about the benefits of increased surveillance: academy financial mismanagement, gaming, bullying and general lack of transparency in particular, as the following chapters show.

A new education muddle?

The result of all of this structural change is bewildering. Even government itself paints a very complex picture. The DfE states that the most common state-funded schools are:

- community schools, controlled by the local council and not influenced by business or religious groups;
- foundation schools and voluntary schools, which have more freedom to change the way they do things than community schools;
- academies, run by a governing body, independent from the local council – they can follow a different curriculum;
- grammar schools, run by the council, a foundation body or a trust – they select all or most of their pupils based on academic ability and there is often an exam to get in.[68]

The official list only covers lines of accountability, categories of students catered for, affiliations and selectivity. There are several permutations possible within and across each of these categories. Steve Courtney[69] mapped school types. He included legal status, curriculum, pupil selection, academy types and multi-school provision as well as branding and their locus of legitimacy (the authority they claimed as a school of this type). Courtney's mapping reveals between 70 and 90 different types of school in England. Questions about who appoints the governing body, who owns the school assets, the forms of accountability and to whom, and the values of the institution, led Courtney to conceptualise a tripartite system made up of corporate, religious institutional and public schools. He argues that schooling in England cannot be described as public and that the state public school is only part of the overall state provision.

Courtney's definition of 'public' recognises that all state schools now operate in marketised conditions, but with strong central accountabilities. However, local authority maintained schools occupy land and assets that are in public ownership, Courtney says, and the local authority school is subject to admissions and planning processes that take a holistic approach to a geographic area. This contrasts with academies, which are: accountable to their particular communities through trustees, satisfaction and performance measures; can be selective about admissions; are able to dispose of land and assets; and have replaced relations with a local authority with a range of contractualised services. This means, Courtney suggests, that, '(w)hilst there remains a considerable, if variously corporatised expression of "public" schooling within current provision, discursively such schools are marginalised: comprehensive is the type that dare not speak its name'.[70] While Courtney's analysis is not the same as Sidney Webb's 1901 educational muddle, Webb would recognise this new fragmentation and the resulting concerns about equity and efficiency.

But the Conservative government, rather than being concerned with the current education 'muddle', with its multiple providers, rationales and administrative procedures, is considering adding further diversity. They want to expand the number and spread of free schools[71] and selective grammar school places. Some local authorities did not abandon grammars in the 1960s when comprehensives became common, but previous governments firmly refused their expansion despite ongoing lobbying.

Grammar schools are a highly divisive public question. After the Conservative May government announced it would entertain expanding the number of grammar schools, the Commons Education Committee called on the government to publish an impact study detailing the consequences of:

> introducing new grammar schools on the wider school system, given the potential consequences for school-funding, the supply of teachers, and the overall health of schools in England from expanding selective education. The Government must also set out how new grammar schools will help close the attainment gap within the wider school system, not just for individual pupils.[72]

These parliamentary concerns emanate from a view of schooling as a public good – funding and teachers are to be distributed fairly, schools should be accessible to everyone and there is to be greater parity of outcome. However, the Conservative government has found a way to game this concern by allowing existing grammar schools to add places and campuses, rather than open new grammars per se.[73]

But while there is opposition, there is also support for the Conservative government, and some agreement that the only way for schooling policy is onward. Writing in the *Times Educational Supplement* (14 May 2019),[74] Leora Cruddas, chief executive of the Confederation of Schools Trusts (CST), argues that the problem in English schools is that the system is 'in the middle' – it is 'half reformed'. It is not a single system. But rather than return to the old structure of local authorities, the way forward, Cruddas suggests, is through 'the group of schools that has the capacity to enable a step change in education. Groups of schools working together in a legal entity whose sole purpose is education are able to embrace cutting edge quality informed by the best research, almost unheard of 20 years ago.'

Groups of schools – the MATs that are CST's members – have the autonomy to innovate and to work for the public benefit, Cruddas asserts. Local authorities, by contrast, have conflicting roles as employer, improver and regulator, when they would better serve as 'democratic overseers' with a particular obligation to see that the most vulnerable children are schooled, that there is a school place for all children and that there is local coordination and planning. This would leave the MATs to focus on effectiveness via curriculum development, professional development, sharing good practice and managing teachers' workload. Cruddas' recommendation comes despite evidence that, to date, MATs have had little overall positive impact on student attainment,[75] their key effectiveness criteria (see Chapters 6 and 7).

However, if a new school system of corporate schools, as Courtney dubs them, were to emerge as the means of resolving the current education muddle, it is important to ask what benefits and problems might be produced. Indeed, what benefits and problems do we already see?

Fully academising the system may not be enough to resolve the education muddle. Cruddas' recommendation is to rationalise provision and to clean out the muddled middle tier. But this ignores several key middle-tier functions and the role of the centre itself. Academising all schools will not, for instance, ensure that schools are available where there is need. Local authorities can try to encourage free schools, but are 'responsible for providing the site for the new school and meeting all associated capital and pre-/post-opening costs'[76] – hardly an incentive. And as recent research on free schools shows, they continue to be established in areas where there is already excess capacity, where there are less at secondary level than primary and where they are less likely to cater for the most disadvantaged children and young people.[77] Good forward planning is still required to ensure equity of provision. And it is not clear at present, nor in Cruddas' revised structure, where this occurs. An educational system comprises more than just legislatively uniformly governed schools.

Chapters 8 and 9 examine proposals to resolve the educational muddle. Chapter 3 moves on to further consideration of the overall organisational changes in the public sector.

Reforming public infrastructure

British bureaucracy is growing out of control

> Philip Jones, former head of
> the Confederation of British Industry,
> reported in *The Telegraph*, 18 January 2009

Scrapping regional bureaucracy will save millions

> Communities and Local Government Secretary
> Eric Pickles, 17 June 2010

Politician's love/hate relationship with quangos

> *BBC News*, 14 October 2010

The UK's civil service needs reform for government to work better

> Chris Johnston, Opinion Column,
> *The Guardian*, 15 December 2013

Civil service stressed and floundering amid Brexit paralysis

> *The Guardian*, 13 March 2019

Government and governing depend on a sound organisational infrastructure. Anti-corruption measures often target government administration, leadership and management. A central administration can be both a source of corruption – through, for instance, cronyism and bribery – as well as a means of tackling corruption in wider society. But governing infrastructure can also be corrupted – where the consequences of organisational practices work counter to public expectations, entitlements and policy promises.

Chapter 2 introduced 'the education muddle' and the early 20th-century development of a unified three-tier school system: a central administration, a middle tier of local authorities, and schools. This central administration – the bureau – was itself a response to corruption. By the time Sidney Webb wrote about the need to rationalise the schooling and local authority muddle, the British central civil service administration had been reformed; it was ready and able to do the coordination and planning work he proposed.

This chapter addresses the history of schooling again, but this time focusing directly on organisational infrastructure and changes to it. I take as my premise that a school system is not just schools and a middle tier, but it is how three tiers work together that matters. The first part of the chapter signposts the development of the top tier, the central bureau, highlighting the processes and structures intended to prevent not only corruption but also inefficiency and ineffectiveness. I then show how growing concerns about efficiency and effectiveness, sometimes also seen as integral to equity, paved the way for the introduction of a new form of public management: governing at a distance. The chapter argues that the infrastructure of funder-purchaser-provider (FPP) assisted by digital platforms makes a marketised academy-based system both possible and logical. This market-oriented governing infrastructure is often recommended to states at the bottom of the corruption league tables as the solution to their corruption problems. But is this recommendation borne out in practice? I conclude by examining some of the literatures about this approach to governing in order to identify potential points where corruption, corrupt practices and/or anti-corruption measures might occur. These points are taken into the remainder of the book, and inform the analysis of the current fragmented school system: the new education muddle.

A fragmented and corrupted civil service

The Victorian civil service[1] was a highly desirable occupation. It was a civilised job for a civil young man. Indeed, some

20,000 university graduates who apply each year for 'fast track' civil service entry still see it as such. But entry to the early Victorian civil service, and promotion within it, were haphazard. Until the mid-19th century, young and largely middle-class white men were employed by particular departments; they stayed in that one department for life, and it provided the only career path available to them. Recruitment and selection involved friendship networks and payment, today understood as patronage, cronyism, nepotism and bribery. 'Indolence, stupidity and incompetence'[2] proliferated. But as governing an industrialising and urbanising Britain became more complex and ambitious, the civil service was tasked with more and more planning, coordination and service delivery. Change was inevitable.

Reform of the civil service is usually linked to the mid-19th century and the Northcote–Trevelyan Report.[3] The organisational problem, as presented by Northcote and Trevelyan, was that of fragmentation, patronage and inefficiency. The solution was a unified civil service where entry was to be based on merit, through more open competition.[4] The civil service executive was to be separated from more mechanical functions and also have some separation from political decision makers. How much separation and over what continued to be an issue for debate.

The Northcote–Trevelyan report began by arguing that government relied on the civil service to get its work done:

> The government of the country could not be carried out without the aid of an efficient body of permanent officers, occupying positions duly subordinate to the Ministers who are directly responsible to the Crown and to Parliament, yet possessing sufficient independence, character, ability, and experience to be able to advice, assist, and, to some extent, influence, those who are from time to time set over them.[5]

The report's use of the term 'character' (lately back in fashion) was Victorian code for someone who was honest rather than someone reliant on patrons and cronies. This reference became the basis for subsequent claims that the report established the fundamental civil service ethos of integrity, honesty, objectivity and impartiality.[6]

The Northcote–Trevelyan report became the basis for ongoing efforts throughout the remainder of the 19th century to move towards open entry examination for a unitary civil service. Employment was to the civil service, not a department, making transfer between branches possible. The service was also organised into a hierarchy of grades with clear separation of tasks. This reformed structure took time to embed.

The impartial bureau?

By the end of the 19th century the British civil service had, in common with other services in other countries such as Germany and France, four key characteristics:

- A division of labour based in expertise. The civil service was divided into specialised units, branches and/or divisions. In a large department such as education, organisational units typically covered curriculum, finances, facilities, staffing, policy and planning. Within each division or directorate there were further subgroupings, each responsible for different aspects of activity. The various specialist divisions usually came together through directors who typically met as an executive team, themselves answerable to the most senior public servants and deputies.
- Hierarchies of organisation with clear lines of accountability and delegations. Public sector organisations typically had a multi-layered pyramid structure. Designated supervisory relationships and responsibilities ensured that work was checked and also fed into actions and decisions. Promotion and pay scales were organised around the work value of each level of organisational activity. There was clarity about who did what, when and how.
- Written protocols, guidelines, rules and regulations. Administrative handbooks were the means of ensuring that there were standardised expectations and procedures. Clear expectations and processes were intended to ensure

conformity and unity, understood as the basis of ensuring fair and impartial treatment. This organisation was also stable and sustainable: staff could come and go without due process changing.

- An impersonal ethos. Cronyism and favouritism were to be kept at bay through the use of technical standards and explicit criteria for merit and qualifications in recruitment and promotion. When dealing directly with the public, there were to be no exceptions made on the basis of association, although criteria such as hardship or illness might constitute a standards-based judgment for exceptional treatment.[7]

Weber famously described these four elements as an organisational structure with 'a shell as hard as steel'. This is most commonly translated as an 'iron cage' of bureaucracy,[8] a term with negative connotations. But a hard shell is equally impervious to external threat as it is potentially inward looking, defensive and slow to change. A steel shell prevents corrosive outside influences.

Weber argued that bureaucracy – the office – although imperfect, was likely to be the most rational organisation for the complex tasks required of government. The bureau ensured that government had timely access to relevant expertise. It was the most efficient way to ensure that public resources were used and processes conducted in a fair and even-handed manner.[9] Nevertheless, this form of bureaucratic organisation was not without its problems (discussed later in this chapter).

By the early 20th century, the steel-shelled British civil service had four main functions: to advise government on the development and implementation of its policy agenda; to efficiently and effectively manage the use of government assets and resources, including through the provision of public services; to make delegated decisions in the name of government; and to carry out the everyday administration of government departments.[10] These duties were managed through an organisation in which, by design, authority did not reside in any one person but was dispersed throughout various branches and executives. This was the central administration, management and leadership capable of ending the education muddle – building a national state school system through the inclusion of a middle local authority tier and a range of diverse schools. The new 20th-century school system depended on the centre for planning, resourcing, regulation and auditing.

But was this stable and sustainable bureau uncorrupted?

How much the civil service had rid itself of cronyism is contested. Some argue that the demarcation between the civil service and government was a defining characteristic of international 20th-century public administration which held fast until the reforms of the postwar period.[11] Yet Trevelyan and his coterie notably failed to condemn practices of patronage,[12] and even until the late 19th century the most senior civil servants were political appointments who were regarded as 'servants' of the monarch. The 'Mandarins' of the civil service had much in common with elected politicians – shared school and university education, gentlemen's clubs and social networks. Even if they were not overtly in cronyist cahoots, they shared a mindset and experiences.

Senior British civil servants were known to have a particularly close relationship with government. They acted as 'counsel' to their ministers, providing a check against the exercise of arbitrary power through personal connection and dialogue. They were expected to 'know the Minister's mind and thus legitimately act as his or her *alter ego*. In other words, such senior civil servants were seen to be 'fused' with their Ministers such that they in effect created a unity for decision-making purposes.'[13] According to Du Gay, this arrangement 'accorded senior civil servants a particular role – as Office statesmen, albeit statesmen in disguise – with an extraordinarily wide scope to their official activities, including policy formulation as well as implementation'.[14]

Ministers of course had the last word on policy making, and were responsible for the delegated decisions made by civil servants. Even so, the mandarins wielded considerable power. The coalition of background and class interests of both politicians and civil servants at the highest level can thus be understood either as collusion and/or coalition, or as checking and balancing. Nevertheless, any cosy politician–bureaucrat nexus may have been heavily mediated by a civil service code of ethics.

The 20th-century civil service was generally understood by those in it, and by government, to have an explicit values commitment to the 'public good'. O'Toole[15] argues that the civil service was guided by an *ideal* which, as he puts it, was and is

> that those in official positions of public authority regard the interests of the whole society as being the guiding influence overall public decision-making, that their personal or class or group interests are to be set aside when making decisions, and that they are public servants purely out of a perceived duty to serve the public.

O'Toole traces this ideal back to Plato's[16] explication of the role of rulers who acted to serve and protect the interests of the commonwealth. O'Toole recognises that the ideal of a dispassionate and disinterested public servant probably never existed in its purest form, but suggests that it was a highly influential norm against which the actions of the civil service were judged. 'Public good' offers an alternative and moral evaluative mechanism to that of scientific measurement which, he proposes, later dominated the civil service along with the corrupted politics of self and group interests.

Postwar public administration: strains in the bureau

In order to deliver on the postwar welfare state promise, a very particular kind of public administration was required. Rather than simply deal with money and 'stuff', the civil service was to nurture and manage all of the resources of the nation in the long-term interests of the public.[17] This was to be accomplished through an expanded centralised welfare state bureau in which national and local public services were subject to a regime of vertical and horizontal audit and monitoring, independent branches managed appeals against unfair treatment and audit and appeals were both seen as integral to fairness and due process.

The promise of universal public provision and equitable distribution of public goods relied heavily on the belief that a bureau organisation was ideally fit for purpose. While this might initially have been the view of postwar politicians, media and the public, it was not to hold for long.[18]

The first wave of postwar civil service reform in the US, UK and France, was concerned with both efficiency and effectiveness; strategic policy making and evaluation was to become more 'rational'.[19] In the UK, the Fulton Report of 1968[20] launched the first substantive postwar critique of the civil service. The report drew on new developments in social science disciplines as well as business practices. It began by stating that the civil service was a 19th-century invention ill-suited to the demands of the second half of the 20th century. It was in essence corrupted, its moral purpose lost in rules and cumbersome process.

During the 1960s and 1970s, the problematisation of a corrupted civil service *inter alia* singled out:

- Role specialisation – the civil service was seen to lack particular forms of expertise that it needed. Where specialisation existed, it produced silos of underutilised experts who had difficulty communicating and working together. Trained reluctance to act outside of one's area was the sign of an organisational incapacity to act with appropriate speed and efficiency.
- The hierarchy of organisation – clearly defined roles and lines of accountability were seen to produce staff reluctance to go beyond what was permitted. When combined with written rules and regulations, initiative and creative problem-solving were stifled. Some staff shirked their responsibilities and covered up mistakes while others mindlessly followed orders; to compensate, more monitoring and supervision were instituted instead of increased delegation. Ambition decreased in the face of those promoted to grades and tasks beyond their competence. The solution was to include staff in decision making and allow them to feel responsible.
- The impartiality required of civil servants – neutrality was seen to produce a technical or mechanistic approach to tasks. Implementing rules became the goal rather than meeting service users' needs.

- The 'wise counsel' counselling role of senior civil servants – providing a check on short-term political agendas – often masked self-serving behaviours. Mandarins acted in the interests of the civil service, not the elected government. It was sometimes argued that civil servants had established an illegitimate and rival power base and wanted to usurp government.[21]

The Fulton Report was not only diagnostic but also pointed to particular kinds of solutions. As Chapman[22] summarised at the time, the Fulton Committee believed that:

> Accountable management means holding individuals and units responsible for performance measured as objectively as possible, it requires the identification of those parts of the organization that form convenient groupings (or 'centres') to which costs can be precisely allocated as the responsibility of the man in charge. Such accountable units should be organized into separate 'commands' which would correspond to the 'budget centres' which have been developed in industrial organizations.

Here, then, were the key targets for reform: the amateurishness of the civil service should be transformed and replaced with a more businesslike approach, focused on making sure that it delivered and was answerable for what it had been given a budget to do. Additional expertise was required in order for it to do its job.

The rhetoric used in and around the 1968 Fulton Report provided the direction for much subsequent reform, with 'lack of service' and 'self-serving' particularly at issue in ongoing political and media commentary. The civil service was characterised in popular media and in political debate as run by elitist 'posh' white men – lazy, self-serving and incompetent – who presided over a bloated, inefficient and unsympathetic civil service. Satirised in the BBC television series *Yes Minister*, elected politicians were depicted as hapless pawns of the devious Oxbridge wit and stalling tactics of the archetypal mandarin, Sir Humphrey. When Sir Humphrey said,

> Minister, the traditional allocation of executive responsibilities has always been so determined as to liberate the ministerial incumbent from the administrative minutiae by devolving the managerial functions to those whose experiences and qualifications have better formed them for the performance of such humble office, thereby releasing their political overlords for the more onerous duties and profound deliberations which are the inevitable concomitant of their exalted position.[23]

viewers knew that this was pompous, patronising obfuscation of the worst order. The public ground was well prepared for a civil service with a more subservient attitude.

However, as was the case in schooling (described in Chapter 2), concerns about the civil service were not of a piece. Not everyone saw lack of businesslike practice as the key issue. Some critics were concerned with processes; it *was* sometimes difficult for members of the public to even contact, let alone influence, the civil service. Others saw that a public service ethos and mission had been corrupted. Social movement activists and social scientists alike pointed to the inequitable nature of a civil service dominated by a clubby cabal of Oxbridge humanities graduates[24] with a poor track record of employing and promoting women and people of diverse racial and ethnic heritages. The civil service record on disability was equally abysmal. But it was not simply employment that was inequitable – many policies and practices were also discriminatory and needed to change if the ethos of 'the public' and 'public good' were to be genuinely inclusive. The *Yes Minister* portrait contained more than a grain of truth.

However, the views of the civil service as ineffective and inefficient neatly coalesced with the neoliberalist logics and imaginaries outlined in Chapter 2.

Enter modernising government

In 1993, David Osborne and Ted Gaebler published a book called *Reinventing Government: How the Entrepreneurial Spirit is*

Transforming the Public Sector. Filled with enthusiasm for change, they argued that the public sector needed to be much better at delivering its core outcomes. Osborne and Gaebler asserted that government needed to stop rowing the boat of state and start steering. Government needed to make others do the heavy work. Governing should be distanced from government services.

Osborne and Gaebler effused about the transformative potential of a single-minded focus on outcomes, competition, a wider range of providers, a focus on the customer, being driven by mission not rules, preventing rather than curing, decentralising to the lowest point and earning rather than spending. These precepts rapidly became policy reform mantra and provided directions for public service reform around the world. A contemporary reader will no doubt see these tenets as commonplace organisational slogans.

Osborne and Gaebler presented, in their own words, a 'simple and clear map' for those who were bunkered down in their own partial work universes:

> those who are today reinventing government originally set off to solve a problem, plug a deficit, or skirt a bureaucracy. But they have bumped into a new world. Almost without knowing it, they have begun to invent a radically different way of doing business in the public sector. Just as Columbus never knew he had come across a new continent, many of today's pioneers – from governors to city managers, teachers to social workers – do not understand the global significance of what they are doing. Each has touched a part of the new world: each has a view of one or two peninsulas or bays. But it will take others to gather all this information and piece together a coherent map of the new model they are creating.[25]

The reader of the 21st century is likely to be startled by two aspects of this opening gambit. The first is the colonialism inherent in the reference to Columbus and a 'new world'. It is a telling metaphor. Like Columbus, Osborne and Gaebler intended to invade, settle and take over – their dream was for a market rationality and entrepreneurial logic to colonise the public sector. The second is the elevation of non-local knowledges – external expertise is essential to building a new policy settlement. 'Others' will put the big picture together using the limited experience and understandings of those practitioners who are already at the frontiers of change.

These allusions to pioneering, exploration and yet-to-be-conquered territory called to international quangos and national policy makers. Osborne and Gaebler's book was allegedly popular with Bill Clinton. Clinton presumably also gave credence to the popular image that Osborne and Gaebler drew on – the public service as self-serving, inefficient, rule-bound, out of date and out of touch. The book was also of interest to aid organisations and reforming governments in countries with known corruption problems.[26]

Osborne and Gaebler were not alone among economists, business commentators and public administration scholars focused on new forms of governing. Stoker[27] defines governance as a capacity to get things done which neither rests on the power of government for command nor the use of its authority. Governance blurs the boundaries and responsibilities for tackling social issues across public, private and third sectors, and ensures that the relationships involved in collective policy action are dependent on each other, as well as on the power derived from being part of governing. Governments which engage in governance develop and use new tools and techniques to navigate, direct and guide. This in turn requires a new constellation of institutions and actors that are drawn from, but are also beyond, government. These are not autonomous self-governing networks of actors but are all tied, via new tools and techniques (see FPP later), to centrally determined government goals and practices. The move to governance was once described as a hollowing out of the state,[28] but is now more often described as a new creeping centralism[29] through which top-down power is diffused, but is paradoxically enlarged and augmented rather than diminished or diluted.

The new governing via steering required a modernised public service with a new organisational structure, one in which the civil service became intimately connected to measurable outcomes and businesslike practices. Christopher Hood[30] explains NPM as a reversal of the two cardinal doctrines of the civil service:

> lessening or removing differences between the public and the private sector and shifting the emphasis from process accountability towards a greater element of accountability in terms of results. Accounting was to be a key element in this new conception of accountability, since it reflected high trust in the market and private business methods (no longer to be equated with organized crime) and low trust in public servants and professionals (now seen as budget-maximizing bureaucrats rather than Jesuitical ascetics), whose activities therefore needed to be more closely costed and evaluated by accounting techniques. The ideas of NPM were couched in the language of economic rationalism, and promoted by a new generation of 'econocrats' and 'accountocrats' in high public office.[31]

The new structure adopted to operationalise NPM was the funder-purchaser-provider model, or FPP as it will be called from now on. FPP is intended to stimulate competition among providers by separating the processes of commissioning and delivering. FPP was introduced in the 1980s into the NHS in the UK, and was the guiding principle of public sector reforms in New Zealand in the 1990s. Health services and education in other locations – Sweden, Finland and Italy for example – also now use a purchaser-provider model.[32]

FPP rebuilds organisational infrastructure, allocating specific tasks to each 'actor'. The *funder* is the elected government – it determines policy and quantum of overall funding and funding for specific programmes such as capital works, system-wide technology provision, an improvement initiative such as a literacy programme, or an electorally sensitive programme such as sex education or music provision. In accountability terms, the funder for education in England is a trio of ministers.

The funder may appoint a series of arms-length bodies to carry out independent auditing of both purchase and provision.

In education in England, Ofsted and the NAO scrutinise operations. Dispersing of funds is given to a specific agency, the Education and Skills Funding Agency (ESFA). ESFA also has a monitoring role and is able to issue financial improvement and closure notices to schools. Such arms-length bodies are able to simultaneously distance elected politicians from decisions, render the majority of decisions a matter of technical/organisational expertise and largely remove decisions and processes from public scrutiny or input.

The *purchaser* is the relevant arm of government, a central civil service department; for schools in England this is the DfE. The purchaser has two main responsibilities:

- Providing advice and feedback on operations to the funder.
- Working with the legal and administrative frameworks for, and the procedures of, procurement. Contracting and commissioning is a core function of purchasing. Purchasers often supplement the expertise of the civil service with specifically contracted advice, usually via consultancies. Some purchase functions are contracted out, and private organisations thus become proxy principals for the state.

In education, as in other areas of the public sector, purchasers often have a regional presence. In schooling, the out-posted civil service role falls to Regional Schools Commissioners who are responsible for ensuring that the funder's decisions – about, for instance, termination of academy contract or rebrokerage of contracts – are carried out.

Providers are contracted to provide specific services; the process of contracting is usually carried out by purchasers and signed off by the funder. In education, providers can be local authorities, individual schools, networks of schools or registered trusts and charities. Mass academisation under the Coalition and Conservative governments transformed school provision. Providers are responsible for what is specified in their contract – this may be education in general, or specialist services. Providers are able to determine how they will deliver the contracted services but they must deliver what they are funded to do. The contract effectively reduces the capacity of each provider to determine priorities.

Within FPP, local authorities became anomalies, as they are both purchaser and provider. In England, the Coalition and Conservative governments want local authorities to be removed from the middle tier altogether, and to become providers with special responsibility for 'unprofitable' services and mandatory functions such as providing education for excluded children. However, as long as they run mainstream schools, local authorities also take on some purchaser responsibilities.

The FPP model needs a special-purpose quality assurance technology connecting provider, purchaser and funder. This technology becomes the new 'steel shell' of the organisation, holding it together. This technology is now data, digitised and algorithmically driven. Ongoing provider (school) self-evaluation uses funder-decided, purchaser-developed categories and measures – in schooling, testing and examination are converted to benchmarks and improvement targets. Independent external monitoring of school results and processes verifies or contradicts provider-level judgments. These two sources of information are fed upwards to the funder, via the purchaser and its hands-off agencies.

FPP materialises and activates the economic rationalities of governing through the development of competing service providers, regulated via digital algorithms and audit technologies. Initially FPP was implemented within the silos of departmental systems, but the advent of government-wide digital platforms meant that changes in one system flow into others; information from one system is also picked up and used in others.[33] Digitised FPP meshes together various state systems: Treasury and budgeting, welfare, organisation, regulation, information, legal and bureaucratic.

FPP separates senior civil servants from ministers, achieving what civil service reforms from Northcote–Trevelyan onwards did not. The civil service is linked to the private sector, entangled in new networks of knowledge, association and practice. The FPP brings new forms of expertise and new businesslike practices into the civil service and public providers. The shift is often described by advocates as a move from the paternalistic client-orientation of welfarism where the professional always knows best, to a customer service focus. Power relations are said to be reversed: customer dissatisfaction is expressed through 'voice' (complaints and bad reputation) or 'exit' (choosing another service). Customer loyalty becomes the driving force for decision making.[34] The system thus moves from 'provider capture' to discipline through the market. Policy emphasis shifts from inputs – in schooling this is usually money[35] – to one where customers (parents and communities) are in control via consumer choice (through, for instance, educational vouchers).

Practices associated with a more businesslike culture bring significant changes to everyday life in the civil service – and in schools. New language is adopted: core business, strategic partnerships, delivery, satisfaction. Marketing, managing reputation and public relations become part of purchaser job descriptions and budget allocations.[36] Collecting, using and disseminating information from 'customers' in order to provide 'value' is integral to self-evaluation. Entrepreneurial profit-making activities become acceptable provider practice.

The new British bureau

Charged with becoming more businesslike, smaller and somewhat more equitable, the second wave of civil service reforms were folded into the policy agenda of a newly elected and energised Conservative government with Margaret Thatcher at the helm. Ushering in the new form of 'steering not rowing' governance,[37] the state sought to divest itself of its recent history of welfarism and universalism. Instead it turned to what is often called marketisation: the infiltration of market principles to all aspects of society.

A second wave of civil service reform from the 1980s onwards was concerned with cost-cutting and the overall effects of public administration on the economy. These concerns were 'connected to the global economic disturbances of the 1970s and the spreading belief that governments had become "overloaded" and that Western welfare states had become unaffordable, ineffective and overly constraining on employers and citizens alike'.[38]

These reforms occurred through a series of reports, policy initiatives, reviews and structural changes (see Box 2.1). The notion of a universal public service with standard conditions of employment was replaced by independent units which operated in a contestable context.[39]

The first move by the Thatcher government was the *Next Steps*[40] report which argued, again, that the civil service should emulate the best practices of business – confining itself to core functions and contracting out the remainder in part by creating new agencies. Private financing of public infrastructure would alleviate some immediate costs, as would making large numbers of non-core civil servants redundant. All government departments were to develop business plans in order to make them more 'customer focused'; new measurement-oriented forms of monitoring and performance management would ensure that staff complied. The ongoing problem of 'amateurishness' in civil service leadership would be augmented by opening up positions to non-permanent employees and consultants.

The subsequent New Labour government was strongly committed to equity and social justice in social policy,[41] as seen in its introduction of a small number of academies intended to lift educational opportunities for children in inner cities (Chapter 2). But its Third Way also espoused strong economistic logics, including continuing the Conservative agenda of 'modernising' the civil service. Prime Minister Blair identified a series of civil service targets for efficiencies, with cost-cutting seen as integral to producing value for money. The targets for reductions and contracting out were:

> 'back office' (for example human resources, finance, IT support); 'procurement' (i.e. purchasing the necessary capital and equipment and other resources to enable the delivery of public services); 'transactional services' (for example, the payment of benefits and the collection of taxes); 'policy, funding and regulation' (separate workstreams for the public and private sectors); and the 'productive time of front-line public servants' (i.e. the time spent on professional activities such as teaching or nursing rather than time spent on non-core activities, implicitly associated with bureaucracy)[42]

Reform of civil service work practices centred on the allied notions of strategy, performance and delivery. A raft of special advisers, think tanks, lobbyists, 'experts' and specially contracted staff were employed to provide 'independent' sources of expertise. Advice itself became a market, via growth in the regular use of consultants;[43] both commissioned and unsolicited experts provided a stream of advice on the next moves government must make to become ever more economistic in their outlook and practice.[44] Experts were hired to help civil servants engage with visible planning via the use of benchmarking and targets, regular monitoring, contestability via the publication of performance results and performance-based reward and punishment through the use of Key Performance Indicators (KPIs), particularly at executive levels. The missionary rhetoric of delivery underpinned all interventions.

The health services provide a helpful illustration of these changes. New private providers were invited into NHS services to deliver particular functions, from operations to pathology.[45] Regardless of provider, all treatment followed evidence-based protocols developed by an independent quango – their calculations used epidemiological statistics and clinical trial research (effectiveness) and judgments about 'value for money' (efficiency). These protocols determined who the patient saw and for how long, when referrals were made, what treatment and medication were on offer and how much the provider was paid. Patients could not challenge treatment protocols, nor could providers. Health practitioners were required to not only follow protocols but also provide digital audit trails which demonstrated that they had done so. Individual health records were aggregated in order to evaluate the quality of the service provided. Services could then be compared, and such comparisons became the basis for public league tables and for decisions about continued funding.[46] A market in health was created where some people who could afford to could 'jump the queue' by paying for services. However, as Chapter 8 suggests, there may be room for rethinking the benefits of the FPP model in health services.

But this is the logic that now underpins the contemporary civil service and produces its quotidian realpolitik. Civil servants are 'taught' to evaluate and calculate worth and risk through a variety of actuarial tools.[47] A new datafied civil servant mindset is produced and reproduced through performance and repetition.[48] Procurement, measurement, evaluation and audit also dominate providers' practices, as well as frame the ways in which ordinary citizens experience their public services.

The shift effected through FPP in the civil service, and in democratic processes more generally, can be glimpsed in the differences between the television series *Yes Minister* and *The Thick of It*, a later satire of contemporary government (it ran from 2005 to 2012). *The Thick of It* is set in a superdepartment responsible for social affairs; this covers just about all of everyday life. A still-hapless minister, policy advisers and civil servants are all at the mercy of the foul-mouthed Malcolm Tucker – a prime ministerial 'enforcer'. Dialogue centres on spin and various deceptions of the media, the public, the Opposition and backbenchers. The popular programme flagged up a new political reliance on impression management and push-polling, as well as the diminution of power of the permanent civil service compared to politically appointed central advisers.

The return of cronyism and fragmentation?

Civil service leadership continued to be seen as a problem by the 21st-century Coalition and Conservative governments. A 2014 Conservative think tank report[49] reflecting on the recent history of second-wave public sector reform claimed multiple achievements, but, *plus ça change*, suggested that the civil service was impeded in its quest to deliver sound advice and public satisfaction. Resonant with concerns first registered in the early 19th century, the authors proposed that inexpert leadership combined with an inadequate notion of what a future civil service might be, as well as inadequate and contested stewardship of a civil service ethos, were the major problems. Reform had not gone far enough.

But had other problems identified in the Northcote–Trevelyan report – fragmentation and cronyism – been resolved? There are mixed views about whether this is the case.

Fragmentation in the civil service – the purchaser as opposed to provision – may no longer be an issue. Margetts and Dunleavy[50] argue that while there was initial organisational fragmentation through NPM, the most recent civil service reform, digital-era governance, has moved away from the disaggregation of large bureaucracies and the introduction of competition and incentivisation. Rather, they say, although there has been a shift to 'economic motivations' through privatisation, user charging and private finance initiatives (PFIs), the widespread use of web-based platforms, including social media, has brought about:

- reintegration, reversing the fragmentation brought about through NPM;
- needs-based holism (client focused structures for departments and agencies);
- digitalisation at the heart of the government business model, with algorithmic platforms that allow users to access and choose services for themselves.

The introduction of standardised digital platforms in the civil service has been directed towards stronger surveillance, standardisation and control. But we might well ask whether the problematic educational muddle is now only made *somewhat* coherent through the integrated digitised platform which stitches it to the central civil service purchaser and political funder. And is this form of coherence sufficient or adequate?

In contrast, the jury is out on cronyism.

Sylvia Horton[51] suggests that because civil servants are now denied anonymity through parliamentary inquiries and are subject to media attention, they no longer feel obligated to defend the government. They act independently and in the public interest. Veronesi and colleagues[52] also query the subservience of the civil service – they set out to test the contention that branch-level public sector managers subject to NPM are incompetent and self-serving. Their study of acute hospital trusts in the NHS suggests that managers do not engage in 'rent-seeking' behaviour, but have a positive impact on organisational performance.

Du Gay argues that, despite mandarins and politicians being similar in background and political persuasion, they are not easily manipulated:[53]

Because the ethic of office regulating the conduct of mandarins makes them likely to greet the panaceas of all political parties with a degree of caution, inevitably this leads them to embrace party political programmes with less fervour than party enthusiasts would wish. This is part of their job, and in fulfilling it they can be seen as servants of the state. This statist role, though, makes them ideal targets in the eyes of party political enthusiasts, who have found it easy to represent them as a historic residue with no 'mandate', and therefore as illegitimate actors in government, or as hopelessly old fashioned bureaucrats rather than 'can do' entrepreneurially minded leaders and deliverers.[54]

Supporting evidence for this view from the UK[55] and beyond[56] suggests that senior civil servants do still have considerable influence in agenda setting, as well as in the implementation of policy agendas.

Countering this view, Richards and Smith[57] say a new form of cronyism now exists between government and the civil service. Because NPM politicised the relationship between the civil service and politicians, ministerialisation[58] – or the expectation that civil servants are accountable to policy makers, rather than acting as a check on political short-termism – has become the norm. Due process and long-term public interest gives way to what the minister will approve; the public service ethos and mission are corrupted. O'Toole[59] concludes that the ongoing reform of the civil service has stripped it of its public good ethos and returned it to the fragmented state which preceded the Northcote–Trevelyan report of the 19th century.

NPM and corruption

Researchers do not agree about whether NPM is a cause of or remedy for corrupt practices.[60] There is some evidence that, because FPP multiplies the points of contact between the public and the private, corruption may actually increase in the short and medium term, although it may also gradually reduce over time, as regulatory controls are put in place.[61] One of the rare investigations of corruption in decentralised school systems, a UNESCO study of Australia, Brazil, Poland and the UK,[62] concluded that:

> The introduction of formula funding for schools and the delegation of spending decision to them can prima facie increase the possibility for fraud as many more people have direct access to funds. ... Conversely, formula funding acts to reduce the likelihood of fraud as one of its essential components is public access to information.[63]

The report suggests that well-designed financial systems, monitoring by school governors and the education authority, trained staff and independent audit are crucial to avoid such corruption.

Those who study public management systems note a plethora of recorded cases of corruption arising in centralised systems of government, such as the one which brought the welfare state to fruition. Another study of school corruption, undertaken in the US by Segal,[64] argues that corruption can occur in both centralised and decentralised systems and it is having the right balance of delegations, perusal and audit that counts. Close control, she suggests, often produces waste, as does trusting decentralisation with few checks. Community controls can give power to narrow self-serving groups. Management can frustrate corruption controls. A culture of public service and integrity is thus vital, she argues.

Decentralisation, building on the principle of subsidiarity – which underpinned the first waves of steering not rowing styles of government – has been advocated as an important anti-corruption strategy. Decentralisation is said to bring accountability and decision making closer to the people served. An evidence review of anti-corruption measures by Hanna and colleagues[65] provides empirical support for the notion of local participation and accountability, concluding that it works best as an anti-corruption strategy in local communities with high levels of participation, and when decision makers and service providers are held accountable by service recipients.

However, local engagement and participation is not generally the case with the marketised FPP model. One of the consequences of the FPP model is that it contracts and privatises functions which were previously more open and public. The FPP model relies on arms-length bodies with little or no public involvement – in education Ofsted, the ESFA and the NAO are significant bodies which make decisions with variable engagement with the education profession or parents. The academised school system is similarly managed by boards and trustees, who have to make only some of their decisions public. One group of scholars sees this sequestration of participation and accountability as depoliticisation[66] – they are alarmed by a nation state where the public are effectively removed from decision making about matters of public concern. A 'democratic deficit' leads to public alienation, they contend.[67] If FPP cannot or does not effectively use public oversight as an anti-corruption tactic, it must instead rely on regulation. The consequences of a lack of democratic oversight are explored in Chapters 4–7.

While the literatures suggest caution in assuming that organisational structures create or remediate corruption, they do point to places and processes that are important to examine: audit, controls, information, decision making and accountability. Chapters 4–7 address these pressure points. However, the literatures also indicate potential difficulties in finding easy solutions to systemic problems. If new assemblages of civil servants, philanthropists, experts, consumers and civil society organisations make formerly public matters technical, as well as produce barriers to wider coordination and forward planning, feedback and policy activism,[68] then the question of how to generate debate and new ideas for a public school system are not simple or straightforward. Chapters 8 and 9 tackle this issue.

4

Costly measures

Sponsors lose control of 119 failing academies

BBC News, 15 June 2016

11 academy trusts fold after schools rebrokered

Schools Week, 11 February 2017

GMB Scotland reveals Ayrshire Councils pay staggering £32 million a year to private companies for just a dozen schools

PoliticsHome.com, 7 April 2017

Defects found at 72 more Scottish school buildings

BBC News, 13 April 2017

PFI firms to get £4.8 billion from schools by 2020, study shows

The Guardian, 19 February 2018

Efficiency is commonly described in disparaging terms as bean-counting, nit-picking, micro-management. My early studies in educational administration were highly critical of planning and the quest for efficiency,[1] epitomised in the notion of the 'efficiency expert' who, clipboard in hand, conducted time and motion studies on unwary employees and made recommendations that invariably screwed workers more tightly to alienating work. More recently, government rhetoric has equated inefficiency with a need to save money;

as Chapter 3 explored, alleged inefficiency in the civil service has been semantically glued to questions of 'bloat' and necessary redundancies.

However, efficiency does not necessarily mean cost-cutting. Scientists understand efficiency as the ratio of input to output. Efficiency is often explained by reference to machines. A machine is not a source of energy, and does not store energy, so machine efficiency refers to the amount of energy dissipated through its operation. A machine runs at maximum efficiency when its output of energy is only slightly less than the input. Of course, it is exactly this kind of definition that critical management scholars have argued is not applicable to organisations.[2] Running a hospital, for instance, ought not, they suggest, be subject to simple input–output measures, as neither input (sick patients) nor output (well patients) are measurable in the way that energy is. But the notion of efficiency as minimal waste reduction is, this chapter suggests, still useful.

In public policy, the notion of efficiency is almost always sutured to that of effectiveness. Effectiveness (addressed in Chapters 6 and 7) is taken to be the achievement of designated outputs and outcomes. Effectiveness measures how well the desired outcomes are achieved, while efficiency addresses the process. While efficiency and effectiveness are usually rhetorically united, the two do not necessarily work together. It is possible for a practice to be effective but in a highly inefficient way. It is also possible to achieve high levels of efficiency and low levels of effectiveness.

It is not surprising that efficiency has been a prime concern of management theorists and managers. F. W. Taylor[3] is generally regarded as a key figure in the history of modern management theory. An engineer, Taylor saw the organisation as a machine which could run more or less efficiently. His concern was to eliminate waste of time, effort and money in order to maximise profit. Taylor's efficiency was to be achieved through a new alignment of manager and management.

Taylor understood inefficiency to result from unacceptable variations in individual decisions made by workers. He reasoned that if workers had the responsibility for deciding what to do each day and to what standard, then there would inevitably be inefficiencies, as some would work slower or less effectively than others. Taylor's answer to this problem was that responsibility for task management should be taken away from workers and given to a manager-planner. The organisation was to be divided up into owners (those who decided what work should be done), heads (those who planned and managed the work) and hands (those who did the work). The planner-manager would be responsible for 'grouping together all of the traditional knowledge which in the past has been possessed by the workmen and then of classifying, tabulating, and reducing this knowledge to rules, laws and formulae which are immensely helpful to the workmen in doing their daily work'.[4]

Codification and documentation was the new 'management science'. Taylor advocated: (1) the use of science (calculation) as the basis for decisions; (2) workforce development that ensured maximum operational efficiency; and (3) the separation of executive decision making from the execution of those decisions.

Taylor's underlying premises – an organisation is rational, the separation of managing and doing is best, scientific calculation must be organised around tasks – runs deep in corporate organisations. And the civil service. The FPP model embodies all of Taylor's three principles. FPP is the latest in a long run of instantiations of the separation of executive decision making from management and execution. In FPP, the purchaser becomes a Taylor-like planner-manager with responsibility for ensuring uniformity, or as close to uniformity as possible, in key aspects of service provision. The provider does what they are told. And Taylor's commitment to rationality and science is manifest in the new civil service steel shell of digital audit and monitoring.

However, there are important differences between businesses which use Taylorist principles and the civil service. Rather than seeking profit as in business, good government prizes value for money.

Value for money and the cost of change

Value for money goals appear regularly in budgetary speeches that condemn debt and promise responsible spending and wise use of public funds – the common wealth. Governments (funders) place high rhetorical stock on planning to minimise waste and maximise value for money. Civil servants classify, tabulate and codify in order to produce regulations which specify what money can be spent on and how it must be spent. They create monitoring systems which show where over-spending and unnecessary expenditure occurs. But when organisational infrastructures are formed and reformed, as is the case with the shift to FPP, value for money calculation becomes more difficult. Change inevitably brings additional costs (money) and often takes time and effort that does not appear in a ledger.

Any financial measurement of major organisational change is likely to miss some opportunity costs. But some can be anticipated. A parallel is helpful here. If a business entrepreneur makes major changes to their existing organisation, they plan for a period of initial loss, calculate risks and target a break-even point. Entrepreneurs driven by belief rather than such forward planning often go under, heavily in debt. But of course, government uses an ongoing supply of taxpayers' money rather than a finite budget. They are also held to account less often, through election cycles not annual shareholder meetings. Nevertheless, because it is using public money intended to support public provision, government is more obligated to risk assessment than free market entrepreneurs. Governments are expected to prohibit profligate spending and misuse of funds. When government executive decisions create inefficiencies they are not, as Taylor argued was crucial, working to maximise benefits.

It is a vulnerable government which hides what it is doing with public money, and/or creates new structures and practices which have high inbuilt waste and/or are very costly to implement. Governments are expected to plan very thoroughly for ambitious change. Such plans might perhaps be available to its investors – that is, the general public. However, I could find no public 20-year plan which shows a total estimated cost for changing a school system run by and through local authorities to a mixed-market system of academies. Nor is there a cumulative account of how much the shift to a contestable school system has cost, year on year. And there is no incremental calculation of how much public money has been shifted to the private sector through contracting out services. In other words it is almost impossible to judge the efficiency, and value for money, of the changes outlined in Chapter 2.

This chapter, however, offers some insights. I look at the 'input' costs of changing the school system through activating an FPP model. I explore academy programme start-up costs, conversion costs and ongoing waste. I suggest questions about value for money and due process arise that from aggregating what we know about the costs of cumulative government changes to schooling. I also ask whether, and if so how, the notion of corruption and corrupted practices might apply to the question of value for money and efficiency.

Start the academy engine

Academies were initially launched by New Labour in 2000. While this story was told in Chapter 2, it is revisited here and retold with an emphasis on costs: those of money, effort and time.

The first academies were in inner cities, and a policy replacement for the more modest Fresh Start scheme in which persistently 'failing' schools were closed and reopened under new leadership and management, often with a new name and investment in new equipment and maintenance. The first academies appeared in the 2000 budget as a specific policy initiative with dedicated expenditure. However, this first intervention failed to leverage significant improvement in schools at the bottom of the league tables. The gap between the top and the bottom of the school league table remained unacceptably large. Labour decided that a more radical approach was needed. A much larger incentive – substantial investment usually in the form of new buildings and equipment, staffing and an enhanced budget for an initial period of time – was to accompany compulsory closure. Labour's budgetary lines then included the costs of school buildings and start-up costs.

Congruent with their Third Way philosophy of joining equity goals to neoliberalist strategies, Labour also sought to extend the involvement of the business sector[5] in school governance. Sponsors were invited to support academies to develop innovative practices in leadership and management, governance, curriculum and pedagogy. Sponsors were asked to provide a cash and in-kind contribution to an academy in exchange for naming rights and a powerful say in the new governing body. Early sponsors were individual business people, churches, the voluntary sector and universities. External 'experts' were contracted to add project management knowledge apparently absent from the civil service; consultants steered all aspects of academy establishment, from the design of the building and focus of the curriculum to the appointment of staff and governing bodies.

Labour's academies were comprehensive, but they could offer a subject specialisation for which they could select up to 10 per cent of students. They had flexibility in staff pay and conditions, and at the outset they began by offering higher headteacher salaries than their local authority counterparts. While academies retained a parent and a staff member on their governing body, they were also able to vary its composition and appointment practices.

The first academies provided two quick political wins for the Blair government. Advocates for the potential of the public sector to both deliver services and create profit for the private sector had a tangible example of 'success', through academy building and project management. At the same time, there was a social justice outcome. Inner-city communities benefited from their new architect-designed and well-equipped schools. Despite concerns about the processes of tendering, costs of consultation and some of the building designs, there was widespread agreement that getting rid of grim Victorian relics in poor repair and interwar and postwar buildings no longer fit for purpose was important in hard-pressed inner-city communities.[6]

But the actual costs of this early academy programme are unclear.

The House of Commons Education and Skills Select Committee (2005)[7] estimated that establishing 200 academies would cost £5 billion. But the first academies appear to have cost more than their counterpart local authority schools, according to the Commons committee, a fact contested by the DfE. In April 2006, the BBC[8] reported that academies were built to similar specifications as other schools but cost more. The DfE rebutted these concerns, saying:

> It is absurd to compare the average cost of a 1,300-pupil academy, built in high-cost, inner-city areas, with the £15m, historic average price tag for a 900-pupil secondary school in a moderate cost area ... You might as well equate the cost of a two-bedroom house in a market town with a four-bedroom house in central London.

The DfE refused to provide precise cost comparisons. Because most of the academies built were through PFI schemes (see later in this chapter), construction costs were commercially sensitive, they said. However, some information was available to the BBC from a 2005 question asked in Parliament: this showed academy costs ranging from £16.5 to £38.2 million each. In 2007, the NAO confirmed that the early academies had cost on average £3 million more than was budgeted for, with the government covering the shortfall, not sponsors.[9] The NAO also reported that the DfE provided each academy with additional start-up funds to cover the costs of establishing a new school: this averaged £1.6 million across the first 12 academies.

Early on in the academy programme, it took the combined efforts of media, Parliament and an arms-length statutory body to come somewhere close to getting information about actual costs. This difficulty in getting accurate financial information was to become a familiar pattern.

Sponsors for Labour's academies were also less forthcoming than initially envisaged. In 2006, the government required each sponsor to pay into an endowment fund which their academy could draw on for running costs. Also in 2006, the BBC[10] reported that the biggest total percentage contribution by an academy sponsor in 2005 was 14 per cent and the smallest 6 per cent; this contribution was to be paid over the lifetime of building costs rather than as a one-off payment. In 2009 *The Guardian* reported[11] that 13 of the then 90 academies had seen none of their sponsor's cash. Again reporting from a question in Parliament, *The Guardian* claimed that sponsors had only paid £98.1 million, or two thirds, of the £145 million they had pledged. By 2011 the government had abandoned its requirement for sponsors to make any cash contributions at all.

The 2009 *Guardian* report focused particularly on the United Learning Trust (ULT), a Christian charity, as an example of the way that academic expenditure was managed. The ULT, it said, had contributed only half of its promised £20 million to match the government expenditure of £300 million on 12 schools. *The Guardian* revealed that the ULT had also been banned from taking on more academies until the standards in its existing schools improved.[12] But, using documents at that time available on the DfE website (now removed), *The Guardian* claimed that the government had also entered into side agreements to allow the sponsor ULT to continue to support its projected 17 schools. Box 4.1 shows an extract from *The Guardian* report that indicates the ways in which initial start-up plans and cost estimates apparently blew out.

Box 4.1: ULT academy financial blowout

For the Manchester academy, the 'side agreement' between the then education secretary, Charles Clarke, and the company set up by the ULT to run the school, says: 'The secretary of state recognises that the company is not able to pay its full contribution during the period when capital costs will be incurred'.

Therefore, it says, the government will pay an additional amount of £1,503,572 less some professional fees and any sponsorship contributions which the ULT had received from third parties. This money was to be taken back by the government through an annual reduction in the cash the academy received in future for its core budget. The ULT would not incur interest on this loan.

Similar arrangements were made for Northampton academy and academies in Salford, Paddington, west London, and Swindon, for which the government agreed to meet all of the ULT's sponsorship commitment in the short term.

In October 2005, this was extended through a 'master side agreement' between the government and the ULT, relating to future ULT academies.

In the meantime, the government had also reduced the amount it required the ULT to commit to the sponsorship of academies from £2m to £1.5m each. But for six ULT academies listed in the parliamentary answer, the commitment appears even weaker than this: the company running each school must only make 'reasonable endeavours' to raise the sponsorship originally pledged.

The Guardian headlined one[13] of its reports on ULT, 'Are academies just a ludicrously expensive con-trick?', referring to academies' lack of headway made against standards, the rationale for the academies initiative and the justification for expenditure. Questioning whether academies are a 'ludicrous expense' and poor value for money also began early.[14]

Labour's goal was 400 academies by 2010. Their aim was not simply to introduce further competition into school provision, but most importantly to improve schooling for the most vulnerable. However, the Coalition saw things differently; they had their eyes on a full FPP model and wanted to move from a quasi-market to a fully competitive model. And they wanted to move quickly. When the Conservative/Liberal Democrat Coalition won office in 2010 there were only 203 academies, with a further 100 planned to open. The Coalition not only endorsed the academy programme, but also decided to accelerate its progress as well as reduce costs. Despite lacking robust evidence that academies were effective, let alone an efficient way to run a school system, in July 2010 the government introduced legislation that made it possible for any school to convert to academy status. It also decided to introduce more variation into the system through new school types: free schools, university technology colleges and studio schools.

The Coalition's 2011 Academies report to Parliament claimed that 59 per cent of secondary schools either were, or were on their way, to becoming academies.[15] While there was a detailed breakdown of test and exam results overall and by population group, *no* detailed costing of this shift was provided in the report.

Effectiveness was promoted as the key criterion for academic expansion, not efficiency or value for money.

The costs of conversion

The Coalition government established some ground rules for any school wishing to become an academy. Schools that were good or outstanding could convert to become a stand-alone academy. Schools which did not have a good inspection grade could also convert, but were required to join an existing academy trust in order to get the support they needed to improve.

Early 'converters' received generous start-up allowances. An online 'ready reckoner'[16] allowed schools to calculate how much better off they would be in the short term as an academy. The conversion windfall was a major incentive for schools to take the plunge. A 2011 Association of School and College Leaders (ASCL) survey[17] of 1,471 of its members showed that nearly half had already converted and three quarters of this number were driven by the belief that their school would be financially better off. Heads were also attracted by the promise of freedom from the bureaucratic imposts of local authorities. Some saw additional funds as the way to save jobs while others did not want to be the last local authority school left standing.

Despite the Secretary of State for Education, Michael Gove, telling schools that initial start-up funds were not permanent, and that they would not always be on offer, schools were disappointed when they were withdrawn. In a piece entitled 'No money in academy status these days', *The Guardian* reported in 2012[18] that part of the reason for loss of start-up funds appeared to be changes in the way that local authorities calculated their costs; the amount passed on to schools to buy back local authority (or competitor) services was reduced. According to the *Guardian* report, the funding gap between academies and local authority schools was decreasing. The funding cut also meant that some academies were going into deficit – the DfE denied there was a funding shortfall, but did acknowledge that the central funding system needed improvement.

There were also some accounting errors made early in the conversion process. The *Financial Times* (2011) reported that:

overfunding was worth more than £100,000 over a full year for a 1,000-pupil secondary school in 74 of the 150 boroughs in 2010–11. In 28 local authorities, the error was more than £200,000. In 10 boroughs, the expected potential benefit of conversion was greater than £300,000 a year. In June, Mr Gibb also said the errors led to 'academies getting too much, or indeed too little, funding'. But underpayment worth more than £50,000 a year to 1,000-pupil schools affected schools in only three boroughs. Overpayments on that scale applied in 112 local authorities.[19]

The Opposition was quick to note the mistakes made, and the potential for them to be continued by a Coalition government guarantee to smooth over any bumps in funding decreases. The *Financial Times* reported that the shadow education secretary demanded that Michael Gove apologise to the House of Commons 'for squandering taxpayers' money' – an illustration both of funder politicians made responsible for purchaser civil service mistakes and the political mileage to be made out of inefficiency.

Over time, funding and accountabilities for academy converters changed. These progressive changes have produced considerable disparity, and arguably inequity, across the country, as fiscal changes are never retrospective. The House of Commons Public Accounts Committee (PAC) reported in 2018[20] that,

> Between April 2010 and December 2017, the Department spent an estimated £745 million on the one-off transitional costs of converting schools to academies. Spending in 2016–17 was £81 million. Schools converting without a sponsor receive a flat-rate grant of £25,000 to help them pay for costs including legal fees, new systems, and finance and administration costs. Legal fees typically represent the largest share of these costs. The costs that schools actually incur vary. The Department told us that it believes that the £25,000 grant is not sufficient to

cover all costs for the average school, but that it wants to incentivise schools to complete the conversion process as cost-effectively as possible. Academy trusts that sponsor underperforming schools receive much larger conversion grants.[21]

The exact details of such larger conversion grants are not easily or readily obtained. However, 'incentivisation' cost issues go beyond these sums. There are hidden costs to conversion. Local authorities must support their maintained schools wishing to convert. Schools are now variously charged for this local authority support; *Schools Week* reported in September 2018[22] that schools had 'shelled out' some £3.8 million to local authorities in conversion costs over the last five years. These 'penalty payments' ranged from a few hundred pounds to £40,000, according to the response to a Freedom of Information (FoI) request sent to local authorities. These school costs are indicative of the marketised payment-for-services approach that all local authorities now use.

There is also the matter of schools in deficit. When the Conservative government announced its intention to convert all schools to academies, the Local Government Association argued that this would cost the council taxpayer £320 million.[23] This was not simply the cost of conversion per se, but also clearing school debts. While central government can choose to repay the local authority for expenditure on converter schools and recover the sum from the new academy, this is not the case for sponsored academies, where debt always remains with the local authority.[24] Local authorities generally do also retain any accumulated debts of their converting schools, and in some cases this is a considerable sum. In June 2019, one local authority went as far as trying to stop a trust taking over a school on the grounds that it would create a trust monopoly in the town; the school in question also had a debt of £2.3 million which would revert to the local authority.[25]

In most cases government sees converter school debt as a problem arising from local authority mismanagement:[26] 'it is a local authority's responsibility to ensure that a school is managed correctly and the local authority has the power to intervene where it has concerns over the financial management of maintained schools'. In other words, if the local authority caused the problem by failing to intervene in school mismanagement, then it should bear the consequences. Conversely, converter school surpluses are treated as the result of good school (not local authority) management and they are generally carried into the new academy. This practice means that some converters start off with significant inherited wealth – a greater bank balance than others. The geography of conversion ledger imbalances and any connections with ongoing financial difficulties (see Chapter 5) is yet to be mapped and calculated.

Compulsory conversion can also take a long time. Delay produces costs of a different kind. The *Times Educational Supplement* reported in March 2018[27] that two primary schools were to be closed as no MAT was prepared to take them on. In January 2018, *The Guardian* reported[28] that a primary school in special measures and subject to a compulsory academisation order had waited two years for a sponsor. The school's buildings were due for demolition and replacement under the previous Labour government, but funding disappeared when the Coalition came to power in 2010. The report described 'mould on the ceiling, smelly toilets, chipped paintwork, overheated and stuffy classrooms and chilly and unwelcoming corridors'. Morale at the school was 'rock bottom' with the head reporting feeling unwanted, 'criminalised' by the experience and unable to provide a satisfactory explanation to parents for the government's inaction and about the school's future. This may be an extreme case, but the uncertainty surrounding a school waiting for a sponsor almost always produces further decline – community confusion, fewer enrolments, premature staff departures and loss of enrolment-tied income are costs which are hard to measure.

A 25 September 2015 report from *BBC News*[29] claimed that responses to an FoI request sent to all local authorities in England showed that some £32.5 million had been paid out in academy conversion costs since 2010. The report stated that 'education chiefs in Birmingham' had refused to write off £1.3 million owed by converting academies, worried that their education budget would run out. A Birmingham City Council spokesperson is quoted as saying that the policy was unfair as all children in the authority suffered when budgets were strained by the costs of conversion. The Isle of Wight council agreed, saying that 'other schools missed out when £1.4 million was paid for a school to become an academy'. The NAO estimated, based on averages, that in 2016–17 the cost to local authorities of deficits from schools that were directed to convert with a sponsor was approximately £7.8 million.[30]

As well as the exact sums involved, the question of due process also arises from these kinds of reports. While clear guidelines on conversion do exist, it seems that what actually happens can and does vary in part because of location and different histories. Converter academies and their local authorities are not given a clean slate, nor have they all received the same financial incentives. In 2018 the NAO expressed concern about the ways in which conversions were managed. Although the DfE improved its scrutiny of financial health of converter academy proposals, the NAO reported that in 2017:

> in designing and implementing the conversion process, the Department has focused on supporting large numbers of schools to convert, rather than allowing only the strongest applications to proceed. Of 2,173 applications from schools to convert without a sponsor between September 2014 and August 2017, regional schools commissioners approved 1,964 (90.4%), deferred 196 (9.0%) and rejected just 13 (0.6%).[31]

In other words, increasing the number of academies was a priority, but efficiency and value for money was not. A telling quotation, highlighted in the NAO press release[32] and thus clearly intended as a headline, was this statement from the NAO chief Amyas Morse:

> It is unclear how feasible it will be for the Department to continue converting large numbers of schools to academies. There is extensive variation across the country, leaving many local authorities with responsibility largely for primary schools. To cut

through this complexity, the Department needs to set out its vision and clarify how it sees academies, maintained schools and local authorities working together to create a coherent and effective school system for children across all parts of the country.

These are the words of a civil servant committed to frank advice about efficiency and the importance of planning and risk management. There are echoes in his words of both Webb's concern about muddle and Taylor's concerns with the science of good planning.

But these concerns – a lack of long-term forward planning, the existence of some procedures and rules which change over time and aren't always followed – reappear in relation to the rebrokerage of academies. A pattern is emerging.

Ongoing risks

Whenever there are ongoing costs which take funding away from core business – the raison d'être of change – there is an efficiency concern.

There are very considerable core business costs in a national education system. There is always, in any service involving people and plant, a given set of predictable ongoing expenses. There are salary costs, people need holiday and sick leave, and they get appointed, promoted, trained and occasionally made redundant. Equipment needs replacing, buildings must be maintained and occasionally new ones need to be built. In a school, wages and wage-associated costs form a substantial part of their budgets too, as they should. The costs of building maintenance, equipment and utilities are smaller but significant. The national education budget also bears the costs of inspection and regulation, as well as forward planning via research and development.

But the current academised school system, now operating in a cost-cutting environment, has new inbuilt and ongoing expenses – new FPP budget lines it didn't have under the former local authority-based system. These arise directly from the ways in which purchasing has been understood and implemented.

Here I discuss two new costs which undermine efficiency: (1) rebrokerage of academies and (2) PFIs.

Rebrokerage

Brokered schools are 'failing' local authority schools which are legally compelled to become academies. Rebrokered schools are already academies and are typically of three types:

- academy schools that belong to a failed trust (see Chapter 5);
- stand-alone academies that are struggling and thus perceived to be in need of the guidance of a sponsor;
- individual academy schools within an existing MAT that are deemed to be better off in a new trust as the existing one isn't doing the job required.

Rebrokering involves finding a new sponsor for a school or set of schools. Official statistics[33] report that 628 schools moved trusts between 2013–14 and 2017–18, representing an increase in rebrokering, from 0.5 per cent to 3.3 per cent of all open academies. Of these movers, 185 received additional funding totalling £22,892,700. But there was a 12 per cent reduction in funding granted for rebrokerage from 2016–17 to 2017–18. Of the 255 academies that moved in 2017–18 only 49 were given additional funding: 206 received no additional money.

The government spreadsheet[34] for the 2017–18 financial year reports that over two thirds of the 255 trust moves were initiated by the trusts themselves; 20 schools were closed, and 61 were moved after an intervention, usually a poor Ofsted judgment. The spreadsheet does not say, but we might assume, that some of these 61 required rebrokerage. The figure of 49 listed as in receipt of additional funding (no actual sums are given) indicates where funding was given for rebrokerage.

Rebrokerage of a 'failing' school is not an easy matter. A 'failed' school is not necessarily attractive to a new sponsor. By definition it has test and/or exam results as well as inspection grades that are persistently below par. It may also have a poor reputation and falling rolls. Many 'failed' schools also have debts and/or significant staffing issues such as high staff turnover or leadership vacancies. Any MAT considering taking on a school in such circumstances is likely to take an actuarial stance – they calculate the risk of taking on both a cost (support required) and a risk (image and overall performance). Sometimes of course a sense of moral responsibility prevails, and/or there may be a logic to taking a school over – it is in the same geographical area, it is a feeder school, it has the potential to offer a new specialisation and/or complementary curriculum.

Rebrokerage never means returning an academy to its local authority. Once an academy, always an academy. Any local authorities wishing to take on 'failing academies' cannot do so unless they establish an arms-length legally constituted MAT. This ruling is a matter of some concern to local authorities and their peak association who insist that they could and did do a better job than some of the current MATs. Local authorities are, however, expected to bear the costs of running repairs to buildings, replacement of equipment and anything else deemed necessary to keep an academy waiting for a new sponsor operational.

Media have taken a keen interest in rebrokerage numbers and costs. *Schools Week* has attempted to monitor and calculate the number and costs of rebrokerage: it suggested in 2017 that more than 100 academies are rebrokered each year, and that this has cost up to £30 million in sweeteners, clearing deficit budgets and funding for improvements.[35] In February 2018, *The Guardian* quoted a DfE spokesperson as unable to say how many 'orphan schools' (schools waiting rebrokerage) there were.[36] *The Observer*[37] tackled the problem in July 2018, suggesting systemic reasons for the number of schools requiring rebrokerage: these included poor financial controls over school spending (see Chapter 5) and a lax academy approval process.

In May 2017, *Schools Week*[38] claimed that leaked emails showed that the academies minister had asked the DfE to present figures in a way that might obscure high rebrokerage costs. The Local Schools Network[39] noted that a subsequent DfE Annual Report[40] combined conversion and rebrokerage costs together, making it difficult to disentangle the two. And in September 2017 *Schools Week* reported that the DfE did not publish all of the costs associated with the transfer of individual schools (see Box 4.2).

Box 4.2. Costs of rebrokerage

The true cost of transferring academies between trusts is likely much higher than the £7.1 million figure claimed by the Department for Education last week – because many payments were simply left out. The transfer market for schools is expanding; the figures showed that 165 schools were passed from one academy trust to another last year. By comparison, just 15 were moved in 2013–14. The DfE claimed that these 165 academies received funding totalling £6.2 million, up from £4.2 the year before, with another £900,000 spent in legacy payments. But campaigners have accused the department of massaging the figures, as they don't include costs relating to redundancies or deficit payments which take place when a school in financial difficulties is taken over. Also missed were capital costs, such as ICT hardware or building works, as were payments resulting from so-called 'diseconomies of scale', for instance when a school is in an area on its own or has a small population.[41]

In July 2019, *Schools Week* again noted the DfE failure to report all costs associated with academy transfer.[42] Reporting on the latest DfE figures, showing 307 academies moving to a new trust in 2018–19 – an increase of 3.3 per cent on the previous year – its headline point was that this was a 'record number'. While the DfE spent some £31 million since 2013 on rebrokerage, the total of 2018–19 grant funding had decreased. But, *Schools Week* said, this figure excluded 'deficit funding, statutory repayments, capital costs and diseconomies of scale'.

Nor does the DfE comprehensively and regularly report the range of times taken for and associated costs of rebrokerage. As in conversion, waiting for a new sponsor creates problems for the school concerned. In February 2017, *The Guardian* reported that there were 60 orphan schools for whom no sponsors could be found because of their debt and level of problems.[43] An FoI request by the *Times Educational Supplement* in October 2017 suggests there were 42 schools that had been without a sponsor for over a year.[44] In September 2018, *Schools Week* reported on one school which had been waiting for a new sponsor for 20 months.[45] It initially belonged to a MAT which collapsed (see Chapter 5) and was £1.3 million in deficit. *Schools Week* reported a DfE spokesperson as saying that the new MAT 'is carefully liaising with the school ahead of transfer to ensure minimal disruption for both staff and pupils'. That's 20 months of careful negotiation. An Ofsted report praised the work of leaders and staff in ensuring that students were making good progress. This is indeed high praise, given the insecurity and anger that can result from not knowing what will happen in rebrokerage.

Key to efficiency concerns is the fact that rebrokering seems to now be a permanent fixture of the organisational infrastructure. Rather than a fixed stage of change/development, instability is hardwired into the school system. As long as some schools are judged below average in terms of attainment, their providers, be they local authorities or academies, can also be seen as inadequate sponsors. In such cases, rebrokering has to occur – with its concomitant waiting times, uncertainty, local authority costs and case-by-case national government financial sweeteners.

A school system dependent on rebrokerage is an inherent risk as well as being inefficient. Anticipating unpredictable numbers of schools needing rebrokerage creates problems for planning as well as having potentially serious consequences for budget overspends. But exactly the same kind of constitutive costs and risks can be seen in PFI projects.

PFIs

Together with selling off and contracting out, the state has made extensive use of PFIs to divest itself of the costs of providing public services. Alternatively known as PPPs – public–private partnerships – the PFI is a way for the government of the day to avoid capital costs on buildings and plant. PFIs are also said to offer access to project management skills the civil service lacks, as well as the security of dealing with only one supplier, not several contractors and subcontractors.

PFIs follow standard purchaser-provider processes. When government determines that a new school building is required, it prepares a specification, allocates a budget and puts the job out to tender. There may be some sweeteners on offer, such as tax relief or cheap energy supply for a period of time, in order to attract the substantial initial cash outlay. The work of the successful bidder is monitored by the purchaser. The building is 'owned' by the private provider and leased back by the state. As landlord, the private provider can specify not only how much is to be paid in rent, but also how the building can and cannot be used. Any 'rent plus' agreements can include using specific linked contractors, for example for maintenance, catering and cleaning (the initial approach taken in the UK).

There are trenchant critiques of the PFI approach.[46] A 2011 House of Commons Treasury Select Committee report[47] noted the potential benefits of PFIs, including allocation of risks to bidders, achieving cost efficiencies, potential to deliver innovation and timely delivery. Risks included the high costs of finance, reduced contract flexibility because of the long pay-back time, high termination costs and the ultimate risk responsibility of the public sector. But the select committee bluntly stated that PFIs offered poor overall value for money. Costs to government were greater than if government had simply borrowed the money itself. The committee's conclusions were damning:

> Evidence we have seen suggests that the high cost of finance in PFI has not been offset by operational efficiencies. Much more robust criteria governing the use of PFI are needed. ... In our view PFI is only likely to be suitable where the risks associated with future demand and usage of the asset can be efficiently transferred to the private sector. Owing to the current high cost of project finance and other problems related to PFI we have serious doubts about such widespread use of PFI. There are certain circumstances where PFI is likely to be particularly unsuitable, for example, where the future demand and usage of an asset is very uncertain and where it would be inefficient to transfer the related risks to the private sector.
>
> We believe that a financial model that routinely finds in favour of the PFI route, after the significant increases in finance costs in the wake of the financial

crisis, is unlikely to be fundamentally sound. The Treasury should seek to ensure that all assumptions ... that favour PFI are based on objective and high quality evidence.[48]

In response to these concerns, the government instituted a review of the PFI process which led to trials of a new approach called PF2. PF2 changes the pure PFI model in some important ways – the government becomes a minority equity investor in any new project. Treasury manages the equity investment, not the purchasing department. Bidders are required to develop secure long-term financing plans. 'Soft services' (rent plus) such as cleaning and catering as well as some aspects of maintenance are no longer to be included. The North West Priority School Building Programme is the largest of the trial PF2 schemes and is expected to produce 10–12.4 per cent equity return for the government.

However, the original PFI schemes and costs remain. In January 2018 the NAO[49] reported the good news that over 90 per cent of government capital investments were public and that the use of PFI initiatives had been reduced since the financial collapse of 2008. The bad news was that 'there are currently over 700 operational PFI and PF2 deals, with a capital value of around £60 billion. Annual charges for these deals amounted to £10.3 billion in 2016–17. Even if no new deals are entered into, future charges which continue until the 2040s amount to £199 billion.'[50]

What's more, PFI costs are not stable but are affected by inflation. In October 2019, *The Scotsman*[51] reported that the total cost of the UK's PFI initiatives had risen by an unanticipated £4 billion since they were signed off. This was because PFI payments were pegged to the retail price index, a flawed measure according to the governor of the Bank of England. This weakness is acknowledged by government.[52]

The NAO reported other inefficiencies too, most particularly a lack of expertise in the civil service to identify and manage savings accrued from PFI projects. The NAO noted that even though purchasers hired a variety of consultants to find the missing savings, an opportunity was missed through lack of coordination to provide lessons across the civil service. The NAO also observed that PFI debt is recorded off-balance in national accounts and does not appear in UK debt statistics. Nor does it count as an upfront cost in departmental capital budgets. This style of national account management runs counter to European statistical guidelines. It also makes any transparent calculation of value for money very difficult.

But perhaps the most damning conclusions from the NAO was that 'there is still a lack of data available on the benefits of private finance procurement'.[53] In other words, PFI was and is driven by belief rather than evidence. These are words to make any responsible senior civil servant extremely worried. But in early 2018 the Conservative government decided to scale up its trial of PF2.

Schools which have been built through PFI arrangements provide extraordinary stories of the scheme's costs and prohibitions. Some of these stories make it into the media. In March 2016 *The Telegraph*[54] carried a story of a Liverpool PFI new school which had failed to attract sufficient pupils, had been closed but continued to cost £12,000 a day. Liverpool City Council would have to find £25 million to buy itself out of the PFI deal. And a PFI school survey by the *Times Educational Supplement* (21 April 2017) revealed the extent of PFI life cycle costs (see Box 4.3).

Box 4.3: Life cycle costs

One teacher, who asks not to be named, cites an example: 'We are a PFI school with an annual PFI bill of £132,478. We have been paying £88 [a year] for the installation of a new sink for 14 years now. With nine years left on the PFI contact, that sink will cost £2,024'. At Bristol Metropolitan Academy, a single blind for a room will end up costing £8,154 under PFI. Oasis Academy Brislington, also in the Bristol area, will pay £2,211 for an external water tap over the course of a contract.

For some schools, even getting the gates open to allow children to use the toilet before a school trip is a costly exercise. One secondary in Oldham – Newman RC College – was charged £48 after security opened the school to allow pupils to visit the lavatory. The same school had to pay more than £400 for caretakers to fit some notice boards.

Such charges are not unusual. Tim Gilson, the head at Malmesbury School, in Wiltshire, said: 'We had some benching put in the canteen, just along one wall, about 20 yards. We have to pay about £40 a month for the facilities management cost of that bench, on top of the cost of putting that bench in and all the materials. It's a monthly charge that continues for the length of the contract'. With 13 years left on his school's PFI contract, the secondary will be charged £6,240 just for the management of the bench.[55]

The worst PFI stories are of course those where there has been mismanagement and/or corruption during the development of the project. It is impossible to ignore the Scottish case of a wall collapsing at a new Edinburgh primary school, funded through a PFI scheme. Seventeen further schools built under the same PFI scheme were closed for inspection, but only one other was found to have the same building fault. An independent report[56] laid the blame for the poor quality building on Edinburgh City Council, the purchaser, which had 'failed to provide adequate supervision or scrutiny of the contractors and sub-contractors'.[57] This is an instance where, as the NAO report[58] suggests, the final risk of PFI falls on the public purchaser not the private provider.

Similar stories emanate from other locations. Bruce Baker runs a website – School Finance 101 – specifically dedicated to tracking public and private school funding in the US. One blog post entitled 'We bought it twice but we still don't own it'[59] maps the ways in which publicly funded charter schools purchasing publicly owned facilities adds up to 'patently stupid public policy'. Diane Ravitch also follows charter schools and their real estate deals. She reported recently that Andre Agassi profited from charter school real estate deals – she claims that Agassi bought a building in the Bronx for US$4.3 million which, in a related party transaction (RPT) (see Chapter 5), he sold three years later to his charter school chain for $24 million.[60] Kenneth Saltman argues that Agassi's behaviour demonstrates that, far from operating in an unfettered market, FPP allows a profit-making enterprise to rely on and benefit from business-friendly government regulation, laws and tax incentives.[61] While this kind of RPT would be considered illegal in England, the point made by Saltman that private sector profit depends largely on public policy and public money is pertinent.

Local authorities are beginning to swing away from PFI and other contracted-out arrangements. On 29 May 2019, *The Guardian* reported that councils are bringing many services back in-house.[62] Concerned by the catalogue of failure of contracted services and their expense, local authorities are looking for a pragmatic way to cut costs and improve quality. More widely, there are emerging public and think tank discussions about alternative funding models, where government enters into partnership with social investment bodies to create collective ownership of public assets.[63] However, the costs of earlier projects remains.

The ongoing cost of expertise

At points during this chapter the use and/or cost of consultants has been mentioned – for instance, either as managers of the purchasing function or as advisers to the funder. Consultancy is a significant ongoing expense that is built into the FPP model. The FPP operates on a 'core plus' staffing model for both purchasers and providers. It is seen as uneconomic for purchasers to employ permanent staff with expertise that is not needed all the time. They 'buy in' supplementary skills and knowledge when needed. The purchaser use of consultants is also, as is the use of consultants by providers, a means of creating and supporting a market of experts. FPP promotes a narrative that hiring in experts is the best way to save money and to ensure that the civil service, known since early Victorian times to be wanting in expertise (Chapter 3), has access to the latest and best in world-leading knowledge and a global 'talent pool'. Buying in experts at the level of purchaser also means that the funder – the relevant minister – can distance themselves from advice if they desire.

But consultants do not come cheap. Building Schools for the Future, the Labour scheme which provided accommodation for the first academies (see earlier in this chapter) cost local authorities some £4 million on average in upfront costs for design, lawyers and consultants, according to official statistics.[64] A later 2018 DfE Annual Report stated that spending on consultants in 2016–17 amounted to £12.1 million, and £14.6 million in 2017–18.[65] The breakdown of these amounts is not provided, although assurances that procurement was carried out according to Cabinet Office procedures is. Consultancy. uk reported in September 2018 that spending on education consultancy was 196 per cent higher in 2016–17 than in 2002–3. With perhaps surprising candour, consultancy.uk reported that while 'spending on education support staff rose by 138 per cent over the same period, and spending on back office functions was 105 per cent, spending on teachers rose by a mere 17 per cent in real-terms'. The report also queried how much the expenditure on consultants would ultimately benefit students.[66]

Doubts about consultants and their value for money are borne out by researchers. For example, Kirkpatrick and colleagues[67] conducted a four-year study of NHS acute care trusts and found 'a significantly positive relationship between consulting expenditure and organisational *inefficiency*'.[68] Gunter and Mills examined the range of people who are consultants, their networks and practices, concluding that an effect of consultants in schools is to sideline teachers' professional knowledge in favour of instrumental approaches which can be packaged and sold in the absence of local authority support and quality control.[69]

How then are schools (providers) to know which consultants to use? The DfE Schools Commercial Team currently offers a review of 'deals'. It claims that deals are 'assessed for compliance with procurement regulations, ease of use, suitability and value for money'. As of May 2019, it recommended one professional consultancy service which specialised in the procurement of training, construction, ICT and consultancy, two facilities consultancies and one for printing. Perhaps there are no 'deals' to be done on curriculum, pedagogy or assessment consultants.

Patterns and questions

Before moving on, it is worth noting the pattern evidenced in this chapter: policy which is not thoroughly costed and has inbuilt inefficiencies, and the difficulty of getting easy access to comprehensive information. This is a pattern not confined to education. The alternative web-based news site Byline News attributes £3.5 billion lost in failed schemes in the Departments of Employment and then Transport, under the rule of Tory minister, Chris Grayling.[70] Concerns about waste and value for money associated with the FPP organisational structure run wider than schools.

It also worth noting the government response to current school financial difficulties. A team of consultants (School Resources Management Advisers, SRMA) has been appointed, at an apparent cost of £2.3 million,[71] to offer advice to schools on where and how to trim their budgets.[72] Schools have been told that if they apply for funding for repairs to unsafe buildings they will have to agree to a visit from the SRMA.[73] But central concern with schools being wasteful does not stop there. The *Times Educational Supplement* reported in November 2018[74] that Lord Agnew, the then academies minister who bet schools a bottle of champagne that he could find savings in their budgets,[75] took a very hands-on approach to school spending. The *Times Educational Supplement* elaborated:

> For months now, I've been hearing stories of how Agnew enjoys nothing more than sitting in his large DfE office going through MAT trustee board minutes and budgets, then demanding to see whoever was in charge. He also likes to hold very regular meetings with groups of MAT CEOs. … One Westminster insider put it like this: 'He wants to be chair of the board for every MAT in the country'.

This description is not of a control system (see Chapter 5) so much as one which is both commanding and controlling. As the *Times Educational Supplement* put it, 'It is not without irony that Agnew, a Conservative politician and long-term Michael Gove supporter, appears to be so unenthusiastic about the autonomy that academies were supposed to enjoy as a result of years of Conservative reform.' Schools being told to watch their photocopying expenditure may find this form of control a bitter irony indeed. Given the costs of rebrokerage, public–private financing and consultancy now built into the system Agnew presided over, they might be forgiven for asking whether the focus on school budgets is a distraction from the total budgetary blowout of current government policies.

Finally, it is important to consider whether the kind of inbuilt inefficiencies detailed in this chapter constitute a form of state corruption. While there are no personal corrupt activities, it is arguably a dubious moral undertaking, and a dereliction of public duty, to waste large sums of public money and to hide the extent of it. The responsibility for this lies directly with the elected governments who advocated and instituted FPP policies. However, the existence of the ongoing debt, and its attendant risk, suggests a less than healthy system.

But the efficiency story does not stop here. Chapter 5 examines even more inefficiencies in risky policy undertakings.

.

5

Market mentalities
and malpractices

Academy founder facing jail over fraud
Daily Mail, 1 August 2016

Accounts reveal shocking financial mismanagement
at defunct academy trust
Schools Week, 7 June 2017

Collapsing academy trust 'asset stripped' its schools
of millions
The Guardian, 21 October 2017

One in three academy trusts reviews pay after
government warning
Schools Week, 24 January 2019

Academy chain boss now earning £210,000
despite crackdown on high salaries
The Independent, 4 February 2019

Control systems are a critical aspect of management. Control
systems are intended to produce consistency in the key
functions of an organisation, and they thus enhance efficiency
and effectiveness. Control is a fundamental underpinning
of any scientific approach to management. Control systems
are generally applied to strategic thinking and planning,
management and operations. Most organisations set objectives

and standards and evaluate performance against them. They have mechanisms to manage ongoing activities to ensure that they stay within set parameters. In the contemporary civil service, internal regulatory controls are used to 'see' risks before they become too damaging, as well as to ensure that the organisation functions at maximum efficiency.

Control of money has always been important in the civil service, as in business. Control systems operate around how much money is spent and who spends it, as well as how it is accounted for. An efficient use of funds is one where there is minimal waste and maximum benefit. The ethos of the civil service (see Chapter 3) is (or should be) that spending wisely in the long-term public interest is also a moral duty.

While there are critiques of the rationalist and causal approach embedded in control systems, it is not unhelpful to use them to evaluate an organisation which uses them. How well does the organisation do in its own terms? This chapter addresses the question of control, again focusing on money. I examine some of the financial practices and control systems that are in place to manage a marketised school system. I ask how rational these practices actually are. The chapter examines efficiencies of scale and salaries for seniors leaders and their staff. It then focuses on mismanagement, unethical behaviours (some of which are criminal and some of which might be better described as corrupted), RPTs, management of assets and asset stripping and fraud.

Businesslike school practices

Chapter 4 argued that the Conservative policy goal of wholescale academisation was the way to achieve a fully competitive school provision. A system of MATs signals the end of a quasi-market constructed through parent choice and league tables. However, the current school system is a 'mixed economy' with some schools in local authority control, together with stand-alone academies, as well as MATs. One of the arguments in favour of a uniform system of academies is efficiency.

Self-managing stand-alone schools and small academy trusts are not particularly cost efficient. While they have their own budgets and can decide priorities for spending, they have few economies of scale. Solo academies have freedom with salaries but they still have to buy in services, such as psychological supports for students and school improvement and professional development. These are services that local authorities once automatically provided for their schools, evening out costs over schools with varying needs. While academies are given funds redirected from central government allocations to the local authority, they are under no obligation to use the local authority provision; they have a range of providers to choose from. Most of the services now provided by companies for back office functions, school improvement and student support are not social enterprises – each expects to make a profit. Public funds that might once have gone into neighbourhood schools now go to private profit margin. Privatised services are also of variable quality, and schools, be they stand alone or in a MAT, have to spend time evaluating what is on offer.[1] Assessing quality is a bigger burden for lone schools and small trusts.

The large MAT, on the other hand, is able to combine the budgets of several schools. Their aggregated purchasing power may mean they get better deals for basic, common supplies and equipment. A MAT, like a local authority, is also able to procure additional necessary services at scale; such additional services procured in bulk might range from supply teachers and special educational services to professional development programmes. However, networks of self-managing local authority schools are also able to work together to procure at scale.[2] There are of course some services which are simply more economical to provide centrally, although until recently the government has been reluctant to consider these. However, a recent decision by the Conservative government to offer a free job advertisement service to schools in order to help them save money is perhaps indicative of a limited move in this direction.

But there are some school services which are simply better if they are not contracted out. Increasing numbers of schools, academies and MATs are, for instance, taking back their school kitchens, seeing school dinners as integral to their social and health education curriculum. Rather than looking for the cheapest meal deal, they want higher-quality catering that they can control. This is perhaps another sign of some rethinking about what constitutes best value for money – is it more important to save money or to educate? There is anecdotal evidence too that some MATs are considering a move away from the cheapest rates to focus on what a school budget might do for a local economy, to support local businesses and provide employment for local families.

And there are other issues that query a simple calculation of MAT efficiency. Like the local authority, the MAT has its own running costs. A MAT centralises some functions across all of its schools. In addition to leadership and business management, many larger MATs employ staff with specific responsibility for targeted areas of school improvement. There is a service charge levied against each constituent school – the MAT administration top-slices school budgets. Without a specific national data collection on top-slicing, it is almost impossible to know whether the MAT top-slice is less than what an individual school would have paid directly for the same services from another provider. There is also an unanswered question about internal customer satisfaction if the central MAT is the monopolistic service provider to its schools: does the central MAT do what schools actually want, need and value? Without such information it is difficult to compare private provider or local authority value for money versus that of MATs.

It is also unclear how big a MAT needs to be in order to achieve economies of scale. In 2017, *Schools Week* reported the then academies minister, Lord Agnew, a former academy trustee and founder, as saying that the 'sweet spot' was somewhere around 20 schools.[3] Speaking to a northern headteachers conference, he offered 5,000 to 10,000 pupils as the ideal. He pointedly noted that the region had 66 MATs with two or fewer schools, and 86 stand-alone academies. Agnew argued that improved efficiencies would offset the loss of autonomy that expansion of MATs meant. While there was no intention to regulate for larger MATs, he said, this was a clear indication of government thinking about efficiency.

However, there are other value for money questions associated with optimum MAT size: these are to do with autonomy, equity, geography and public participation.

Autonomy

As Lord Agnew signalled, there is debate about how much autonomy an individual school in a MAT retains and how much it is subject to a new form of centralisation. There is now research[4] as well as media reports[5] which suggest that MATs have restricted what it is that their constituent schools can do. (This is, of course, not universally the case.)[6] In the name of efficiency some MATs have taken control of individual school budgets and reduced the capacity of site headteachers and middle leaders to make decisions about spending. In the name of improvement, a MAT centre can be highly prescriptive about the curriculum, teaching methods and/or disciplinary processes. In some instances – for example the move by the E-Act trust to take charge of school exclusions in order to reduce them[7] – there is divided opinion about whether executive MAT control is a good thing. In the E-Act instance the divide is between whether the means – reducing school autonomy – justify the ends of inclusion.

Equity

In 2016, *Schools Week* investigated MAT top-slicing and found highly variable practices.[8] Some MATs charged a flat fee, others had needs-based payments in recognition of variable improvement support demands: the CfBT Trust, for example, used Ofsted grades so that outstanding and good schools paid 3 per cent, schools requiring improvement 4 per cent and inadequate schools 5 per cent. *Schools Week* reported that some MATs were accumulating cash reserves so that trustees had some discretionary funds for particular innovations or interventions. While only a few trusts pooled each school grant and then allocated cash to each school, *Schools Week* suggested this would eventually become more popular. They also reported calls for transparency about top-slicing, and some calls for a form of regulatory control over variation between MATs, perhaps through a delineation of a MAT 'core school offer'.

Geography

Critics suggest that some MATs with clusters of schools in areas that are separated by considerable distances lose out on networking and sharing good practice; staff find it difficult to attend common professional development. There are reports that MAT leaders are constantly on the road when MAT commitment to the larger geographical community around each school is reduced; they are thus actually less available and visible. Defenders of MAT geographical 'spread' argue that if large MATs of 20 schools or so are concentrated in a single area then this can become a small monopoly – an instance of 'provider capture' that is very like the local authority the MAT sought to replace.

In 2016 the government issued advice for MATs[9] that Regional Schools Commissioners (RSCs) wanted to avoid the geographic isolation of individual schools and were looking to support MATs with place-based clusters of schools. The DfE also provided a case study of two separate MATs in the same location that worked together to share trustees and professional development, with one of the trusts providing back office functions for both. DfE advice suggests that control of geographical spread is exercised at the RSC (purchaser) decision-making stage – but there is little transparency about such decisions (see next section). There is no control through explicit funder regulation about location and size.

Public participation

A large MAT can reduce the opportunity for local parents to have a say in school policies and operations. Academy legislation replaced elected school governors with trustees selected and appointed for their management experience. Academy trust school governors act only in an advisory capacity to the board of trustees. They are trust committees rather than bodies which hold trustees to account. This change has led to considerable concern about the loss of democratic participation in academy governance. An overall democratic deficit is produced, argue lawyers, journalists and educational professionals.[10]

There is evidence for this concern. A 2018 National Governors Association survey saw:

- 91 per cent of governor respondents saying that academy school-level committees were responsible for monitoring pupil progress and attainment;
- 71 per cent for monitoring key strategic priorities;
- 66 per cent for stakeholder engagement;
- 63 per cent for determining school-level policies;
- 60 per cent for managing the school's budget; and
- 57 per cent for headteacher appraisal.[11]

These are all functions that 100 per cent of a local authority school governing body would carry out. This survey data also suggest that in some cases, general and policy information that school governors/committee members get is less than they would have seen when they were legally in charge.[12] Such moves push parents into the position of consumers rather than decision makers. When local accountability is reduced, so is the capacity of local schools to create 'little democracies' which strengthen horizontal social bonds.[13] As *The Guardian* commented on a 2019 report from the National Governors Association, 'Academy schools risk being rejected by local communities if their management is remote and motivated more by rapid growth than improvement'.[14]

None of these size and scale issues are settled. Debate continues about whether the old local authority system with self-managing maintained schools was more efficient and/or better, or just different from the still-forming academy-based system. But perhaps one of the more contentious places where a businesslike approach has taken hold in both academies and in the local authority sector is in relation to the ways in which leaders are seen and rewarded. Salaries and performance bonuses draw attention to the question of control systems as well as value for money.

Enter CEO

Once the person who ran a school was uniformly called a headteacher. This term replaced the gendered terms headmaster and headmistress only comparatively recently. But now there are also 'chief executive officers' and 'executive headteachers'. These two new titles signify a head who has a line management responsibility for other heads. Heads of multiple schools understandably earn more than they did when they were responsible for only one.

There is little doubt that salaries for senior leaders in schools have escalated rapidly. While most media attention is paid to salaries in the academy sector, local authorities have also match-funded in order to retain heads, particularly those running primary federations. In 2019, Lord Agnew reported in the House of Lords that headteachers in maintained schools are paid an average of £88,000 compared to the £92,000 paid to an academy school head.[15]

Academies are required to report in their accounts the number of staff paid over £60,000, as well as trustees who are paid and how much. The PAC (2018) noted that there were 102 instances of trusts paying salaries in excess of £150,000 with insufficient justification or a link to school performance.[16] It is worth noting that the PAC concern was expressed in moral as well as efficiency and economic terms: money spent on high salaries was money not spent on children's education, and overpayments skewed the market and created unnecessary year-on-year increases and pension contributions. At a time when schools were experiencing budgetary cuts, individual trusts were clearly not being 'sufficiently rigorous' in efficiency measures.

Trustees *are* advised by the DfE not to let executive salaries grow at a faster pace than that of teachers. Academies are, however, exempt from national salary awards. Since 2012 they have been able to employ unqualified or less qualified staff if they deem them suitable. In contrast to the figures on school leaders' salaries, teachers' salaries in academies are lower than their maintained school counterparts – £38,000 (local authority secondary) compared to £36,500 (academy secondary) according to the 2016–17 school workforce census. Senior academy teachers are nearly level pegging with their local authority counterparts, getting £63,700 in maintained schools and £63,600 in academies.[17] The pupil–teacher ratio[18] in maintained secondary schools is 16.4 compared to 16.9

in academies, suggesting that the total teacher salary bill in academies is also less (academies pay less for fewer staff) than in local authority schools. Data on qualifications suggest that local authority maintained secondary schools have only 0.2 per cent of teachers with non-educational qualifications compared to 0.6 per cent in secondary academies. However, there are no data on how these disparities play out geographically, or by academy chain. Recent research also suggests that academies not only pay less for teachers and educational support but also more on back office costs.[19]

Schools Week has pursued the question of salaries for several years. In April 2018 it reported that 92 academy trusts had multiple staff on salaries of £100,000 to £150,000.[20] Of these, 56 trusts had fewer than 10 schools and 11 had one each, the implication being that high salaries were not related to the scale and perhaps complexity of the job. A few academy bosses have begun to refuse annual salary increases,[21] but in March 2019 *Schools Week* reported that 23 academy 'chiefs' still earned more than £200,000.[22]

The highest paid, the Harris Federation (48 schools) head, has a salary package of £550,000.[23] In November 2019, news of high salaries made it into the tabloids – *The Sun* reported four headteachers earning over £200,000, three of whom worked in local authority secondary schools; *The Sun* claimed the majority of heads on six figures were from academy trusts, with the number from local authorities small and stable.[24]

Schools Week has attempted to make some sense of these figures by looking at them as per pupil costs.[25] Their calculation (based on some 200 or so of the highest academy salaries) revealed a range of £521 to £68 per pupil. They also compared school salaries to those in the NHS and to annual turnover. Their conclusion was the average academy CEO salary was less than those paid in the NHS, perhaps because NHS services generally had considerably more turnover. The average academy head salary was also less than that paid in the charity sector.

It is not surprising that academy trustees from the private sector bring with them expectations about the work that leaders do and how it should be rewarded. Business trustees live in the world of personal assistants, glossy foyers and executive training.

They are familiar with corporate practices of performance bonuses as well as salary benefit packages which might begin with a leased car necessary for travel from site to site. The rationale for these arrangements is that if high salaries are not paid, then headteachers will migrate to the private sector. There is, however, little evidence produced for such migration, other than to educational consultancies.

The government is concerned about high salaries. The ESFA has written to academies asking them to justify their levels of pay. An initial letter to 94 trusts produced limited results. In 2019, *The Guardian* reported that fewer than one in four trusts had taken action to curb pay[26] (see Box 5.1).

Box 5.1: *The Guardian* reports on salaries

This week's letter is the fourth from the DfE on the subject. In 2017, the department wrote to trustees of academy trusts running just one school with at least one member of staff earning more than £150,000 a year; in 2018, it wrote to a further 87 multi-academy trusts paying staff more than £150,000; and in February this year, the DfE wrote another letter to 28 trusts, including some with two or more staff earning above £100,000.

Trusts receiving the latest letters will have to provide information on 12 aspects of their pay policies, including a rationale for setting salary levels and evidence that its decisions are in line with the government's guidelines. Those trusts that ignored previous requests have been asked to provide details of 'succession planning for highly-paid staff where trusts intend to reduce the level of salary in future'.

Teaching union leaders said the effort reveals 'how utterly feeble' the government's powers are to moderate academy executive pay, with a recent investigation finding that 23 chain chief executives were paid more than £200,000.

The letter from the ESFA dated 9 May 2019 expressed concerns about high salaries, and reminded trustees that they had an obligation to ensure value for money through processes that were 'transparent, proportionate, reasonable and justifiable'.[27] Trustees were reminded that they needed to take into account:

- the educational performance of the organisation;
- ensuring effective financial performance of the trust and a healthy, balanced budget;
- the number of pupils being educated in the trust and the degree of challenge in the roles of the highest paid.

The language used in the letter is significant. There is a focus on performance (effectiveness) – measurable in the first instance as test, examination and inspection results – and a calculation to be made about numbers and challenge (efficiency). Later, the letter talks about pay being 'defensible relative to the public sector market'. The letter was described as a 'strengthened position' vis-à-vis salaries.

However, it is not clear what leverage the government has in 'successful' academies and MATs other than asking them to report and releasing information about salaries and sites. Just a few days later a *Schools Week* headline read '31 trusts fail to justify pay – but DfE admits it's powerless to act'.[28] If the report is right, then it suggests there are no control systems about salaries, neither through salary banding, nor through purchaser input into trust decision making. We might nevertheless suspect that a trust paying high salaries and asking for debt relief or permission to expand would face demands for a trade-off. This kind of control is of course largely hidden from public view.

It is not hard to whip up outrage about high salaries, even if they are paid to only a minority of heads, particularly in a country in the midst of deep cuts in public expenditure and daily reports of escalating homelessness, child hunger and high-street failure. Educators in particular are acutely aware of the difference between teacher and senior leader pay scales. The average teacher salary is between £25,000 and £36,000 per year, with leading practitioners such as heads of department being paid between £40,000 and £61,000.[29] Teachers in London get an additional location allowance. It was hardly surprising that in early 2017[30] teacher unions began campaigning on the stark and growing gap between heads and classroom teachers.

High salaries are likely to remain an issue for the government. They sit alongside other media reports which also bring considerable public and professional angst, scrutiny and critique.

Financial management and mismanagement

Academies are legal entities, run by registered charities. Academy funding arrangements are a 'purchaser' contract.[31] The DfE 'buys' educational services from the trust and the trust guarantees to 'deliver'. The particular academy curriculum offer is always part of the negotiated funding agreement. MATs enter into supplementary financial agreements for each academy as well as one overall financial agreement. Like local authority maintained schools, academies are funded by annual direct block grants calculated on enrolments; these are allocated by the ESFA. They may receive supplementary high-needs payments, for example for students with special educational needs, and Pupil Premium funding for children in receipt of Free School Meals. Academies may also receive additional funding or in-kind support from personal or corporate sponsors.

Academies are funded for the academic year while maintained schools are funded for the financial year; as noted earlier, academies receive a top-up which allows them to purchase services from the local authority or elsewhere (this is not new funding but funding the local authority no longer gets). Academies may also receive capital funding. While they pay business rates for purchases, they may be refunded for some of these because of their charitable status. They no longer receive top-up insurance funding.[32]

Any trust board is expected to have its own control systems about, *inter alia*: appointment, oversight and performance management of executive leaders and other key staff such as business managers; management of risk appetite, toleration and mitigation; ensuring compliance and propriety in financial matters and value for money; and providing accurate documentation and effective communication to key stakeholders. Trust boards are expected to be transparent, self-regulating and evaluating, and to be clear about delegations and decisions.

Trustees are expected to conform to the seven principles of public life, which emphasise values such as openness and honesty.[33] But these principles are subject to interpretation, as are most definitions of ethics and corruption (see Chapter 1). It is interesting to note that the recent academies minister, Lord Agnew, one of the founders of the Inspiration Trust, was involved in some discussion about potential conflicts of interest. Appointed in 2017, he resigned immediately as chair of the trust, but stayed on as a trustee: he left the trust almost a year later.[34] In November 2018, pointed questions were asked in Parliament[35] about the transparency of the formal statement required of politicians about conflict of interest,[36] and the potential for partisan decision making in relation to particular academy trusts. However, concerns about favouritism, as opposed to those about transparency, may have been alleviated by the DfE's decision in March 2019[37] to consider termination of funding for one Inspiration Trust school after a poor Ofsted grading.

There are regulations about academy control systems. Academies are required, for instance, to publish their audited financial reports annually. Some do not. A 5 March 2018 letter to academies from the newly appointed head of the ESFA, Eileen Miller, reported that for the year 2016–17, 90 per cent of academy accounts returns and 95 per cent of financial statements were submitted on time.[38] Ten per cent equates to about 550 schools that did not submit their accounts by the due date. (We could be forgiven for asking what figure under 100 per cent is an acceptable level of compliance.) Miller informed schools that the ESFA would take a firmer stance on noncompliance. In September 2018, a list of trusts that did not meet deadlines for two or more of their annual financial returns was published.

Some academies in breach of financial guidelines are issued with financial notices to improve. Notices to improve are the result of deficit, failure to report as required, governance and administrative failure to plan, control and make savings. Fiscally failing schools are always put on a short leash by the ESFA; delegations are revoked and all transactions must be ESFA approved. They are usually required to prepare an action plan for improvement which includes repayment of any loans. Notices to improve may also include school-specific requirements such as reconstituting the trust board, recalculating pupil number projections, consideration of joining a MAT and making efficiency savings. In May 2019, the gov.uk website[39] showed that ESFA had issued 42 open notices to improve, the earliest of which dated from August 2014, and 47 closed notices. Included in the notices to improve were three closed academy trusts, perhaps an indication that final investigations are ongoing and time consuming.

The former academies minister and academy trust chair, Lord Agnew, claimed that academies are now much more transparent than local authority schools.[40] However, both media and researchers have expressed concern that, even with timely returns, the level of financial detail required of academy trusts is insufficiently transparent.[41] In early 2019, the ESFA published new guidelines and resources to help academies comply with their contractual agreements. There are now tighter regulations about the timing of returns, and processes that trusts are advised to use in relation to procurement and asset management. Information was updated in the *Academies Financial Handbook* for 2019[42] with a new requirement to self-evaluate.[43] Academies must now send an annual report about internal controls to the ESFA and enhanced guidance about, *inter alia*, providing audited accounts to trustees, processes of approval for some transactions and provision of better public information about financial notices to improve.

It has of course taken some years to get to this point, and the sequence of few controls, schools being caught rule breaking and then increased control represents an after-the-event approach to regulation which might be challenged given the sums of public money involved. It is worth reprising some of the concerns that have led the ESFA to become increasingly focused on the control of finances. These are to do with assets, RPTs and financial malpractice.

Assets

There are specific concerns about academy assets. The arrangements related to academy assets are complex, particularly the leasing and disposal of land and property. At present academies lease school grounds and buildings from local authorities for peppercorn rents. In 2015/16 the DfE reported that some £43.3 billion of assets had been transferred to the care of academy trusts[44] (the veracity of this calculation remains subject to an NAO query).[45] These are assets that in theory can be sold off by academies and trusts in order to raise funds. There are safeguards around the disposal of school land, with local authorities needing approval from the ESFA for any transactions; the government can overrule ESFA decisions and has done so in a few instances. Academies need consent from the secretary of state for the sale or reuse of any land. Most of the land that is sold comprises 'surplus' playing fields or schools that have been closed.[46] However, the National Education Union is concerned that the current safeguards around school land could be overturned by an Act of Parliament, particularly at a time when schools are acutely short of cash.[47] In February 2017, the *Times Educational Supplement* reported that sales of school land were at a seven-year high.[48]

But schools often have other valuable assets, such as art collections, and it is a matter for trustees whether these assets are kept in perpetuity for the school or not. Deciding, for example, whether a valuable sculpture should be sold to a museum or left on display as its donor intended is more than a financial matter and goes to complex ethical questions about generational responsibilities and entitlements. Both the sale of playing fields and artworks are not simply questions of efficiency, but speak to wider questions of public interest.

RPTs

As explained earlier, the FPP infrastructure exponentially proliferates the points at which the public and private come together in contractual arrangements. Both purchasers and providers are engaged in a wide range of procurement activities. Who is chosen to supply goods is a matter for due process, with public expectations that probity and transparency will prevail over self-interest.

Self-interest is a matter of public concern, with politicians in local and national government routinely expected to declare their interests[49] (see Chapters 1 and 3). The same standards are expected of all providers and trustees, and under the Charities Act they are required to register their interests on an annual basis. However, it is also possible for trustees associated with schools to win contracts. According to a House of Commons briefing paper: 'Academy sponsors, and companies and individuals related to academy sponsors, may provide contracted services to their sponsored schools, as long as this is provided "at cost" in the case of transactions over certain financial limits. The goods or services also have to be procured fairly and openly.'[50] How 'cost' is determined is unclear and this ambiguity has the potential to be amenable to self-interested interpretation.

Schools Week reported in February 2017 that over a third of academies had been involved in some form of RPT.[51] Of these, 23 academy trusts had breached rules and made illegal payments to the tune of more than £4 million. *Schools Week* claimed that 17 of 26 dubious RPTs were to companies owned by trustees, eight were for consultancy services and three paid to firms linked to the trust chief executive.

In 2018 the House of Commons PAC noted that purchaser DfE RPTs controls were 'too weak to prevent abuse'.[52] The PAC reported that in 2016, 40 per cent of academy trusts engaged in business with either an organisation or person with whom trustees, governors or senior leaders had a personal connection. This equated to £120 million of expenditure. The PAC asked the DfE about this and were told that 'related party transactions can be beneficial to academy trusts, for example, where a trustee provides goods and services free or at a reduced cost'. The committee curtly noted, 'We are not convinced that this is always the case'. They went on to say that,

> in most cases, ESFA only becomes aware of potential issues when it receives the trust's accounts at the end of the year. We are concerned that the rules are difficult to police, as the Department's processes are not robust enough to prevent abuse and that such abuses only come to light after the fact, often as a result of the year-end audit, or whistle blowing.

These arrangements between academy trusts and related parties should arise by exception, rather than with the current frequency.[53]

The PAC recommended that RPT and financial reporting rules should be tightened and that academies should be prevented from entering into RPTs without approval from the ESFA. The committee repeated its concerns about RPTs in their January 2019 report.[54] They were particularly concerned about MATs which were subject to investigation and the regulatory loopholes and lack of sanctions that existed in the system (see Box 5.2).

Box 5.2: The Public Accounts Committee on related party transactions

We heard that, despite a catastrophic failure of governance, Durand Education Trust had a considerable liability to the executive headteacher. ... This arose from a related party transaction whereby a company owned by the former headteacher was contracted to manage the accommodation and leisure facilities on the school site. The witness from Durand told us that the previous executive headteacher was entitled to a lump sum payment when the contract was terminated. ... [T]his payment was potentially worth £1.8 million but, after a statutory inquiry by the Charity Commission, the trustees and previous executive headteacher had agreed to reduce the amount to £850,000. ... [M]ost of Durand Education Trust's income from its assets, approximately £400,000 a year, was therefore going towards covering this payment.

The Charity Commission described to us how it had intervened in relation to the contract with the former headteacher of Durand Academy. Given its concerns that the contract had not gone out to tender, the Charity Commission had directed the trustees of Durand Education Trust to benchmark whether the payments in the contract were reasonable. It had then ensured that the trustees capped the termination payment in line with the benchmarking exercise. It told us that, because of its intervention, the payment that the former headteacher received was £1 million less than it might have been.

The Charity Commission said that the consultants commissioned by the trustees of Durand Education Trust had identified a number of options for benchmarking the value created through the contract; they selected the private equity model as the most appropriate. The Charity Commission ... had concluded that it could not direct the trustees of Durand Education Trust to use an alternative benchmarking methodology since there were plausible reasons to use the private equity model. ... [It] might have thought that the amount paid to the former headteacher might be lower but, if it was not outside the bounds of reasonableness, it did not have a legal basis on which to challenge the payment.

We asked what sanctions the Department or the ESFA could use against chief executives or trustees who had, for example, misused public money. The Department told us that it could ban individuals from teaching, as it had done in the case of the former headteacher at Perry Beeches Academy. It could also ban individuals from being school governors, but the Department admitted that this was very unusual.[55]

The ESFA continues to investigate incidents of illegal RPTs. Three more examples will suffice to make this point:

- Bright Tribe,[56] an academy chain closed in 2018, was subject to investigations about RPTs to companies run by its venture capitalist founder as well as for making false claims for building and maintenance grants. After a police investigation, the Bright Tribe case was referred to the Fraud Squad[57] with the possibility that the government would attempt to recoup £1.8 million from Bright Tribe for improper use of funds.[58]
- In February 2019, *Schools Week* carried a story of a special school that had paid hundreds of thousands of pounds to consultants, including one who served as its chair of trustees and chief finance officer.[59]
- A later report, in May 2019, recounted the result of one investigation in which a former chair of two free schools paid more than £500,000 to his own company.[60]

From April 2019 the ESFA required that academy trusts must (1) notify the ESFA in advance of entering into any RPT, regardless of the value of the transaction, and (2) seek the prior approval of the ESFA if a proposed RPT exceeds £20,000 as a single transaction, or where a proposed RPT of any value takes the total value of RPTs with that related party to more than £20,000. This guidance was reported by the press as academies needing government approval for RPTs, but this inaccurate. There is a mix of report and approve in the controls. The approach taken is one of risk mitigation, and limited support for the autonomy and self-regulation of trusts. This latest regulatory change does strengthen the role of the ESFA.

This tighter control approach has arguably been a very long time coming. It is probably as much a response to lobbying by the many 'honest brokers' in the academy system who have been dismayed to see the way in which a minority of trusts has abused procurement, as it is to media and political (funder) concerns. There is widespread unease about private snouts in publicly funded troughs. And when a self-employed behaviour consultant[61] is appointed to chair a national 'crackdown' on behaviour,[62] questions of expertise and conflict of interest – not the same as RPTs unless some kind of causal connection can be demonstrated – can only add to the general whiff of corruption.

Financial malpractice

There are repeated incidents of financial mismanagement and academy trusts in debt reported in the press.[63] It is often not clear from public information whether these are cases of insufficient funding, poor accounting or profligate spending.[64] The National Governors' Association alleges that some independent auditors are not being thorough enough and are allowing financial problems to build up;[65] the quality of costly private expertise is letting providers and purchasers down. More worrying are practices that are clearly corrupt and/or criminal.[66]

Unethical and corrupt behaviour is of course not a new phenomenon. There have always been some people who have chosen to defraud and embezzle funds for their own purposes. In my 20 years of being a headteacher these, together with safekeeping violations, were the most difficult situations I had to deal with. It is always shocking when an entrusted professional chooses to use school funds to buy travel, cars and luxury goods for themselves.[67] Two examples of the criminal are in order:

- The appalling behaviour of the collapsed Perry Beeches Academy Trust headteacher who paid himself two salaries via an RPT arrangement resulted in a well-deserved Teaching Regulation Agency verdict of professional misconduct.
- A 2019 *Schools Week* report alleged that the ESFA was owed £5.7 million by the failed Schools Company Trust, of which £3 million had to be written off.[68] RPTs were also being investigated, as were salary and expenses payments.

A non-criminal, but ethically dubious, act was perpetuated by the Wakefield City Academies Trust (WCAT) which, apparently on DfE advice, transferred millions of pounds from school reserves into central coffers before announcing that its 21 schools needed a new sponsor.[69] It had previously been in the spotlight for RPTs involving its chief executive.[70] WCAT schools will not see any of this money back despite some being funds raised by parents of individual schools.[71]

These examples suggest that tighter ESFA guidance for academies on spotting fraudulent behaviour is needed as well as welcome reassurance that the public interest is being addressed albeit belatedly.

Many of the fiscal efficiency concerns discussed already in this chapter come together – and when this happens, the provider is no longer able to provide.

Provider collapse

Failure is built into competition. Any race always has winners and losers. Markets by their very nature eliminate the weakest – those who start with impediments, who cannot manage risk, who face unanticipated obstacles, who don't appear attractive enough to their designated 'buyers' or who simply can't cut it. Markets are, despite the rhetoric of their advocates, fundamentally inefficient at scale. While individual units might become more efficient in order to survive, there is always some overall loss. We have only to look at the failure rate of small business to see this – smallbusiness.co.uk reports that 91 per cent of start-ups survive their first year but four out of every ten do not make it past five years. Markets are predictably a waste-producing model – wasteful of effort, and wasteful of money.

It is crucial to remember that when we speak of market failure in education, we are talking about public money. We are discussing a publicly funded whole, not individual autonomous schools and trusts. We are talking about human services, and young people whose life chances may well be damaged if their school or educational service is a market casualty.

It is difficult ahead of time to predict exactly where market failure will occur, when, where and with what consequences. In the corporate world, careful capacity assessment at the start, ongoing monitoring and comprehensive 'insurance', is the usual way to manage market risks and inevitable failures. Overextended organisations, or those that get going quickly without the necessary checks, are a good bet for potential failure.

There are dramatic instances of failure in marketised public services:

- The collapse of the Swedish profit-making school company JB Education. JB Education closed four of its schools in February 2013. It then announced that it would sell 19 of its high schools and close its remaining four, leaving some 10,000 students without a school place. This decision was precipitated by JB's owner, private equity company Axcel, which decided that it could no longer cover the education company's losses. However, the Swedish government has not introduced legislation to prevent this kind of failure happening again. Rather, it has focused its attention on the national decline in achievement in international testing and increasing inequity in student attainment. For-profit schools continue to be debated within the country with competing evidence about their capacity to produce better results.
- An Australian company, ABC Learning, was floated on the stock exchange in 2006 as one of the largest preschool providers in the world. ABC went into voluntary liquidation in 2008[72] and sold off most of its centres to another Australian company, GoodStart.[73] ABC was highly profitable until its

investments were affected by the US mortgage crisis which caused its debt to spiral and profits to fall. ABC had not been without controversy, and was often accused of profiting on the back of government childcare subsidies and poor wages.[74] The Australian government response was to regulate the market by tightening up early childhood quality audit measures, rather than shift back from demand-side subsidies to public community-based early childhood provision.[75]

- In England the government has had to take back two of the country's train lines, as their owners failed to deliver the services for which they were contracted, while incurring significant debts. Closer to education, the UK construction company Carillion also went under, with significant debt. Carillion held a number of government contracts including managing nearly 900 schools through PFI arrangements. When it went into receivership it was reported to hold 420 public contracts, with its 2016 income from public sector revenue totalling £1.72 billion; subcontractors were owed some £1 billion.[76] At the time of writing, Carillion's contracted work was still proceeding and wages were still being paid through the official receiver. And in December 2018, Interserve, one of the biggest companies providing catering and cleaning to hospitals and schools, was rumoured to be in crisis. Another building contractor, Kier, also needed to hastily raise cash from new investors. *The Independent's* chief business commentator wrote in response to these events: 'The notion that the private sector is always better than the public sector simply doesn't stand up to close scrutiny. These jack of all trade companies are masters of none. Interserve's woes only serve to underline that point. Yet public contracts, and public money, continue to be showered upon them.'[77]

It is not surprising that the same kinds of woes have been seen in the government's academy programme. There are regular reports about free school closures and investments in schools that never opened.

In December 2018, *Schools Week* reported that while the Labour Opposition claimed 100 free schools had closed, the minister responsible, Nick Gibb, reported the total figure as

41, made up of 13 free schools, 7 university technical colleges and 21 studio schools.[78] *Schools Week* suggested that more up-to-date official government data put 55 mainstream and alternative provision schools actually closed since the start of the programme in 2010, but of these 15 were rebrokered.

Schools Week also suggested that the DfE spent more than £23 million on failed or never opened studio schools.[79] Studio schools were intended to be a new kind of 14–19 year old vocational provision. They were clearly more interesting to policy makers than to families, who they largely failed to convince. *Schools Week* reported examples of studio school market failure on the ground: £241,886 was spent on two studio schools – Digital Studio College Derbyshire and the Aldridge Centre for Entrepreneurship – which never actually opened. Almost half a million was written off against the Harpurhey Studio School, which opened in 2011, but converted to an alternative provision academy in 2012, before closing a year later. The same kind of failure appeared in the free school sector. Bolton Wanderers Free School closed after apparently paying its sponsor football club £300,000 per year for rooms in an otherwise empty stadium. It had a £380,000 debt and a £200,000 pensions deficit when it was 'handed back' to the government.[80] In November 2019, one free school closure made the news: IAG had been stuck in temporary accommodation for three years waiting for planning permission for a new building. *Schools Week* reported that by the time the DfE decided to close the school, it had spent £1.1 million on the temporary site and plans for the new school with a further £3.2 million in running costs.[81] In June 2018, *Schools Week* put the overall cost of free school projects at £115 million.[82]

These figures give some sense of the waste that has been and is *still* being incurred in pursuit of stimulating diversity of provision, and academising a school system. But the story doesn't stop there.

City technology colleges intended to focus on technical education are in trouble too. In October 2018, 50 were open, with ten having closed or been converted to another type of school. However, students in the colleges were failing to produce the high levels of attainment it was suggested they would, and the schools also had high drop-out rates.[83] In July 2019,

The Guardian[84] reported that £64 million had been spent on university technical colleges (UTCs) that had been closed. The report stated that

> Research by the Price Bailey accountancy firm disclosed to the Guardian reveals that 31 out of 40 UTCs with published accounts owe money to the DfE's education and skills funding agency (ESFA), including 25 schools owing a total of £8.6m after educating fewer pupils than they received funding for through their general annual grant.

Not surprisingly, the headline accompanying the story was of a political 'vanity project' that was 'piling up debts'. A related 2018 report by the Education Policy Unit[85] found that UTC students scored a full grade lower in GCSE than comparable peers at mainstream schools. This lack of effectiveness may of course be equally related to the kind of student attracted by the promise of 'technical' education.

There are also cases of MAT failure. Prospect Academies Trust (six schools) was the first chain to close claiming that its incapacity to support the improvement of schools was due to scattered geography. There is quite a closure list: the Collaborative Academies Trust (eight schools), the Schools Company Trust (three Pupil Referral Units) and the Salford Academy Trust (four schools) all handed in their schools for rebrokering. The WCAT, which ran 21 schools (only four were rated as good or outstanding by Ofsted), asset stripped from individual schools to balance the books across the chain (see earlier in this chapter). The trust had been known to be in difficulty for some months before it gave up its schools, and doubts had been raised about RPTs.[86] Other chain collapses also centred on finances: the Lilac Schools Academy Trust (nine schools) spent money on consultants while in receipt of emergency public funding, and the Education Fellowship Trust (12 schools) and Perry Beeches Academy Trust both seriously mismanaged their finances. The University of Wolverhampton academy trust top-sliced £376 thousand from a school with a million-pound debt and then handed it over to another trust together with its debt.[87]

In late 2018, *Schools Week* estimated that 91 academy trusts had closed since 2014 at a cost of some £6 million in start-ups, as well as unknown amounts for rebrokerage and writing off debts.[88] *Schools Week* reported a range of different views on the ethics of closure. Leora Cruddas, chief executive of the Confederation of School Trusts, praised the DfE for its responsible action in closing down schools; Andy Jolly, a transparency campaigner, suggested that people were walking away from failed trusts without scrutiny; and a DfE 'shut-down specialist' said that it is too easy to focus on unacceptable mistakes. However, she said, the mistakes happened because 'people have lost sight of the moral imperative' (failure was a result of bad apples and not the system).

The total sum of wasted investment on market failures is unknown. A known contributing factor has been insufficient planning and regulation at the outset. A self-evaluation report issued by the now closed Robert Owen free school[89] (the closure resulted from a poor Ofsted grade and a financial warning) named four areas which it said anyone opening a free school should attend to: ensure the local authority is not hostile to the project; have experienced public relations staff; don't open too early; and establish clear communication with civil servants. These recommendations suggest a lack of consistency, due diligence and due process on the part of the purchaser and political enthusiasm from the funder, as well as haste and naivety on the part of the free school sponsors.

Waste not

It is important to pause at this point in the book to consider efficiency understood as waste. It is important to ask whether the costs of the academy dream have been worth the expense. Converting a school system, from local authority-based maintained schools to a mixed economy with academy trusts, has inbuilt inefficiencies and has demonstrably been wasteful of time and money. Financial control by closure is certainly inefficient – and potentially immoral. Failures are very damaging to students and communities.

The situation in England is not unique. The same concerns about waste and fraud are evident in the US, where the charter school system follows FPP logic, although the infrastructure and legal framework is somewhat different. The US federal Department of Education is reported to have spent US$1 billion on charter school waste and fraud.[90] A detailed analysis, tellingly entitled 'Asleep at the wheel',[91] attributes the charter school overspend to charters that were opened or closed quickly, a flawed grant process, grants given to schools with known enrolment problems, ignoring warnings from the Inspector-General (a body like the UK's NAO), insufficient oversight by the department, flaws in contractual processes and falling quality in applications. The similarities in this account with the situation in England (outlined in this chapter and Chapter 4), suggest that inefficiencies are integral to the logics of FPP and are not simply a national problem.

However, advocates continue to argue for their vision of a school system which operates like a market, despite mounting evidence that the organisational infrastructure incurs significant cost. It is important to ask whether a system in which there has been very poor planning and there is still an inbuilt ongoing potential for recurrent waste works in the public interest. It is important to ask whether this is now a system which is, in the moral sense, corrupted, if not actually corrupt. In other words, do we really have a case of some bad apples, or do we have a flawed system?

It is vital to conclude the chapter by restating that the book does not argue that all schools are engaged in unethical financial practices. They clearly are not. The vast majority of schools are staffed by people who are more likely to dip into their own pockets to pay for additional 'stuff' than take anything from their school budget or plant. Reports of staff routinely buying classroom consumables and breakfast for hungry children, and paying for school excursions, are commonplace. The argument made in this chapter and Chapter 4 is that reforming the school system has incurred significant cost, and contains ongoing elements which run counter to efficiency. It suggests that this is a corruption of a public service which operates in the public interest.

The effects of effectiveness

DfE: school improvement has 'arrested or reversed' in some academies

Schools Week, 23 January 2019

State funded academies deliver poor exam results

Financial Times, 20 December 2018

Schools staying with their local council more likely to remain good/outstanding

Local Government Association press release, 23 May 2019

The problem isn't the framework, it's high stakes accountability

Schools Week, 19 January 2019

Schools to get curriculum review grace period under new Ofsted inspection framework

Schools Week, 14 May 2019

John Chubb and Terry Moe's book *Politics, markets, and America's schools*[1] addressed ineffectiveness in the US school system. Chubb and Moe argued that declining educational quality (as measured by test scores) could be attributed to a power imbalance in the school system – state control needed to be balanced by parent power and school autonomy. Effectiveness, achieved through clear school goals, rigorous academic standards and high expectations, good discipline, regular use of homework, strong leadership, teacher participation in decision making and parent support, was dependent on separating schools from bureaucratic interference. Public schools should become like private schools (higher quality, better test scores) directly accountable to parents.

Chubb and Moe argued that accountability to parents and competition was the only way to reduce the dead hand of inequitable monopoly. State-administered schooling must give way to a competitive devolved system. Chubb and Moe's quality solution was for school autonomy, with schools free to select students and to create their own curriculum; charter schools (schools set up by any group capable of doing so); and a voucher system which would allow parents to choose any school for their children.

Critics took issue with the research underpinning these proposals – a comparison of public and private schools which omitted significant questions of social context and resourcing – as well as with the untested solution that Chubb and Moe proposed.[2] Chubb and Moe advocated a full market system as more effective than any other. But no such system was in existence. Whether a marketised, deinstitutionalised system would provide more equitable education was thus a matter of belief, critics said. Chubb and Moe offered a policy solution which had no basis in evidence.

However, the school system in England is perhaps now the test bed *sine qua non* for the argument made by Chubb and Moe. This chapter examines the evidence for the full market model. I examine how the new academised school system is faring in effectiveness and in the measurement of effects. This chapter discusses effectiveness as assessed in policy as well as the scholarly research, particularly where the research speaks to the measures of effectiveness used by policy makers. The chapter lays the groundwork for the discussion of corrupted practices and corruption that follows in Chapter 7.

Effectiveness

Effectiveness is defined as the degree to which something is successful in producing a desired result – in other words how successful it is in reaching its stated outcome.[3] Measuring the effectiveness of something as complicated as schooling is a complex task and one that is also highly contentious. What is seen as effective is always up for debate. Questions – such as what counts as effectiveness? Who decides what is effective? How is effectiveness to be evaluated? Who decides on the processes of evaluation? What are the effects of effectiveness? In whose interests does this effectiveness work? – always come to mind.

Effectiveness depends on an articulation of outcomes. An outcome is directly derived from aims – or purposes. What is seen as effective also depends in large part on expectations of what *can* be achieved. For instance, if the purpose of the school system is seen to be getting students into employment or employment-related training, then effectiveness might be measured by the percentage of students either getting a job or going on to further or higher education. If these figures are disappointing, policy makers might respond accordingly; they might decide to add incentives, set targets, punish those who fall below a set minimum level or fund new programmes, organisations or institutions. However, critics may argue in response that education can only create job readiness and not actual jobs. But then, how is job readiness to be measured? The policy maker must decide whether to stay with what can be measured, even though it is hard to influence, or opt for something harder to measure but more achievable.

Of course, this example is partial. Preparing students for employment is only one of the expected outcomes of the school system, not its sole purpose. Schooling has mixed mandates – educating young people for citizenship, family life and employment, at the same time as supporting them to fulfil their personal ambitions, as well as ensuring that the next generation has the knowledge and skills to live well. Different people, from policy makers to professionals and parents, have different views not only about what such outcomes mean and which of these outcomes is more important, but also what kind of schooling might allow them to be achieved.

Given this complexity, it is not surprising that effectiveness measures are vexed and contentious, as they have to attend to a complex array of expectations and aims as well as what is possible. It is also not surprising then, that when government changes, measures of effectiveness change too. When Labour lost office, the Coalition instituted a new national curriculum to be measured through examinations. These moves, intended to ensure that all children had access to a 'traditional' body of important knowledge, changed outcomes and measures of effectiveness. Exams and tests were not the only things that were adjusted. In 2019, Ofsted moved to a more broadly based inspection framework focused on the whole curriculum. While tests and exams remain, schools also have to demonstrate a more holistic approach. This change might be understood as a readjustment in effectiveness measures to prevent systemic skewing through a narrow focus solely on exams and test results[4] (more on this later).

Measuring effectiveness

Schooling in England is subject to three major types of effectiveness measures. Some are multi-purpose, having more than one function:

- Measures to evaluate overall system health and evaluate individual school and MAT performance. Examples include:
  - student attainment – aggregated tests and exam results, with development of rubrics and targets for aggregated measures used for league tables, and as the basis for triggering policy change and/or purchaser and provider intervention;
  - attendance and discipline – performance against targets, also used as evidence for systemic improvement/ intervention by both purchasers and providers;
  - special needs and SES data – used to judge 'value added' by schooling and allocate targeted funding;
- Measures to promote a competitive school market through inter-school competition. Examples include:
  - publication of league tables using aggregated test and exam results, publication of inspection grades;
  - identification and promotion of best practice examples, judged best against designated standards to show principles of effective practice;

- Measures to manage people. These operate primarily at the provider (school or MAT) level but form part of inspections carried out by the funder. Examples include:
  - student psychometric testing for special needs which triggers funding for purchase of services;
  - student predicted tests and exam results which trigger school remediation;
  - student discipline infraction scores used to remove students from roll;
  - student grades used as measure of teacher performance;
  - actuarial risk management practices used to permit or restrict activities.

Every one of these measures is contentious.

Critiques of measures of effectiveness in schooling are various, but three concerns are worth mentioning at the outset. These are (1) the influence of context, (2) insufficient evidence and (3) inadequate measures.

The influence of 'context'

School effectiveness research began by showing that the wider social context, sometimes measured through family income and educational levels, has a stronger influence on students' test results and educational outcomes than their schools.[5] Schools do of course make some difference[6] – the provision of early childhood education, for example, can make a significant positive difference to later educational outcomes.[7] But, in the UK, school improvement has been insufficient to change social mobility patterns in the 20th and 21st centuries, the exception being in the immediate postwar period. Educational achievement remains stubbornly strongly correlated with the educational levels and socioeconomic circumstances of families; this relationship has been highly resistant to change.[8]

The reasons for inequalities produced and reproduced through schooling are complex. The British educational sociologist Michael Young invented the term 'meritocracy' to describe the ways in which those who were successful in schooling understood their success as resulting from their effort.[9] The meritorious did not recognise their advantage, which arose from the correspondence between family knowledges and associations, and what was valued and tested in schooling. The French social theorist Pierre Bourdieu saw meritocracy as a 'misrecognition' which disguised the ways in which the sorting and selecting practices of education reproduced the social status quo.[10] Belief in meritocracy also meant that those who are unsuccessful in school are seen and see themselves as deficient and lacking in merit.

System school effectiveness measures often ignore socioeconomic context. Schools differ in important ways, and offer very different experiences to their students. Schools vary in school mix, location and reputation; real estate costs and transport are in part responsible for the production of various school populations.[11] And schools are variously able to provide resources – schools possessed of large, well-manicured leafy campuses, classrooms with the latest materials and equipment and well-remunerated staff teaching small classes are routinely pitted in league tables against schools which struggle to maintain buildings, budgets and morale. Schools which serve communities made poor by the loss of factories, mills and mines have welfare demands that wealthy schools cannot imagine. Yet they are routinely compared with those where students have every advantage at school and at home.

About two thirds of the variation between schools in GCSE performance can be explained by the characteristics of the school populations.[12] Some researchers argue that these kinds of contextual differences make any straightforward systemic effectiveness comparison between schools and their students highly unreliable.

Insufficient evidence

There are different ways to approach measures of system and school effectiveness. One is to combine measures so that there is only one set in operation. An alternative is to separate measures out so that evaluating system effectiveness is not the same as judging the effectiveness of a unit (a school or MAT). Measures can also be based on a representative sample or a census.

In the US, system effectiveness is measured by the National Assessment of Educational Progress (NAEP), a representative sample of students' achievement in various domains. The NAEP may originally have resulted from the sheer political impossibility of getting every state to agree on common tests; each of them also set their own tests in addition to the NAEP. However, the 2002 No Child Left Behind legislation saw the introduction of representative national standardised tests of reading and mathematical knowledge. The NAEP supports a comprehensive longitudinal national 'report card' on student learning which sits alongside other state, regional and district measures. The OECD's Programme for International Student Assessment (PISA) is also a representative, not census, testing regime which allows for systemic comparison across countries. Some market advocates do not favour census testing and advocate representative testing only.[13]

There are complex decisions to be made about system effectiveness measures. A census sample across a system will always be less than complete, as some students will inevitably be absent. The level of absence is usually not an issue because of census scale, unless for instance there is a large organised boycott. Other absences might be due to students being unable to take the test because they are not yet sufficiently competent in the English language or they have special educational needs. In such cases the claims made for a test cannot be 'all students'. However, census tests are not usually dismissed on the grounds of being non-representative of students. They may, however, not be representative of learning. Census tests and surveys are usually slower and more expensive than smaller representative samples. In education, the cost and speed factor of tests and exams limits what can be measured each year. If the same item is measured each year (reading comprehension, for example) then annual comparison is easy, but only against a limited measure.

The question of what is measured and what it adds up to – what is it a proxy for – is crucial to judgments about effects. Regular census basic skills testing, as is the case in England, usually only measures a narrow band of learning, a selection deemed a proxy for literacy and numeracy. By omitting other areas of language, mathematics and other subject areas altogether, a very partial systemic picture of student learning is generated. Perhaps, critics argue, the selection is too partial to use for judgment about anything wider than those things that are tested. Perhaps the tests are not a valid stand-in for learning as a whole. Perhaps they ought not to be the basis of the intervention measures and triggers as they are not robust enough to indicate what schools actually do. One alternative for testing systemic effectiveness would be to have a rolling set of measures which show a wider spread of learning, but only allow comparison across time intervals much greater than a year.

In England, school performance measures do not generally take student background into account but focus instead on the 'value added' by the school – this is a measure of individual school effectiveness. Various forms of census-based 'value-added' measures exist. Goldstein and Leckie examined the most recent English school value-added measure, Progress 8.[14] Progress 8 is a calculation based on learning in eight traditional academic subjects between the tests taken at the end of primary school and GCSE exams. Progress 8 is used to judge the effectiveness of schools, measured against performance targets. Poor performance usually triggers inspection.

Goldstein and Leckie register serious concerns about the statistical modelling process used for Progress 8. An unorthodox calculation, they say, together with the lack of measures of other important aspects of learning, no moderation for pupil background and absence of evidence that there are tangible benefits for student attainment from the use of the value-added approach, means that the measure is highly dubious. They say that:

> The types of automated data driven decision making that the Government currently aspires to, whereby schools falling below a single floor standard are declared underperforming, cannot be supported by the data. Our view is that, for school accountability purposes, the most school value-added measures can be used for is as 'screening devices' to choose schools

for careful sensitive further investigation (Foley and Goldstein, 2012). However, we believe that a better use is simply as tools for school self- evaluation where they can potentially help inform schools on the policies and practices which help different pupil groups to reach their potential.[15]

The issue of whether census testing is useful is crucial to discussions of system effectiveness in general, as well as for schools. W. Edwards Deming (the 'father' of quality management, see later in this chapter) argued that any whole system testing, be it representative or census, not only produced generally inaccurate/insufficient evidence but also put the emphasis on the wrong part of a system. He said that relying on inspection of results, rather than focusing on improvement, was an obstacle to effectiveness as it placed effort in the wrong place. He proposed learning and improvement cycles which relied on an intense programme of education and self-evaluation, where holistic measures were applied at the point of 'production' as part of a plan-do-study-act organisational strategy. This is not a dissimilar position to those who research school effectiveness and improvement.[16]

However, in England census tests and examination results have a dual purpose. They are used, together with inspections, for school self-improvement purposes. But they are also used to trigger systemic sanctions and interventions. Whether highly focused tests of a small band of learning combined with a two-day visit is sufficient evidence to justify closure or forced academisation is certainly debatable. Furthermore, making judgments on the basis of limited census information may be flawed. The narrowness of tested items is particularly important when it comes to questions of equity. While the distribution of test results may stand as an indicator of inequalities, they do not provide adequate information for intervention. Just because tests and exams indicate inequitable patterns of school success and attainment, this does not mean that attending to the particular subject areas that are tested will produce equity in a more holistic sense.

To put it bluntly, even if we were able to raise the 'bottom' of the exam and testing tables, this in itself may do little to change wider educational and social patterns of inequity and injustice.

Inadequate measures

Education Datalab analysed PISA data,[17] which they say shows that 40 per cent of English heads say they use effectiveness-related data every week compared to 10 per cent in most other OECD countries. Their report elaborates:

> 87% of schools in England use educational data to identify how instruction could be improved (compared to the OECD average of 61%), 84% to adapt teaching to pupils' needs (OECD average, 54%) and 81% to guide pupils' learning (OECD average, 64%).
>
> The second area is benchmarking schools' performance. Over 90% of schools in England use educational data to monitor school progress, and compare their performance to other schools and to local/national benchmarks. Again, this is well above the level observed in most other developed countries.
>
> Finally, data also plays a key role in helping shape the organisation of schools and providing feedback to key stakeholders such as teachers and parents. This includes the setting/streaming of pupils, informing parents about pupil progress and in making judgments about teacher effectiveness.

This regular use of data for school improvement is only worrying if the data are inadequate. If measures are to be helpful in evaluating effectiveness, then they need to be up to the task. Yet, test items themselves may favour some students over others. Debates about the nature of tests and their inherent biases are international in nature. Bias matters even more when tests are high stakes.

In the primary school test aftermath of 2016, teachers complained on social and in print media about a test which reduced pupils to tears. The test featured a text about a garden party, where 'two children sneaked away during a garden party at the ancestral home of a girl whose family once married into royalty. They explore the grounds of this "big house", which has its own lake, island and secret marble monument.'[18] The *Times Educational Supplement* reported one teacher as saying that this was a test of vocabulary not comprehension, and others speaking of the lack of relevance to and connection with students who lived on inner-city estates.[19] However, in 2019 the *Times Educational Supplement* reported that the year's tests appeared to have less middle-class bias with a more generally relatable story about a park being closed.[20]

The effects of inadequate effectiveness measures may be very significant. If effectiveness regimes are based on assumptions about a 'level playing field' that does not exist, then they are by nature unfair. It is perhaps not unreasonable to suggest that any school system or school which is effective must be inclusive. If the consequences of a measurement system are the exclusion of any pupils on the basis of their life circumstances, or that of their school context or school mix, then perhaps the school cannot by definition be seen as effective.[21] While logical, this stance is likely to be far too politically unpalatable to take hold.

But tests of effectiveness may have more or less influence on events, given more or less weighting. Understanding that tests may be imperfect can lead to the lessening of the influence of apparently neutral and objective systems of merit and measurement. Box 6.1 illustrates the ways in which measures of effectiveness can be reduced in impact. The example comes from the US,[22] where the dependence on test and exam results used for university entrance is under challenge. This 'letter to the editor' is written by a senior academic in a medical school who succinctly describes the complex confluence of factors that come together to produce inequitable test and exam results.

When tests are put in their place – perhaps when system tests are separated from individual school measures and their limitations recognised, perhaps when inclusion comes to matter – new policy options are opened up. This possibility is taken up again in Chapters 8 and 9.

Box 6.1: College admissions and test results

June 27, 2018

To the Editor:

Even though standardized test scores may provide much-needed financial assistance to low-income students, their use results in merit-based support across all socioeconomic groups which favors students from higher income families. The number of low-income minority students who score high on either the ACT or SAT is small, resulting in a small number admitted to not only upper-tier schools but college in general.

Standardized test scores are directly affected by both race and class. Historically, white students have scored higher on standardized tests than minority students. Even when adjusting for socioeconomic status, the scoring gap persists. For instance, minorities of high socioeconomic status score higher than low-socioeconomic-status minorities but significantly lower than low-socioeconomic-status whites. This is due to multiple variables in the K-12 educational system. Many minority students attend schools that are under resourced, have high student-to-teacher ratios, have no Advanced Placement (AP) courses, and are lacking in tutoring and counselling services. This places them at a distinct disadvantage and generates a small pool of minority students with high ACT or SAT scores.

I support the efforts of the University of Chicago in making the ACT and SAT optional and moving to a more holistic admissions process that takes into account race, socioeconomic status, ethnicity, gender, ableism, gender identity, geographical location, and first-generation status. Awareness, implementation, and adherence to the current Supreme Court ruling in *Fisher vs University of Texas at Austin* will mitigate many of the effects of implicit bias on the admission process. Admissions committee members must also be trained in the utilization of the holistic admissions process. If we do not bring about a dramatic shift in our admissions process, our efforts to diversify and enhance the educational process in higher education will fall way short.

Academisation and system effectiveness

The stakes are currently high for measuring system effectiveness, for everyone involved. Effectiveness measures are particularly significant for the funder: government. The legitimacy of contemporary neoliberalist policy agendas depends on having independent and apparently objective mechanisms which address effectiveness. But these measures also make government vulnerable. The test of any policy change, particularly a big and dramatic change, is whether it achieves what it says it does. And, given that the major rationale for the switch from a welfare state local authority provision model to the FPP academy-led system is that it would be more effective and less inequitable,[23] it is no wonder there are current debates about effectiveness.

Any new evidence about systemic effectiveness is always in the news, and at any one time is the subject of several large-scale research projects. The next section considers some of this evidence.

Has the academy system produced more school choice?

The key to effectiveness was in part to be realised through the promotion of more choice in the system.

Selection and choice is a highly emotive issue in the UK, and nowhere more so than in England. It is often associated with the stigmatisation of particular schools and students. Recall the policy history outlined in Chapter 2, where choice policies were/are interpreted differently at different times. When school choice was introduced by the Thatcher government in the 1980s, it was widely argued that the policy would create unpopular 'sink schools'. There is little evidence that a schooling quasi-market per se created this effect, with educational segregation allied more strongly to costs and availability of housing, transport and work.[24] When New Labour continued with the Tory policy of school choice some people, those strongly committed to comprehensive schooling as the primary way to provide social justice for the poor,[25] saw it as acceptable as long as there was some form of independent mediation of applications. Mediation would ensure parity in access and avoid sink schools. But choice was not the key issue for others in the Labour Party – academisation of inner-city schools was the way to address ghettoised schools and to bring them 'up' to the level of those found in other more wealthy locations.[26] The Coalition and Conservative governments had no such worries, believing as they do in a neutral meritocracy. Choice in recent times is simply a matter for the market to decide.

DfE statistics suggests that one in five pupils don't get their first choice of school.[27] Research at scale and over time[28] says that 35 per cent of families choose only one school and 97 per cent are successful in this one choice. But some of those families do not get a real choice because of where they live. And choice chances are not distributed equally: English as an Additional Language (EAL) students have lower chances of getting their first choice. Researchers also suggest that these statistics may hide the fact the most parents make choices based on what they think is a likely outcome.[29]

There is international evidence that sometimes it is schools that select students rather than the reverse. Two educational economists[30] in a US randomised control trial sent fictitious entry letters to 6,000 schools: they found that charter schools were less likely to respond to any students whose letters signalled they would be harder to teach. This practice happens in England too.

In England, school selection is legal for schools with a specialisation or where a religious criteria which can be applied. Where there is oversubscription – there are more applications than places – there is a decision-making and appeal system in which the local authority is usually involved. There are ongoing arguments[31] and some evidence[32] that through these three forms of selection there is increased segregation of schools. Steven Gorard suggests that the capacity of some schools to determine their own admissions causes more social segregation in schooling than markets and parent choice per se.[33] And when school choice is based on entrance tests, as is the case in areas where grammar schools still exist, some research suggests that expensive coaching and familiarity with test-taking give some students an advantage over their peers.[34]

The Coalition intended free schools to produce more choice in the system, but worrying information about the operation of free schools is emerging. Rob Higham, for example, examined proposals for free schools.[35] He reports that proposers who are most able to negotiate the approval process draw on a range of professional networks, have strongly conservative academic educational aims and on average do not seek to specifically serve disadvantaged communities. On the other hand, the majority of proposers located in highly disadvantaged areas had aims and expertise that did not fit well with what the government was willing to accept. A class bias married with cultural conservatism dominates the free schools that have been allowed to open, he argues. This is hardly supply side 'innovation' or a guarantee of more equitable student learning.

The former chief schools adjudicator, Sir Philip Hunter, has recently argued that the schools admissions system needs a radical overhaul. Hunter says that the statutory school admissions code needs strengthening, that greater powers for the Office of the Schools Adjudicator are needed and that there is a role for Ofsted in examining schools' admissions criteria.[36] He argues that what is needed is different and more regulation.

Whether choice is used as a proxy for system effectiveness or as an indirect factor necessary for system effectiveness, there is some doubt about how successful the new organisation and policy agenda have been.

Do academies lead to improved results?

A review of the international literatures on school accountabilities suggests that a key problem for the type of systemic effectiveness measurement and allied intervention used in England is that 'there is a paucity of data and robust, quantitative evidence about the impact of accountability on the curriculum, standards, and teacher and pupil engagement'.[37]

It is little wonder that finding evidence of effectiveness is a priority for the English government. However there is, despite ministerial press releases which seek to put the best possible spin on information, remarkable consistency in analyses of academy performance in inspections, tests and exams. Perhaps the Education Policy Unit puts it most succinctly, saying that 'academies have not provided an automatic panacea to school improvement. ... [T]here is significant variation in performance at both different types of academies and Multi-Academy Trusts.'[38]

There does seem to have been overall improvement in Ofsted gradings in academy schools, with converter schools more likely to get good and outstanding grades than sponsored academies.[39] This is not surprising as sponsored academies were sponsored precisely because they had poor grades, which triggered intervention in the first place. Converter academies were by definition good or outstanding. This maintenance of relative positioning, despite some dramatic examples of improvement in some sponsored academies, suggests that autonomy and choice are not the key issues they are said to be. Rather, the overall lack of change at the systemic level is probably due to a complex set of factors, including the powerful effects of social and economic contexts.

One study found some differences in the effectiveness of primary and secondary academies.[40] Using test results and exams as their measure of effectiveness, researchers suggested that 'there appear to be no short-term benefits in improved school performance associated with academy status for primary schools'. On the other hand, there was some difference in secondary schools.

The differences in school GCSE performance between secondary sponsored and converter academies that have been open for between two and five years and groups of similar maintained schools are small, and many are not statistically significant. However, the proportion of pupils achieving five or more A★–C grades including English and maths is 2.7 percentage points higher in sponsored academies and 1.1 percentage points higher in converter academies, each compared to similar maintained schools. This result demands an explanation, but perhaps has something to do with school pedagogical and disciplinary preferences (see later in this chapter).

DfE-commissioned research suggests that the longer a sponsored academy had been open, the more likely it was that their performance was in line with the average performance of maintained schools. Given that these academies were sponsored because they were seen to perform poorly, this indicates that many have now caught up. However, researchers also found some longstanding sponsored academies which continued to underperform, and evidence that some had slipped back. The conclusion of the researchers was that overall, and despite the overall unevenness in performance, there was some evidence that 'pupil outcomes in sponsored academies have typically improved since their formation in comparison with sets of similar schools'.[41]

However, a long-term study of a sample of academy chains serving disadvantaged communities and students offered a finer-grained analysis with a strong emphasis on equity as its measure of effectiveness (see Box 6.2, emphases added).[42]

Box 6.2: Hutchings and Francis on academy effectiveness

There continues to be *very significant variation in outcomes for disadvantaged pupils, both between and within chains.* In 2017, disadvantaged pupils in 12 out of 58 chains had attainment above the national average for disadvantaged pupils in all mainstream schools, including three chains which were substantially above that average. However, 38 of the 58 had attainment below the mainstream average, including 8 which were well below average.

The five-year analysis shows that there has been only limited change in the overall ranking of the chains in the analysis. The same small group of chains consistently outperform the national average for disadvantaged pupils, while another small group of chains remain at the bottom of the table each year, and there is little to suggest that the Regional Schools Commissioners are having any success in bringing about improvement in these chains. A small number of chains have shown consistent year-on-year improvement in the ranking, demonstrating that change is possible, while some others have fallen or fluctuated.

Newer academy chains have performed less well than on their first year of inclusion in our study than those already in the study, with almost 8 out of 10 having below average results. This suggests both that *it may take more than three years to bring about improvement in an under-performing school, and also that it takes time for a new academy chain to develop effective strategies for improving schools.*

Those chains that were most successful with disadvantaged pupils also tended to be successful with their more affluent pupils, while less successful chains tended to have poor results for both groups.

The five-year analysis shows that, in comparison to the national pattern, the overall performance of disadvantaged pupils in sponsored academies in our analysis worsened slightly from 2013 to 2016, but is now recovering. This may be because the move to a more academic curriculum has been a major shift in focus for sponsored academies, many of which previously entered their students for a wide range of vocational qualifications. This change in focus has had implications for staffing and resources, and has taken place at a time when schools have suffered from falling budgets.[43]

While Hutchings and Francis do find evidence that there is a small improvement in specific academies, this is hardly a ringing endorsement for the dramatic structural change in schooling which, as already outlined, has cost an enormous amount to bring about. And there are some concerning implications, as commentators have been keen to point out.

In a 2017 public lecture, Becky Francis, one of the authors of the Chain Effects research (Box 6.2), noted that it was 'alarming' to find schools where, despite the academy intervention designed to improve their prospects, attainment remained 'significantly low'.[44] Even though there were improved inspection results, and the energisation provide by academisation and the success demonstrated by some schools, 'results produced by the DfE as well as by the Education Policy Institute and Sutton Trust, academies cannot overall be viewed as fulfilling their role as the "battering ram for high standards" envisaged by Lord Adonis'.[45] Francis concluded that the potential of the academisation programme had yet to be reached, that schools and MATs clearly needed more support if this was to be achieved and that there needed to be more learning from the schools that had achieved success. Overall, she suggested that 'our strange mixed economy of LAs [local authorities], chains and standalones is going to be challenging to maintain'.[46] In other words, the variation of school type which now constitutes the provider mix is not conducive to overall system effectiveness.

Research[47] on free schools is similarly mixed, with primary pupil attainment among the lowest of all state-funded schools, and secondary-level pupils making the most progress. However, much of the secondary attainment can be explained by the socioeconomic status of the school population. This result chimes with international research,[48] which shows US charter schools, which are like English free schools, often outperformed by state schools; they too are seen as 'stunningly uneven'[49] at best.

These two instances – choice and results – raise questions about the effectiveness of academisation on its own terms. If the system is not showing a dramatic change in results (however flawed the measure is), if it is not closing the gap and if it is costing a great deal of time and money, then both its effectiveness and value for money are questionable. And if there are doubts about choices then this policy approach becomes highly electorally charged. But effectiveness issues do not stop here.

One of the other concerns for government is whether effectiveness measures have counterproductive consequences. The remainder of this chapter explores some of the effects of effectiveness measures. Chapter 7 canvasses the range of unethical and illegal behaviours that effectiveness regimes can produce.

Skewing the system

Effectiveness measures can have counterproductive effects. They change behaviours and require extra and new work.

Changing behaviours

Rather than being neutral, any measure points to what is important: what is an acceptable output. Target setting is designed to work in this way. A target is set precisely in order to encourage people to reach it. A reward may be attached to reaching the target, or there may be a penalty for failure. The English school system arguably leans towards penalties and punishment, although there are inbuilt rewards for the few:

personal honours, mentions in parliamentary press releases and being a good practice case in policy texts.

W. Edwards Deming, introduced earlier in the chapter, was scathing about the use of targets and performance measures. He reasoned that they skewed the organisation and had counterproductive effects. Deming used as an example insurance companies setting targets for sales which encouraged staff to focus on signing people up, rather than ensuring they could pay. The use of targets ultimately led to a loss of customers as people defaulted or became disillusioned when they found small print they hadn't been told about. Deming likened this target-setting approach to the ways in which annual performance bonuses could discourage teamwork, as well as fail to take into account exceptional circumstances that might benefit or hinder output. Deming argued that targets not only perverted what people did but also encouraged tinkering. Deming's example of perverse tinkering was that trying to adjust a hot water tap before it reached optimum flow could lead to wild fluctuations in temperature. Target-related tinkering perversely produced more variation rather than the desired levelling of performance. Changing staff behaviour may not always be positive or promote effectiveness.

Extra and new work

If an effectiveness measure cannot be seen, evidenced and demonstrated, it does not matter, it is not 'true'. This performativity principle characterises (post)modern life[50] – being seen to perform well as seen through measurement. Visible performance is not only important to the legitimacy of any arm of government, but is also crucial at each individual point of calculation: school type, school, faculty, leader, teacher, student. When tied to competition and punitive interventions (such as school closures), performative effectiveness measures have a penetrating bite.

The performance of effectiveness requires particular kinds of visibility work. Teachers are required to make very detailed forward plans, keep daily or weekly records of students' attendance, learning targets and attainment and to use standardised and digitised forms of assessment. These records must be produced with little or no notice. Writing and producing such 'evidence' of performance can easily take away from the time and energy needed to be spent on the actual teaching. Perusal and evaluation of performance via documentation, rather than support, then dominates the work of line managers. Performance of effectiveness dominates workload. Effectiveness measures become 'terrors' which strongly steer teachers' professional agency and autonomy – their educational soul, according to Stephen Ball.[51]

But other skewing occurs too. The most common response at school level to effectiveness regimes based on visibly reaching targets is teaching to the test, where the behavioural equivalent to Deming's insurance sales staff can occur. However, at system level, effectiveness concerns lead to policy misjudgment, tinkering and churn – the introduction of new policy measures before existing ones have a chance to bed down and/or their consequences understood, the equivalent of Deming's continued adjustments to hot water flow. The next part of the chapter examines these two phenomena.

Teaching to the test

If tests and exams are very high stakes, teachers understandably focus their efforts on ensuring that children get good results. Of course, a few teachers teach to the test because they do not know how to do anything else. But more commonly, they simply do not have time to maintain practices that they think are important as well as do high-stakes testing work. Experienced teachers in schools committed to a broad and balanced curriculum and with good inspection grades are more likely to be able to combine testing imposts with rich pedagogical repertoires than those who are new or less accomplished.[52] It is hard to ignore the tests and inspections altogether.

There are complex reasons for why teaching to the test may have a pedagogical raison d'être:

- Well-designed tests can pinpoint patterns of error or indicate that individual students who generally work hard, work neatly and/or are dealing with complex ideas do have some areas they need to work on. The reason to test is to diagnose and remediate particular issues in student learning.[53]

- Aggregated and analysed test results may show up patterns in learning that need attention – particular groups of students failing, or common errors indicating lack of coverage. School leaders may use test results to guide allocation of time and budget for teacher professional development or teacher research.[54]

There may also be a moral basis for teaching to the test:

- When tests are used for access to particular resources or are a path to life opportunities, then teachers see doing well in tests/exams as a matter of justice. Even if they know tests/exams to be stressful and/or implicitly biased they see the consequences of failure – through any lack of attention to what is required – as a worse consequence than a narrow teaching focus on how to pass.
- When tests are used to judge the viability of their school – the school will be closed or academised if test/exam or inspection results are poor – then their own job security, and that of their colleagues, depends on good results. In some instances, students might also be disadvantaged if school closure means that they have to travel further to a new school or if there is no guaranteed place for them.

It takes a very brave school and school leader to stick to their educational philosophy in the face of a system espousing uniform and highly reductive approaches to effectiveness, but this does occasionally happen. My colleague Chris Hall and I conducted research in a school where a veteran and very accomplished headteacher refused to institute New Labour's Literacy Hour.[55] The Literacy Hour was a system-wide effectiveness strategy designed to focus attention on 'the basics' and lift literacy performance at the bottom of the attainment graph, as measured through standardised tests. The head summoned the chief inspector, at the time the formidable Chris Woodhead, whom she knew personally, and informed him of her decision not to have a Literacy Hour. His response was that as long as the students still did well on the tests, the school wouldn't be penalised. The school remained outstanding and an example that it was possible for inner-city children to engage in a creative literatures-based curriculum and still do well on standardised measures. But this was an exceptional case.

Much more common is the 'triage'[56] response from schools under pressure to show rapid improvement in their test results. Triage is an orthodoxy about what can be done quickly to become more effective. Schools identify those students who are closest to the target 'pass' mark and apply intensive remediation, often in the form of additional tutoring and after school and holiday classes, in order to get them over the line. The line is not imaginary but visible on tables and graphs of aggregated attainment. The triage approach tends to ignore children who are close to the top and those at the bottom – it doesn't see every child as having a need for additional support. Rather, it is the school's need to be seen as effective that produces narrowly targeted intercession.

An alternative approach used by failing schools is an attempt to moderate effectiveness by controlling variation and standardising aspects of pedagogy. This might be, say, the introduction of 'best practice' teaching methods, or of a more prescribed curriculum, or both. My colleagues and I observed the ways in which a best practice approach could skew everyday life in schools for students.[57] We shadowed young people for a day to experience lessons from their point of view, and saw a uniform display of daily lesson objectives, reductive learning targets and four-part lessons which used quizzes and games as their primary mode of ensuring factual recall. The result was a rhythmic monotony which encouraged some students to underperform rather than the reverse. This was, we argued, a case where saving the school came at the cost of students' engagement and attainment.

Teaching to the test is understandable in a system in which success and failure are judged by results. However, the resulting effects on wholistic student learning are of serious concern, and we know too little about the long-term effects, particularly on equity and inclusion beyond school.

Tinkering with policy

Policy churn is a feature of contemporary school reform.[58] Churn, produced by ongoing tinkering, is an international phenomenon and is usually driven by political impatience and eagerness to get electoral approval. Schools in England have been concerned about rapid changes in policy for some time and the short time frames in which measures of effectiveness are implemented. Schools are cumbersome organisations and changing routines takes considerable time, money and effort. Rapid change generally works against effectiveness in the short term. Three examples will suffice to make the point that tinkering can work against effectiveness: (1) curriculum reform, (2) uniform and discipline and (3) expanding grammar schools.

Curriculum reform

When the Coalition came to power in the UK they decided, as discussed in Chapter 2, to redesign the curriculum in England and scale up academisation. This, together with new kinds of schools, would introduce innovation into the system as well as greater efficiency and effectiveness. These policies have placed particular pressures on schools and have perhaps had some unanticipated consequences.

The new curriculum espoused a cultural and pedagogical approach that is abbreviated to a 'knowledge-rich' curriculum, after E. D. Hirsch.[59] Hirsch's argument was that in order to participate in society and to become socially mobile, all students needed access to the best of 'common culture'. In order to steer schools towards this new approach, a new performance measure was introduced for secondary schools. How much the new curriculum is a good curriculum is not the concern of this discussion. What is important here is the accompanying measure of effectiveness. A response to what was seen as the 'dumbing down' of GSCEs, the English Baccalaureate (EBacc) is a core selection of subjects: English, maths, a science, one of history or geography and an ancient or modern foreign language. Schools were to be held accountable for the percentage of students who achieved these five subjects with grades 5–9. This was the new 'gold standard' for effectiveness.

The government initially intended to make 90 per cent of pupils in England study for the EBacc. It is not surprising that in response to this policy, many schools have reduced the time, budget and staffing spent on non-EBacc subjects. GCSE enrolments in the arts have particularly suffered, with a 35 per cent decline in arts subjects from 2010 to 2018.[60] The minister responsible for digital culture, media and sport reported to a parliamentary inquiry into live music that the falling number of enrolments in music was a result of the EBacc, a phenomenon denied by his colleague, the schools minister.[61] At the time of writing the EBacc is still on the books, but its use as a primary effectiveness measure appears somewhat diminished. However, its toxic skewing effects are still in play, with arts, physical education and computing science in particular being studied less across the country.

Uniforms and discipline

The ratcheting up of academisation and the increase of new types of schools also appears to have strengthened one of the trends made prominent via the earlier policy of school choice – the equation of effectiveness with discipline. An uncompromising approach to student behaviour which depends on a 'tough' approach to school uniform and behaviour infractions is said to improve results. Students are well behaved and thus learn better. The strong discipline approach was endorsed by a former chief inspector, Sir Michael Wilshaw; when in office he was reported as saying that school uniform 'added to pupil's sense of self-worth'.[62] In 2019, the Conservative government allocated £10 million to a new behaviour network which would support 500 schools to develop best practice in sanctions, detention systems and the like.[63] Contentious measures – 'silent corridors' (no running and talking in corridors)[64] and the use of isolation booths[65] and assemblies designed to intimidate[66] – are defended by causally connecting discipline and improved student attainment.[67] While there are other reasons for school uniform, such as reducing cost for parents, and while every school does need to keep and instil order, it is the correlation of appearance and obedience with learning and effectiveness that is of note here. Effectiveness can be made visible through how students look and act.

There is considerable concern about the effectiveness effects of uniform and well-drilled behaviour.[68] There is debate about whether attention to the easily observable takes time and attention away from other more important matters, such as learning, whether the focus on discipline comes at the expense of pastoral support and whether focusing on the observable puts public relations and regulation ahead of inclusion, resilience,[69] character education[70] and a 'growth mindset'.[71] But the more discipline is seen as synonymous with effectiveness the more schools are pushed to comply with politically directed and visible behavioural norms. That diverse students might not all benefit from a singular approach to order is not considered.

Expansion of grammar schools

Congruent with the reassertion of these trappings of 1950s grammar schools comes pressure for reinstalling grammar schools themselves (see also Chapter 2). The formation of the Conservative government was accompanied by renewed calls for the expansion of grammar schools, where entry would be on 'merit' assessed through a competitive test administered at the end of year six. Arguments for grammar school expansion highlighted their effectiveness – their apparent postwar success as agents of social mobility – a meritocratic claim that conflates the socioeconomic context of postwar Great Britain with the workings of selective schools. The grammar school lobby called on a rhetorical combination of the value of parent choice, and objective measures – exams select the most meritorious of the working class who would otherwise miss out on an academically excellent education. Box 6.3 shows how one *Guardian* journalist sought to explain the debate to readers.[72]

Prime Minister May's speech harks directly back to Margaret Thatcher. Labour is accused of being elitist and denying working people their opportunity to compete on an equal basis with those of their peers. Her government, by contrast, would move to institute yet more change in the system.

Box 6.3: Political debates over schooling

The drive for comprehensive secondary education had been part of a postwar consensus that saw education as part of a Scandinavian-style egalitarian social democratic society. Most kids would go to their local secondary school, where they would encounter a range of people from different social and cultural backgrounds, which would help to foster a strong, diverse society in the following generations. This was the general social good for which the comprehensive system aimed. It was inextricably linked to similarly comprehensive provision in healthcare and housing.

May's vision is very different. Parents, she said, had been operating a system of 'selection by house prices' in the secondary system. She would put an end to that by reintroducing 'selection by academic merit'.

'Politicians – many of whom benefited from the very kind of education they now seek to deny to others – have for years put their own dogma and ideology before the interests and concerns of ordinary people,' she said. Her answer was to overturn the nostrums of the anti-selective 'educational elite' and bring back selective grammar schools.

Her government, she said, would be all about creating opportunities for 'ordinary working-class families' – the sort of people who had been ignored and even despised by a national elite of policy makers and other shadowy and ill-defined power-brokers. The chief characteristic this elite exhibited was hypocrisy: they opposed selection and grammar schools, but sent their own kids to private schools or used their higher salaries to move to the catchment areas of popular or successful comprehensive schools, leaving failing schools behind to be occupied by the poor.

Researchers strongly contest the history mobilised in this policy narrative. Gorard and Siddiqui, for instance, argue that:

> pupils attending grammar schools are stratified in terms of chronic poverty, ethnicity, language, special educational needs and even precise age within their

year group. ... [T]he results from grammar schools are no better than expected, once these differences are accounted for. There is no evidence base for a policy of increasing selection.[73]

Gorard and Siddiqui conclude that 'This kind of clustering of relative advantage is potentially dangerous for society'. Introducing more grammar schools in the name of effectiveness for a meritorious few could well produce a less effective school system overall. However, any signs of individual students being more successful in schooling will undoubtedly be used to counterbalance statistics in an ongoing debate about what constitutes effectiveness and how it should achieved and be measured.

Tests and exams, speedy change and tinkering, are not the only skewing effects of effectiveness. There are more dubious consequences too, some of which indicate corrupted practice and some of which are clearly corrupt, as Chapter 7 shows.

Secrecy, lies and gaming

Secretive DfE academy committees finally publish agendas

Times Educational Supplement, 17 December 2018

DfE silent on Education Fellowship Trust's payouts

Schools Week, 11 May 2019

More than 49,000 pupils 'disappeared' from English schools

The Guardian, 18 April 2019

Ofsted closes in on gaming schools

Times Educational Supplement, 4 September 2018

Britain's best school has its SATs results ruled null and void after 'superhead' takes failing primary to top award

The Mail online, 21 July 2018

School effectiveness must be performed and be visible. Test, exam and inspection effectiveness measures (discussed in Chapter 6) depend on a top-down view – funders examine data assembled from various measurements of providers and provision. But governments too are expected to be transparent, their doings open to public scrutiny. A bottom-up view occurs when the public are able to access policies, reports and data that they can use to make their own judgments about government effectiveness. The 'gaze' goes both ways.

The downward funder view can be helpfully traced back to the British philosopher Jeremy Bentham. Bentham designed a Panopticon – a prison built on the principle of centralised inspection. A circular building afforded the prison governor, or a deputised warden sitting in a tower, a view of every prisoner. Although the omnipotent watcher was invisible, prisoners knew they were watched and managed their own behaviour to avoid punishment.[1] Discipline depended on prisoner internalisation of rules, via the application of surveillance. While Bentham's prison was never built in exactly the way that he imagined it, the panoptic gaze has, according to Foucault,[2] become the dominant way in which modern societies are governed and populations disciplined. Recent sophisticated digital platforms and algorithms have provided new panoptic avenues for government to 'see' and monitor a range of public, institutional and private behaviours.[3] They have also afforded sousveillance: the means for people to see themselves through a range of calculating devices.

Bentham also believed it was possible for there to be common interests and common cause between elected rulers and subjects.[4] This depended on two-way accountability: his top-down gaze was matched by a bottom-up equivalent. A republican advocate of liberal values, Bentham envisaged a form of open government in which officials were watched by the people and held accountable for their actions. He imagined this as a Public Opinion Tribunal where the public were able to watch officials in action and hold them to account. He saw freedom of the press as integral to the workings of 'unfettered and inclusive' public debate.[5]

Much of what Bentham envisaged in the Public Opinion Tribunal now exists in modern Western democracies in particular forms. Not only can the public attend parliamentary sessions but their views are regularly polled by political parties. Yet the development of nudge politics – where publicly polled opinions are steered by questions asked and options proposed – is arguably a perversion of open government, where the 'top' attempts to move 'bottom' opinion in particular directions. In Bentham's terms, nudge politics is a device intended to make the ruler's interests those of the people, instead of the reverse.

Bentham was of the view that rulers could and would likely have sinister interests unless they were held to account, and it was thus imperative to avoid creating a false consensus on any issue.[6] The use of sophisticated spin can easily be understood as just such a move.

Bentham was a utilitarian philosopher and his ideas were later criticised for being elitist, exclusive and too focused on government rather than democracy.[7] Nevertheless, his allied notions of top-down and bottom-up openness and the potential for perversion of the goal of open government are salient in this chapter. The degree to which effectiveness works for and against the top-down and bottom-up gaze, supporting a culture of transparency as well as secrecy and deception, is explored through three sections focused on secrecy and lies, gaming the system and management malpractice.

Secrecy and lies

Being open is problematic for governments. There may be good reasons for some information not being public; questions of national security, for instance. But equally at issue is that public trust may be reduced rather than enhanced by seeing what government actually does.[8] And an expectation that government is 'transparent' could paradoxically make it more secretive and guarded. As in the dystopian world of *Nineteen Eighty-Four*,[9] policy makers might speak in code and do the equivalent of passing notes under the table for fear of what telling the truth might bring.

Being open is also problematic for schools. In a competitive enrolment environment the question of risk and trust is a major concern. Schools may be reluctant to make some of their management decisions public for fear they will be misinterpreted.[10] The recent example of a school in Birmingham boycotted by some parents and religious leaders because of its inclusive approach to sex and relationships education is a case in point.[11] But if the production of glossy brochures and websites tends towards advertising the good and hiding the bad, then schools can arguably be seen to be simply following the lead of their government.

The UK government espouses transparency but its practice sometimes falls far short of its rhetorical commitment. Journalists and the public now routinely make FoI requests in order to get information about decision making, costs and statistics, areas where one might expect transparency. The UK website whatdotheyknow.com, run by the charity MySociety, aggregates such requests, and at the time of writing held 591,163 requests to 24,262[12] different authorities.

The Information Commissioner's Office (ICO) guidelines state that public organisations should publish minutes, agendas and background documents. Public organisations are not expected to publish any data that invades privacy, documents older than the past three years, information that is too resource-intensive to publish or lower-level meeting minutes. Public organisations can edit minutes and documents but should, ideally, make their reasons for editing clear. Internal government documents may be withheld only when it is not in the public interest that they be made public. Exemptions to FoI requests are allowed when there are concerns about the conduct of public affairs, personal privacy, information obtained in confidence and commercial interests.[13] FoI requests thus often produce partial accounts and/or redacted documents. Sometimes FoI applicants are referred to multiple publicly available texts which they are expected to analyse themselves.

The ICO does have sharp regulatory teeth. It can secure prosecutions, as it did successfully against Cambridge Analytica for their misuse of data. The Cambridge Analytica investigation began with a subject access request made in the US, demonstrating the potential for individual citizen FoI requests to have significant consequences. The ICO reports to government and the public on the ways in which public organisations respond to FoI requests: it can name and shame secretive public organisations. The ICO also deals with appeals made by the public about inadequate FoI responses and it does sometimes overrule organisations' decisions and compel information to be made public.[14] Appeals against FoI refusal are lengthy and can be costly, but the ICO website reports that since 2005 it has ruled on more than 8,500 FoI and environmental information cases.[15] Each ICO investigation requires a decision which assesses public interest. If the interests of a private business, or an individual with particular business interests, are taken to be more important that the public good of transparency, a decision can come perilously close to 'capture' of the civil service or a charity by a special interest group (a form of clientelism). The ICO treads this fine line in each and every appeal.

It is worth looking at an individual incident to see how the ICO process plays out in real time. The education journalist and former teacher Laura McInerney wanted to get information about free school decisions made by the DfE. Her first FoI request for detailed information about why some free school applications were refused was turned down. She was told that releasing the information would encourage people to copy applications, would put off potential bidders and could be used against schools in the future.[16] McInerney twice asked for an internal review of the decision[17] but was again refused. Her appeal to the ICO was successful. The DfE were instructed to release the information for 'strong public interest' reasons. However, the DfE appealed and took the ICO judgment to a first-tier tribunal.[18] McInerney lost at the tribunal because the judge decided that the DfE didn't have the resources available to redact the documents.[19] Some three and a half years later, the DfE notified McInerney that she could have the relevant documents.

McInerney has been able to reveal this story through social media. Social media is now a significant tool for ordinary citizens wanting to hold image-conscious organisations, both public and private, to account. Anyone can blog or tweet about any concern, including lack of transparency. Traditional media are less frequently able to reveal government misbehaviour. But traditional investigative journalism still functions as a check on government; examples from Watergate to the infamous Australian government whiteboard affair – revelations about undocumented funding decisions which brought down a federal minister[20] – attest to the power of an independent media. But social media adds exponentially to the pressures that can be exerted on public organisations. Social media is, on occasions, Bentham's public affairs tribunal where the ordinary citizen can debate government decisions, practices and directions. Social media is thus also another site for the exercise of government spin, an important aspect of transparency realpolitik.

Consistent use of spin reduces trust in government.[21] The public do generally understand that their elected leaders manipulate information. From Australian Prime Minister John Howard being caught in lies about refugees,[22] to Donald Trump's litany of comments about Clinton, Obama, Mexico and Iran,[23] the examples keep coming. In 2019, in an extraordinary series of interventions, the UK Statistics Authority (UKSA) reprimanded the DfE and its minister, Damian Hinds, for its misuse of statistics. Box 7.1 shows media headlines and extracts from the sequence of UKSA letters.

Box 7.1: Damian Hinds and the UK Statistics Authority

Damian Hinds censured by stats watchdog over school funding claims

Schools Week, 14 March 2018[24]

The Director General for Regulation requested that the DfE improve its presentation of statistics: 'it would help support public understanding if the Department were to publish a consistent and comprehensive set of official statistics on school funding, to which all participants in public debate could refer'.[25]

UK statistics authority has 'serious concerns' over DfE funding claims

The Guardian, 8 October 2018

The Director for Regulation writes to the DfE Chief Data Officer: We have discussed the recent Tweet and blog on schools funding. The way statistics have been presented gives a potentially misleading picture of changes in schools funding. In particular, the graph in the Tweet had a truncated axis that gives an exaggerated picture of the improvements; and the Tweet was presented in cash terms, not real terms. It also did not take account of an increase in the number of school age children in England. In addition, we are concerned about a related blog on school funding (which the Department has now updated). In this blog, the

Department compared spending on education with that in other OECD countries. The comparison included a range of aspects of spending that are unrelated to school funding.'[26]

DfE told to publish official school spending figures amid another stats slapdown

Schools Week, 30 May 2019

The Director for Regulation urges further action by the DfE: 'For a meaningful debate about public spending in any area, it is necessary to have a trustworthy data source. In that context, we note that the Department does not produce a comprehensive set of official statistics on the funding of schools. A wide range of data sources on school funding are currently used to inform debate, by both the Department and others. This in turn can mean that statements using data are hard to verify and replicate, and this creates a risk of undermining the perceived trustworthiness of those making the statements.'[27]

What is most alarming about the letters in Box 7.1 is not that they were sent in the first place, but that various government ministers, including the Prime Minister, were still using the statistics in question some weeks later. The UKSA warned the DfE yet again in May 2019 about its partial and misleading reporting of statistics on school funding.[28]

On 7 June 2019, *Schools Week* reported a further eight uses of dubious statistics recorded in Hansard.[29] Their report juxtaposed the Hansard details with the results of a survey conducted by the campaigning lobby Worth Less?[30] which showed that 99.2 per cent of the surveyed 1,500 headteachers did not trust DfE statements about budgets. It is hardly surprising, given reports that four in five heads contribute to their schools' finances[31] and teachers regularly pay for resources out of their own money,[32] that there is scepticism about claims that there is more money than ever going into schooling.

This kind of statistical spin is not confined to the UK. In the US, the state of Colorado has recently been accused of hiding data on student performance in the name of privacy,[33] and California accused of providing inadequate data about differences between student groups, schools and districts on its data portal.[34] In Canada there are consistent calls for better data on race and school attainment, even though these might challenge the national narrative about success on global assessment measures.[35]

On 13 June 2019, *Schools Week* reported that the DfE's most senior civil servant had promised to do better with statistics, saying that he wanted to build the department's reputation as a 'trustworthy communicator of statistics'.[36] Is this, we might wonder, a case of a civil service mandarin shouldering all the blame on behalf of its funder government? And, if the DfE is to be an honest broker of information, where else, we might ask, is there other information not yet made public? Headteachers are concerned about lack of information from RSCs,[37] and media are concerned that the DfE hides information about schools that are under investigation[38] and are slow in dealing with schools that fail to publish annual accounts as they are obliged to do.[39] How much does the funder–purchaser relationship lend itself to politically favourable information practices?

It is not simply the potential for misinformation created by spin or sins of omission that matters here. It is also that organisational cultures are set from the top. And, when combined with the push for effectiveness, practices of hiding information can bed in. They can influence a whole organisational culture.

MATs and free schools are legally obliged to publish their minutes, accounts and reports, just like a business or charity, but are not compelled to engage anyone beyond appointed trustees in decision making. Here is where the question of parent accountability, the possibility of the upward gaze, comes into play. (As explained earlier, transparency and accountability at the local level are one of the measures strongly correlated with successful anti-corruption practice.) The vast majority of MATs still see some form of parent involvement as good practice, even if they are not required to have parents as trustees. Most trusts maintain individual school bodies where parents are represented, but with more limited responsibilities than before (see Chapter 2). Many also consult parents about policy changes, but they do not *have* to do this – and some don't. MATs that do not make themselves open to parents see their responsibility and accountability as directed upwards rather than outwards to the communities they serve.

Openness is also a matter of organisational effectiveness. Research tells us that organisations with formal processes for achieving consensus, and for bringing top-down and bottom-up values, experiences and imperatives together, are likely to function well.[40] Along with parents, staff can both understand and influence organisational directions. Students may also have a say. But when there are no formal means of reaching consensus and when administrators make autocratic decisions, the consequences include poor morale and passive resistance from staff.

Secretive management, be it at system or school level, morphs easily into spin. Where poor administration and spin coexist in a non- virtuous but mutually reinforcing relationship, Bentham's Public Opinion Tribunal shifts from meeting rooms and considered debate to media investigations, public demonstrations and caustic exchanges on social media. An acrimonious politics of voice and exit prevails.[41] This is probably not the kind of public accountability that either Bentham or Chubb and Moe[42] (see Chapter 6) imagined. These are corrupted practices which erode goodwill as well as undermine effectiveness – the goal they are apparently intended to support.

The connection between a top-down spin culture, lack of transparency, poor administration and its links to effectiveness measures also supports a variety of clearly corrupt activities.

Gaming the system

Gaming means using rules and procedures designed to ensure due process and protection of a system in order to manipulate it to particular ends. The term gaming can alternatively be expressed as bending the rules, rigging the results, abusing or working the system – or simply cheating. Gaming can, for instance, be undertaken by companies wishing to avoid taxation: they employ clever accountants who find loopholes they can use to bump up costs and losses, or move their money to offshore havens. It is perhaps indicative of the English school system culture that the term gaming is now widespread and generally understood. However, there is debate about what constitutes gaming and what is fair use of the existing rules. And it is almost impossible to gauge how much gaming goes on.

Two examples of borderline gaming can be seen in the ways in which schools deal with high-stakes tests and examinations. There were various responses to the introduction of performance targets for GCSEs, and various ways to understand them. A number of schools achieved spectacular success rates against their targets by offering a menu of largely vocational courses. This was seen by critics as a form of gaming as it was allegedly easier for students to get good grades in vocational than in the traditional academic subjects. The 'easy option' judgment stemmed from the greater emphasis on doing and making, group work and moderated teacher assessment in vocational courses. Recent longitudinal analysis by Data Lab nuances these critiques.[43] The longer-term outcomes for young people who took the vocational courses is not much different than those of a comparator group taking a more conventional academic route. Vocationally qualified young adults had slightly lower rates of participation in higher education, and were slightly more likely to be employed at age 29; this can be understood as an expression of their aspirations. But neither of these two results suggest that the vocational students were any less well prepared by their courses. But Data Lab does question whether the courses were overvalued in performance tables and whether schools encouraged so many students to take vocational options in order to boost or game their results.

GCSE procedures have now changed, partly in response to the strategies used by schools to maximise success. The certificate has changed: the option of partial resits and early and multiple entry to examinations have been removed. These changes are seen by teachers as producing a more level playing field which stops 'other schools' gaming.[44]

It is almost impossible to gauge how much gaming goes on. One indication might be taken from a survey of 548 volunteer teachers in secondary schools and colleges:[45] Eighty-three per cent had focused efforts on borderline students and 80 per cent taught what they thought would be on the test/exam; 49 per cent had not covered all of the specified content in order to concentrate on areas most likely to be tested; and 48 per cent had provided wording of sections of course work to students. However, only 6 per cent had opened exam papers before the specified time. The researchers found that teachers were often faced with difficult ethical dilemmas where they had to choose between doing what was right, and doing what was right for the school: performing well on audit measures. They concluded, congruent with corruption research, that 'changes in accountability metrics and qualification design … are no substitute for an ethical school culture'.[46]

A second example of debatable practice centres on whether independent schools are gaming the league tables by offering the International GCSE (IGCSE) rather than the newly redesigned examination-based English GCSE. The IGCSE was designed to accredit the International Baccalaureate (IB), a curriculum which provides access to a range of further and higher education options in a range of countries, not just England. When the first new GCSE awards were made in 2018, it was hardly surprising that there was interest in their effects and outcomes. In late December 2018, media reported a parliamentary Opposition speech which alleged that private schools were 'refusing' to shift to the new reformed GCSEs. The headlines 'Private schools "cheating GCSE system to rig their results"' (*The Independent*)[47] and 'Exam reforms boost private pupils in race for universities: Tough tests are forced on state schools as data reveals benefit to independent sector' (*The Observer*)[48] were followed by 'Labour demands inquiry into how GCSE reform has benefited private schools: Independent schools are offering easier IGCSEs as state schools trial harder exams' (*The Guardian*).[49] Independent schools were quick to defend their curriculum, nominating as reasons parent choice and the pedigree of the IB as a tried and tested international qualification, as opposed to the new and untested GCSE.[50]

The discourse of gaming emanates from a culture of suspicion about manoeuvrings designed to maximise results and league table positions. A further example is the selection of students, discussed in Chapter 6, which is seen as a form of gaming when schools apparently use guidelines related to specialisation, religious affiliation, residence and so on to choose students who will make their school results better. There are indeed reports of individual MATs who say they have no room for students with special needs.[51] The sense that some schools are playing the system is reinforced by a small but steady stream of media reports about schools where cheating actually does occur. Students are helped with test answers,[52] someone in the school marks falsely,[53] changes scripts or removes scripts[54] that would drag down results[55] and native speakers are enrolled in English-language tests not intended for them.[56] Weak teachers are sent home during inspections or excellent teachers shipped in.[57] Governors are sacked,[58] and teachers and heads prosecuted for cheating.[59] Media are quick to point out when some of these infractions occur at schools previously lauded by Tory ministers.[60]

If we are to take all of these media reports to be true, then gaming is widespread and endemic in English schools. Indeed, Channel 4 *Dispatches* claimed as much in 2015, saying that cheating was prevalent in British universities and schools.[61] Ofsted wrote to its inspectors in 2016 instructing them to look out for schools entering students for inappropriate qualifications in order to boost their league table standing.[62] In February 2018, *The Guardian* reported that nearly 2,300 malpractice offences were committed between 2012 and 2016 by staff in schools offering Oxford, Cambridge and Royal Society for the Arts (OCR) exams – this information was produced through an FoI request and was not initially in the public domain.[63] And in October 2018, *Schools Week* reported one academy CEO calling for changes to the ways in which primary tests were administered on the basis of 'a rise in SATs test results being suppressed because of cheating. Provisional data shows 2,688 test results were suppressed this year while the Standards and Testing Agency investigates maladministration, compared with just 723 last year.'[64]

The volume and consistency of this kind of reporting helps to produce and reproduce the impression of a prevalent gaming culture. It suggests that England's move to school choice and competition, based in large part on effectiveness measures such as tests and exams, is having perverse effects.

The government and DfE *are* keen to ensure that regulations about fair play are followed. In this, they depend on being able to detect and prosecute cheating when it happens, and here they rely heavily on whistle-blowers. In April 2017, the Office of Qualifications and Examinations, a non-ministerial body that regulates credentials, tests and exams, sent schools a suite of posters with the slogan *Seen it? Suspect it? Report it* to all schools.[65] The poster was intended to encourage staff to report (alternatively 'grass on') their colleagues. This is surely some evidence of government belief that a culture of cheating exists in schools, but is not right.

In his regular *Times Educational Supplement* opinion piece, Geoff Barton, the General Secretary of the ASCL, attributes gaming to the exam system. High-stakes tests produce cheating, he argues (see Box 7.2).

Box 7.2: Geoff Barton on monstrous exams

All it takes is an online post with a couple of blacked-out questions and a price tag of £70 for the whole paper, and the exam board has to launch a major operation to establish the scale of the breach and deal with the fallout. Here then is the situation in which Edexcel operator Pearson found itself at the end of last week over the leak of an A-level maths paper. And to its credit, it moved quickly in narrowing down the source of the leak to a geographic area, visiting every school in that area, and finding one centre in 'serious breach of correct practice'. ... This was an impressive response to a difficult situation. It should give confidence to centres that everything that can be done is being done.

An exam leak in the era of social media is a wildfire that proliferates so quickly that it is virtually impossible to contain and takes enormous effort to dampen down. And it does not stop there. Exams boards are facing an uphill struggle to remove fraudulent posts on social media from people claiming to have leaked GCSE papers. In some cases, individuals have posted photos of past papers with the date doctored, to try to con candidates into parting with cash.

But what can we possibly do to tackle these issues, given that social media is here to stay?

To start with we need to put things into perspective. The scale of the public examination system is enormous and the number of security breaches is small in comparison. Last year, there were a total of 68 breaches. Of these, 40 were due to schools or colleges opening, and sometimes handing out, the wrong exam paper, while only 14 involved a 'leak of materials'.[66]

In the longer term, we really must rethink an exam season that has grown to monstrous proportions. It has long been a fixture of our national life but the reforms of recent years, with their emphasis on terminal assessment and stripping out of coursework, have upped the ante even further. If we could imagine a different system in which there were fewer exams, and the final papers were only a part of how we assessed and guided young people to their future courses and careers, there would be many benefits.[67]

Barton's solution, and he is not alone in proposing this, is to diversify student assessment and reduce the pressure points where gaming and cheating might occur.

Exclusions and off-rolling

Another apparently popular form of gaming is the removal of students from class and/or the school in order to both make it more attractive to potential families, and better positioned in inspections and test/exams.

The vast majority of schools have a documented procedure for withdrawing students from lessons. Removal from class is intended to isolate the student from the situation where they are in trouble and troubling to others. This is a form of informal exclusion. Isolation is contentious and subject to media discussion about potential psychologically damaging effects[68] and legal action.[69] Formal exclusion is usually the result of a series of documented disciplinary infractions and can be fixed term or permanent, on site or off. While a few schools boast that they formally exclude no students at all, most do. Formal exclusion is on the rise in England, after some years of falling.[70]

Most formal exclusions short of permanent exclusions, such as being suspended from school for a period of time, or part- or full-time attendance at an alternative provision, keep the student on their 'home' school roll. However, these forms of administratively sanctioned exclusion have been joined by an increase in 'elective' home education,[71] and an illegitimate form of exclusion: off-rolling. Off-rolling, as the name suggests, occurs when students are illegally removed from the school roll. Ofsted define off-rolling as: 'the practice of removing a pupil from the school roll without using a permanent exclusion, when the removal is primarily in the best interests of the school, rather than the best interests of the pupil. This includes pressuring a parent to remove their child from the school roll.'[72]

There may be reasons officially recorded for off-rolling. For example, families transfer to another provision without following procedures, they move house or students begin looking for work. But the primary reason for off-rolling is highly likely to be because the students are a potential institutional hazard. Off-rolled students are generally a direct reputational risk for the school through their visible behaviour, or an indirect risk through dragging down performance averages. Rather than students presenting with persistent and unresolved behavioural issues manifest in records, and during inspections and community and parent visits, they are simply encouraged to leave. An Ofsted survey of teachers revealed that most teachers believed that off-rolling was motivated by league table position and the pressure of maintaining or improving position.[73]

Off-rolling – the disappearing of students – is a not a new phenomenon.[74] It has become public only recently. ASCL's Geoff Barton says he only became aware of the word in 2017 (see Box 7.3).

Box 7.3: Off-rolling

[A]s headteacher, you would periodically encounter students whose attitudes and behaviour made it impossible for us to accommodate or contain them. This is where local agreements, managed moves from one school to another, placements into pupil referral units, all gave some limited scope to give the pupil a second or third chance to succeed within our education system.

For students who were supremely disruptive, defiant, violent or threatening, there was permanent exclusion. Sometimes it was the only way to ensure alternative provision was found for the student, that order was restored for the school community, and that our school's values and standards were publicly reaffirmed.

I'm not misty-eyed about the need for some children sometimes to move off-roll from one institution to another. But I worry about the scale of off-rolling I'm now hearing about from the school and college leaders I routinely meet – and, increasingly, from the people I talk to in offices in Whitehall.[75]

The actual number of off-rolled students is hard to determine. An Ofsted 2018 investigation revealed some 300 schools engaged in off-rolling;[76] these schools were not named, as making them public might affect potential inspections, Ofsted said. An Education Policy Institute study located 50,000 pupils with unexplained moves. Education Datalab suggests that it is almost impossible to correctly identity the number of students who are off-rolled, but reported that it had located some 22,300 who had disappeared from rolls altogether.[77] Both Education Datalab and Ofsted say that it is income-poor pupils, those with special educational needs and pupils with low prior attainment who are disproportionately removed from the school roll.[78]

Ofsted have pursued the question of informal and illegal exclusion for quite some time. They know that schools: look the other way when students drift away; attempt to persuade parents to educate at home; or refer young people to alternative provision and then forget about them.[79] Ofsted have continually tried to find ways to make schools more accountable and responsible for the education of students on their roll. A House of Commons library briefing paper on off-rolling[80] notes several government moves designed to close loopholes, including a review of exclusion and alternative provision. They paper says that the lack of tracking data shows the need for new safeguards, sanctions and scrutiny – still more needs to be done. It is important to note that these recommended moves all focus on sanctions; the DfE have also recently begun to promote better in-school early intervention, prevention and remediation.

There is not as yet a positive policy incentive to encourage all children and young people to remain in school, grounded in a commitment to a full secondary education as a universal entitlement and benefit.

Management malpractice

Is off-rolling morally wrong – a corrupted practice? Yes. But there is a logic to it. If schools decide there is less risk attached to off-rolling than the risks of dropping position in test/exam league tables then off-rolling can be seen as a pragmatic actuarial decision. This position contrasts with schools with an explicit moral commitment to inclusion where the response may be to keep students at school and use public relations to mitigate against poor reputation, and perhaps the inspectorial gaze. And if off-rolling is a pragmatic response to the punitive use of comparative effectiveness measures then more regulation may not be sufficient, any more than transparency alone might create a climate of renewed trust in government. Tinkering with exclusion practices and monitoring off-rolling may even simply produce different forms of exclusion. Analogous to tax avoidance, schools and their managers may simply find other ways to manage the risks of competitive student attainment measures.

We could be forgiven for wondering why it is that gaming and off-rolling are relatively widespread. Is it that teachers and their managers are simply unethical people? There are of course, in the school system in England, incidents of fraud and disregard for procedure bordering on the criminal. These are clear-cut instances of unprincipled behaviour. But gaming and off-rolling are more common, and a simple explanation about individual behaviours – bad apples – seem less plausible.

Researchers suggest that of-the-moment and often pragmatic decisions are the norm for school leaders.[81] Scholars of unethical business practices suggest that the decision to engage in an ethically dubious practice is often instantaneous and spontaneous.[82] The wrongdoer thinks to themselves: 'If nothing happens to those who break the rules, then those responsible for regulating behaviours are turning a blind eye', 'If everyone else is breaking the rules, then not doing so is actually a disadvantage. I owe it to my people not to put them at a disadvantage', 'The risk of getting caught is not significant' or 'It is better to be caught in a misdemeanour than suffer a greater ill'. And afterward, culprits tell themselves: 'Breaking the rule was a moment of madness atypical of my usual approach'. Momentary decisions are embedded either in moral passivity or conflicted moralities engendered by the instrumentality of accountability and the apparent rationality of managerialism.

Practices such as off-rolling and gaming are symptoms of systemic structural *and* cultural practices. The shift to dubious leadership can be clearly seen in the ways in which school leader-managers deal with the pressures created by the structure and culture associated with effectiveness. They engage in transactional leadership which, combined with calculation, leads (as Zygmunt Bauman argues[83]) to 'faceless' organisations in which human connections, encounters and accountabilities matter less than numbers and records. Rather than the caring environment rooted in vision and mission, schools in toxic accountability cultures are desocialised.[84] They tend to become 'non-places'[85] where students are known by their potential scores, their funding status (Free School Meals or Pupil Premium) or their 'needs' calculation (special needs). Toxic leadership becomes possible, as well as poor spontaneous decision-making.

Let us move then to see how and why toxic leadership is systemic and not simply about flawed individuals. Previous chapters established that intensified measurement and audit practices reduce the space for autonomous professional judgment exercised by grassroots professionals such as teachers, nurses and social workers – although many of course do maintain ethical commitments and practices. However, they do so under considerable pressure. Digital trails make visible what has been done when, with whom and for how long. The emphasis on being able to evidence and make visible in text the work and achievements of the organisation produces accountabilities at every level. The work expected of line managers is to ensure that those below them reach codified targets and standards. Many line managers thus demand that teachers make very detailed forward plans for teaching, keep daily or weekly records of students' attendance, learning targets and attainment and use standardised and digitised forms of assessment. These records must be able to be produced with little or no notice. This is not a decentralised system but rather one which has recentralised around a core set of activities related to overall performance against systemic benchmarks. 'Performance' and 'delivery' are the important factors. Greany and Higham call this 'coercive autonomy'.[86]

The term managerialism is often used to denote the shift from administrators ensuring that an organisation runs smoothly in the interests of those it serves to leaders ensuring that the organisation can demonstrate it is doing what it is contracted to do. Paradoxically, the move to managerialism has led to downplaying the importance of management. Training materials and promotion criteria now focus on leadership and the capacity to articulate a vision and mission for the organisation, making staff more businesslike and responsible for public image as well as overall organisational performance.[87] The rhetoric of leadership separates out leaders from non-leaders; 'leadership' creates distance between an executive and the rest of the workforce, strongly demarking those who make decisions from those who carry them out. The managerialist work of headteachers, and sometimes one or two of their deputies, is generally directed down to staff as well as to organisational advancement, through the symbolic work of building a narrative about the schools' strengths and achievements, and through entrepreneurial activities ranging from marketing to raising funding to the provision of mentoring or services to other schools.[88]

In contexts where there is strong pressure to perform, designated line managers may adopt highly coercive practices, seek to control rather than empower, intimidate rather than coach and support, respond to challenges personally rather than analytically, micro-manage rather than delegate and order and require rather than discuss and negotiate.[89] Some line managers may even engage in maladministration.[90]

'Destructive' and 'dark' leadership has strong negative effects on staff work morale and behaviour[91] – the exact opposite of what is intended. Peter Milley lists eight forms of maladministration which are used to 'pursue misdeeds, cover tracks and instil passivity':[92]

- disqualification – excluding some people from expressing their point of view through tactics ranging from favouritism and creating a climate of fear to holding closed meetings;
- naturalisation – making something seem natural and fixed, or the result of individual disfunction, rather than structural or socio-historically produced;
- neutralisation – removing discussions of values through, for instance, the use of apparently 'objective evidence';
- topic avoidance – using rules and procedures to prevent discussion or alarmist narratives about potential reprisals;
- subjectification of expertise – preventing the sharing of interpretations of events so that some can be rendered idiosyncratic and exceptional;
- meaning denial and plausible deniability – repudiating accusations through coercive measures which may extend to destroying or hiding records or intimidating witnesses;
- legitimation – giving reasons for administrative actions that are presented as logical or urgent and in organisational interests rather than self-interest;
- pacification – engaging in discussion with the goal of reframing the debate, suggesting there is no longer a problem or that addressing a problem will create an even worse situation.[93]

Such maladministrative practices have a range of consequences, but one of the most important is the impact on staff.

The vast literature on teacher stress almost always discusses combinations of work pressures – workload, time spent at work, heavy demands – and unsympathetic work cultures.[94] Delivery at all costs and/or workplaces that are not organised to support staff are common causes of low staff morale.[95] The same combination of excessive demand, long hours and poor management is correlated with high staff turnover and early career departure,[96] now an acute issue in many schools in England and beyond. Media suggest that half of London's teachers quit within five years;[97] the major teaching union claimed that in 2018, a staggering 80 per cent of teachers have considered quitting in the past year.[98] Some research attributes this professional alienation to the nature of the work rather than its quantity.[99] What matters is what is to be done not how much work there is, with accountability and performativity being the key to poor retention.

Research into bullied teachers almost inevitably lists the same factors as that on stress, but specifically points to the poisonous combination of power imbalances between teachers and their leaders and a fearful environment. Intentional and repeated humiliation, arbitrary allocation of work, favouritism and unfair distribution of privileges erode collegiality from schools and undermine individual and collective well-being (see Box 7.4).[100] They make teachers ill and push them out of the profession.

Box 7.4: A bullied teacher

Because her intimidating behaviour was gradual, subtle and at the same time explosively unpredictable, it was incredibly confusing. Part of me felt I could still win her over, or please her, and make her proud of me again. When she told me I showed a complete lack of commitment to the school, I was distraught. Instead of standing up for myself, I knuckled down and tried to work harder, stay at school later, and aim higher ... until I ended up in a heap.

To some extent, the whole school suffered, although there were two or three of us who were most likely to find ourselves on the receiving end of her most hurtful comments. Colleagues would discreetly let each other know whether or not it was a safe day to say good morning to her. We supported each other but did not seek help or dare to confront her about her behaviour. We were fearful for our jobs and possible future references. And, eventually, the unacceptable became normal.

Countless friends and colleagues have admitted they've also experienced similar bullying at school. Ofsted puts huge pressure on primary and secondary schools, which is passed on to staff by headteachers. Some of those at the chalkface go under with the strain of trying to cushion that pressure from above, to protect the children.[101]

Bricheno and Thornton, in their aptly entitled book *Crying in cupboards*, note that factors which contribute to both direct and indirect bullying include leaders new to the job, pressures to show rapid improvement and moves to reduce the staffing budget.[102] Bricheno and Thornton argue that even when school leaders try to create caring environments, performative pressures create conditions where they respond by creating divide-and-rule staffrooms. Public discussion and challenge make things worse. Heads are often reluctant for teachers to speak up and then do not know, or do not find out, how to deal with complaints. Bullied teachers report that colleagues rarely spoke up for them and were more concerned to protect themselves for fear that they would be next.[103] But occasionally teachers do act collectively to confront bullying.[104]

School leaders pass down to teachers the funder–purchaser demands for greater effectiveness and efficiency, because they too are subject to systemic intimidation, including public humiliation and losing their job if their school fails to deliver.[105] There are numerous tales in the media of headteachers who are suspended[106] and/or held culpable for school failures.[107] Many heads are prevented from discussing the circumstances of their removal because of legal agreements linked to payouts – 'sacked and gagged' as *The Guardian* once put it.[108] There are also instances where heads contest decisions to remove them.[109] But the suspension of a headteacher who starred in a school reality television series for allegedly changing student records,[110] and the resignation of another after inspection results worsened,[111] stand as warnings that *all* heads are vulnerable.

Woodley and Morrison McGill suggest that toxic schools are often subject to repeated restructures, none of which overturn the hierarchical relations between staff and school leaders.[112] Staff are either balkanised, highly isolated individualists or a collective prone to dysfunctional 'group think'. They suggest that it is vital that senior leaders listen to teachers. Putting the human before performance is, they suggest, imperative if unhealthy school power relationships are to be changed.

These organisational failings (secrecy, gaming, exclusion and off-rolling, lack of humanity and maladministration), perhaps the unintended effects of effectiveness, are indications of systemic problems. They are, to return to the major theme of the book, strong suggestions of a system which is corrupted. A system which in its operation fails to act in ways that are congruent with its goals.

Chapters 8 and 9, the final two chapters of the book, address the challenge to humanise and change the system.

8

Rebuilding
organisational infrastructure

Home education rises, with schools left to 'pick up pieces'
Schools Week, 7 July 2017

Our education system isn't working. It's time for a new approach
Huffington Post, 1 December 2017

Education reforms causing greater inequality in schools, major study finds
The Independent, 1 July 2018

English schools are broken. Only radical action will fix them
The Guardian, 9 August 2018

Gove and Johnson make school funding pledges as education becomes key campaign issue
Schools Week, 3 June 2019

Corruption, as defined at the start of the book, is understood as the abuse of entrusted power for private gain, where private can mean an individual or an organisation. It can also be understood as the corrosion of government when elected politicians fail to act in the public interest. Corrupted practices include: patronage (where the object of exchange is a vertical move to assure allegiance and loyalty), patrimonialism (the horizontal exchange of resources and favours including cronyism, blurring of public and private in procurement and partial and arbitrary application of rules) and state capture and political particularism (private interests dictate to or unfairly influence governing actors). All of these practices have featured in previous chapters.

So far the book has elaborated on how a particular take on efficiency and effectiveness produces instances of individual corrupt behaviours within the English school system, particularly fraud, procurement malpractice and cheating/lying. But, I argue, there are many more examples of corrupted practices – off-rolling, gaming, excessive remuneration, secrecy, teaching to the test, toxic management and so on. The case made is that corrupted practices are a result of an economistic (calculating and competitive) logic materialised in the FPP organisational structure. I also suggest that interventions intended to produce more efficiency and effectiveness may in fact sometimes do the opposite.

The previous chapters, taken together, indicate strongly that the education system lacks a structure and culture which supports integrity, even though the majority of people within it do generally act ethically. Schools largely remain principled and dedicated to the interests of children and young people because of the personal commitments of staff. The system runs on goodwill and professionalism. But punitive top-down management and a culture of spin, combined with the contemporary educational muddle of variously administered autonomous units, do not support the institutional practices needed to produce a 'good' school system. The first section of this chapter and the whole of Chapter 9 deal with the question of what is good. My analysis here is guided by the wise words of Australia's Wiradjuri people: *yindyamarra winhanganha*, the wisdom in respectfully knowing how to live well in a world worth living in – surely a bedrock value of and for a public education system.

This chapter examines some remedies, germane to ending schooling scandals, which are prescribed for the current school system. The chapter canvasses four areas for changing the economic rationalities that dominate public policy in England and elsewhere. These are expressed as proposals for changes in the accountability regime, more and better regulation, structural change and the adoption of a code of ethics.

Proposal for change: end perverse accountability incentives

The previous chapters listed some of the toxic consequences which arise from a high-stakes, narrow and digitally integrated accountability system. These included:

- poor measurement design and the use of a small number of proxy measurements for major decisions;
- triage measures designed to get school performance over the line rather than offer support to all students;
- teaching to the test, skewing the learning of all students but particularly those traditionally not served well by schooling;
- bullying of teachers and toxic school work cultures;
- off-rolling and various quasi-legal forms of in- and out-of-school exclusion;
- gaming exams and tests;
- lack of transparency and use of spin.

Previous chapters also offered some remedies. It *is* important for equity purposes to understand how well the system is working in the interests of all children and young people. One of the obvious ways to reduce some of the toxic effects of current accountability regimes is to separate the testing of system equity and effectiveness from that designed to diagnose teaching and learning issues for students and the functioning of individual schools. Once these two are separated, it is possible to consider system measurement using a representative, not a census, sample and perhaps using a rolling range of measures over a number of years. This is more like the testing conducted by the OECD and the NAEP in the US (see Chapter 6).

Another obvious option is to change the emphasis on the punitive – at present there are more adverse consequences for apparent poor performance than rewards for doing well. The negative systemic gaze takes too little notice of contextual factors; algorithmic blinkers screen out anything beyond the attainment of students in a narrow range of tests and often miss areas where schools are doing well. An accountability system oriented towards support rather than punishment would not trigger school closure and academisation after a single inspection but rather offer enhanced support. In England, this would mean ending league tabling of national examinations and the heavy use of market accountability.

School inspection might shift to become more formative in its evaluations, rather than issue summative singular grades which fail to capture the complexity of schools. The OECD reports that most countries do have an inspection system of some kind.[1] Inspection usually evaluates compliance with rules and regulations, quality of instruction, student performance, financial management and the satisfaction and perceptions of students, parents and staff. But only ten countries say that inspection had a high influence on school closure.[2] In other words, the balance of punishment to support is generally different to that in use in England.

Alternative modes of inspection might be canvassed[3] – after all, some countries in the world, including those above England on international league tables, do not have an expensive inspection service. As Sahlberg notes, the much praised Finnish education system has been built on 'ideas of sustainable leadership that place strong emphasis on teaching and learning, intelligent accountability, encouraging schools to craft optimal learning environments and implement educational content that best helps their students reach the general goals of schooling'.[4]

According to Sahlberg, intelligent accountability means that decentralised schools are trusted, and are accountable to the system and to their communities for student learning. Education authorities are held accountable to schools for making it possible for them to achieve educational outcomes. Words such as trust, professionalism, respect and reciprocity are materialised in a high-support, low-punishment approach to schooling.[5]

At school level, accountability measures might use both standard and locally designed instruments, incorporate teacher judgments and be moderated and benchmarked to allow valid comparison against national averages. They would be available for local decision making and inform improvement strategies as well as student (individual and group) support.

These are of course simply possibilities. In the first instance, public discussion about accountabilities is long overdue: to whom, what, how, how often and with what effects. Simple solutions such as replacing Ofsted will simply arouse opposition. Taking time to think collectively about better systems of accountability will pay off not only in terms of a better result, but also in wider ownership and less suspicion of a new regime.

Proposal for change: more regulation

Regulation is a key management function. Regulations make clear what can and cannot be done, and set out the consequences for failure to comply.

In the English education FPP model, some regulation is designed and carried out by arm's length independent bodies – the ESFA for instance has the capacity to discipline fiscal miscreants. Carrying out regulatory decisions is, however, often delegated to the civil service 'purchaser' – the DfE and its outreach RSCs. For example, Ofsted decisions may trigger academisation or rebrokerage which must be managed by RSCs. There are also independent auditors who can investigate regulatory breaches and make compliance orders – the NAO is one such body. Arm's length regulators can also recommend to the funder changes in regulations, and in turn the funder can require that the purchaser investigates further and/or drafts new legislation and/or administrative guidelines. This has been the case, for example, with changes to PFI operations and changes in rules for RPTs in procurement.

As this book has illustrated, regulation in the school system is variable in its effectiveness:

- Regulation appears to be slow. This is the case in some academy financial dealings such as reporting or managing debt.
- The regulatory framework seems to lack teeth. For instance, there seems to be little that the ESFA can do in relation to forcing a few reluctant MATs to reduce excessive CEO salaries.

- Breaking the rules is sometimes ignored. Continued awards of outstanding status to schools where there is known narrow selection and excessive exclusion is a case in point.
- There is reluctance to develop harsher regulatory measures, particularly if they affect special interests. The cases of school and childcare market failure in Sweden and Australia reported in Chapter 5 were not met with changed financial regulations, rather both governments focused on raising quality and performance, an effectiveness approach to the problem.

Transparency, financial probity and the partial treatment of particular staff and students are areas where tighter regulation may be required. Some commentators would certainly outlaw RPTs with trustees altogether.

In mid-2019, the House of Commons Public Accounts Committee nominated the DfE as its top concern, listing both financial strain in schools (a funder responsibility) and a lack of oversight of academies with 'a succession of high profile academy failures that have damaged children's education and been costly for the taxpayer' (a purchaser responsibility).[6] As argued in Chapter 4, the push for rapid conversion led to a lack of due diligence in financial checking and risk assessment. The committee also found a lack of transparency to parents, who sometimes had to resort to FoI requests to get information that should have been available to them (see Chapter 7). These are all areas where further regulation might be pursued.

The business of RSCs and their headteacher advisory boards may also be a case where further regulation about transparency in decision making would go some way to alleviating concerns about a lack of due process. The current heavy use of FoI and the appeals processes (Chapter 7) about new schools and conversion and rebrokerage suggest a system where regulatory information practices are flawed. At least some decisions to redact or refuse to publish information due to commercial confidentiality or lack of public resources could be read as political particularism favouring sponsors. The extensive use of non-disclosure agreements across all types of schools suggests inadequate regulation around discriminatory employment practices.[7]

Regulatory tardiness, powerlessness, inattention and reluctance are not simply about catching those who do bad things. Patchy regulation creates and supports a culture in which calculating the risks attached to rule breaking seems possible and sometimes even the most logical provider decision.

Changing regulations might go some way to shifting the conversation about bad behaviours, alter actuarial calculations about doing bad things and/or move systemic organisational culture towards one where acting with integrity is integral to everyday organisational life. However, arguably government *is* consistently engaged in regulatory change. As has been seen throughout previous chapters, government is moving – often after the event, often quite slowly and sometimes when it is caught out – to tackle some contentious issues, tardy financial reporting and mismanagement, off-rolling and misreporting of statistics.

And there is also the cost of regulation itself, and possible costly consequences. It is cheap to create a new rule, but often very expensive to monitor and pursue rule-breakers. In her book on corruption in America's schools, Segal produces multiple accounts of central authority pursuit of small sums of money, cumbersome central checking which impedes efficient processes, including payment for services rendered, and petty pilfering which is out of reach of centralised view.[8] Simply having more regulation neither tackles perverse incentives to do wrong nor guarantees there will not be unintended consequences, she says. Segal's solution is one which balances regulation with local oversight and accountability. She proposes structural change which finds a balance between subsidiarity and both local and central accountability.

But none of this deals with the fact that there is none so inventive as those faced with a challenging rule. As taxation law shows, there are those who seek to do their own thing, regardless of the effects on others – a case of autonomy at all costs, as Bellah and colleagues have it (see Chapter 9).[9]

Proposal for change: structural realignments

There are already a range of suggestions for structural reform on the English education policy table. These include:

- returning struggling schools to the local authority;[10]
- returning all schools to the local authority;[11]
- strengthening local authorities so that they have a strong improvement capability commensurate with MATs and can manage all admissions and selection procedures;[12]
- opening up academy trusteeships to parents, staff and local communities;[13]
- completing the academisation of the school system so that all schools are on an apparently equal footing;[14]
- introducing more variety in the system, particularly through allowing new grammar schools[15] and 'rebooting' the free school system;[16]
- returning all schools to comprehensive status;[17]
- changing the role of Regional Schools Commissioners so that they are responsible only for commissioning (purchasing), and removing headteacher advisory boards so that there is no conflict of interest in the advice provided;[18]
- creating an annual open hearing between the local authority and Regional Schools Commissioner where local authorities can present the particular needs of their local community (planning for new schools for example);[19]
- creating a national teaching force through which professional issues and working conditions and salaries would be uniform across the country regardless of the provider.[20]

Many of these initiatives assume that structural adjustment is the key to change. However, deciding the particular solution, what structural modifications are needed, is always derived from a problematisation. The current academised school system was also the logical outcome of a problematisation which focused on bureaucratic inefficiency, professional ineffectiveness and a narrow definition of equity. Business approaches, particularly the logics of competition and economistic calculation, were believed to be the remedy (Chapter 2–3). The FPP organisational grammar was the means of creating competition as well as raising standards and ensuring compliance through a narrow band of calculative measures.

It is important not to romanticise what came before the most recent reforms and to ask whether the concerns that led to the FPP and academisation had a basis in reality. We need to acknowledge that local authorities *were* sometimes hidebound by unnecessary and out-of-touch rules and practices. While 1970s schools had responsibility for their own curriculum development, schooling quality was patchy – and as a whole the school system was profoundly inequitable. Competition existed in the pre-choice system too – some schools were almost always perceived as better than others, often because of the population they served. Nor was the previous system a shining light of local democratic oversight. As Newman and Clarke ask, 'When were public services so great that we would like to go back to them? When was the public realm ever wholly open, accessible and inclusive?'[21] Surely we do not want to return to these problems, but to move forwards.

However, the policies associated with quasi-markets and school choice have produced new inefficiencies. The self-promoting and self-protective behaviours of autonomous schools, massaging their public relations and building strategic networks, were a response to league tables based on census testing and punitive interventions triggered by inspections. Schools have been caught, Greany and Higham suggest, in an ambiguous situation. As they put it,

> For higher status schools and their leaders, in particular nationally designated 'system leaders' and those forming MATs as well as for LAs willing to 'reform' themselves, there are new opportunities to influence and reshape local landscapes, albeit while being bound closer to the performance management of central government. ... At the same time, however, school-level actors are being encouraged to enhance their own positions and the positioning of their school(s), both by working entrepreneurially to sell services in new markets in school improvement and by working in new regional and sub-regional governing networks, These governing networks combine the hierarchical authority of RSCs with the processional networks of and increasingly co-opted elite of school leaders.[22]

Perhaps the answer *is* to return all schools to local or regional authorities, to allow MATs to continue but make their line of accountability to local government, not Westminster? While this may be a sensible direction, some new policy and practice would be required to attend to previous local authority problems, such as patchy responsiveness to parents and lack of transparency about decision making. Perhaps a more democratic structure which moved away from the party politics that dominate local government might complement realigned lines of local accountability. Perhaps the answer is to formalise networks that cooperate and reward them.

The pursuit of autonomous interests has been shown to foil local collaborative networked bodies. One example can be seen in the work of local Fair Access Panels, intended to manage the movement of young people needing a fresh start or alternative placement. Fair Access Panel cooperation can be rapidly undone by the self-serving behaviours of one or two schools seeking to put more students into the system than they pick up.[23] This example, together with Greany and Higham's analysis, suggests that structural change is, like regulation, perhaps part of a solution, but not all that is required.

If the problem is, as this book has argued, calculative practices and economistic logics that are operationalised through the grammar of FPP and digital platforms, with accompanying inefficiencies and ineffectiveness, then what new/old structures might suffice? Perhaps the structure of FPP can be unpicked? Perhaps deconstructing FPP will also address corruption directly, by reducing the points of contact between the public and private?

There are already moves in England away from some of the structural elements of a pure FPP model. Many local authorities are bringing their contracted services back in-house. The PFI scheme has been modified to guarantee some state equity and a form of insurance against financial collapse. Some provision has never been outsourced, or has been returned to the state. More renationalisation of key infrastructure is proposed. But perhaps one salient development comes from the highly beleaguered NHS.

The NHS is edging away from a payment-for-services model which encouraged growth in activities (admissions, operations, referrals to generate income). It has yet to abandon a market model, but there are now policy ideas about more joined-up and collaborative approaches, given that FPP has demonstrably failed to address recovery rates (effectiveness measures) and has failed to meet quality targets such as waiting times.[24] The NHS has now focused on Sustainability and Transformation Plans (STPs) which reinstate a locality basis for coordinated planning. Local purchasers *and* providers work together to decide how their collective resources, assets and services can be organised in the most efficient and effective way. STPs are now being trialled around the country. These trials are called the Integrated Care System (ICS). The ICS and STPs have a commitment to better care for patients – their website strapline is 'No trust is an island'.[25]

This NHS initiative does appear to offer one way to produce greater efficiency through the reduction of local competition and through procurement and professional development at scale. It also aims to reduce unproductive organisational skewing through the perverse application of effectiveness measures. But research into the development of the STPs and ICS[26] notes legislative barriers to the realisation of the new integrated local health imaginary:

- Reporting and financial arrangements are based on an autonomous provider with a history of competition.
- Some elements of competition law designed to stimulate marketised behaviour also run counter to full collaboration.
- NHS regulatory frameworks and accountability systems are designed around autonomous units/trusts rather than systems.
- There are conflicting messages from various national bodies.
- Leaders face competing demands.
- There is mounting frustration that inadequate funding prevents negotiated plans being fully realised.

These are both cultural and structural barriers to shifting away from the NHS FPP model. Tellingly, one researcher writes, 'Areas that are making progress are doing so *despite* the statutory framework and because their leaders have invested in developing collaborative relationships to support their ambitions.'[27]

Researchers also say that the lack of a clear narrative about an integrated care system and shifting policy terminology has created suspicion about why it is being promoted. The presence of suspicion calls attention to the need for serious authentic discussion about the ethical or moral basis for any new structural approach (see Chapter 9).

It is likely that the same kinds of regulatory, accountability and legislative issues would arise if there were an equivalent school structural reform, if local authorities and trusts were to collaboratively plan how their joint assets might be used to best effect in the local area. However, the prospect of seeing the slogan 'No trust is an island' writ large across the state school system does also indicate some potential in moving towards more networked services which use a common funding 'bucket' and see their obligation as the provision of schooling for shared communities. However, in considering a locality-based option it is important to recall that when New Labour's poverty interventions were working at a local scale they removed regional and macro forces responsible for poverty from the equation and thus stymied some potential equity shifts.[28]

Nevertheless, schools might learn from these NHS moves. A locality focus could bring together disparate providers, local authority schools and various trusts in a conversation about how their combined resources might best provide schooling for their local communities. Such a discussion might disrupt local competition that supports partisan selection, for instance, and promote the development of a comprehensive local menu of educational options, rather than the current fragmented and duplicating muddle. Indeed, a few local trusts and schools are already moving in this direction. However, without negotiated respite from the kinds of regulation, legislation and accountability that pit schools and trusts against each other, they may struggle to move away from their current competitive positioning.

Nevertheless, the renewal of local accountability which is not subject to partisan interests is important, and not simply as a way to use resources more efficiently and effectively. It is also one of the known ways to address corruption. As this book has shown, as the FPP has been folded into MATs, decision making has been taken away from local communities, and has become less transparent and in many cases more remote from many component schools. The logical solution then is not simply to unpick the FPP, but to restore real control of local schools to local schools.

Proposal for change: a code of ethics

One avenue to counter corrupted practices in the schooling system is for staff to adopt a formal code of ethics.

In March 2017 the ASCL, a professional body representing some 19,000 leaders from all phases of schooling in England, launched an Ethical Leadership Commission. The resulting Framework for Ethical Leadership was released in late January 2019.[29] Chaired by serving headteacher Carolyn Roberts, the commission was designed to address:

> concern about the absence of an ethical framework for education leadership, particularly in the context of a fragmented system in which accountability measures and their consequences are severe, and in which decisions are often taken under great pressure, and with competing demands in play. ... [A] clear set of principles, owned by the profession, was needed to help us all navigate the educational moral maze.[30]

Speaking ahead of the launch at a national conference for governors,[31] Roberts discussed some key ethical behaviours, indicating what they meant in practice (see Box 8.1).

Box 8.1: ASCL ethics

Trust: 'If we hold trust on behalf of children then we can't be off-rolling them willy-nilly. We can't be encouraging parents who are signally incapable of home educating a child to take a child home to be educated because it will make our numbers look better at the end of the year. That's not holding trust on behalf of children. The safest place for children to be is in school.'

Wisdom: 'Proper schemes of work, not exam tricks.'

Kindness: 'If you have to give someone some really bad news, don't say at 3.30pm on a Friday, "I want to talk to you on Monday", because that's their and their family's weekend gone. Do it on the Monday. Have a thought for how other people live.'

Justice: 'Schools that have zero-tolerance behaviour policies, and they are very popular at the moment and I'm not saying that they are wrong, some children will fall out of that system. Where will they go, and who's thought about that, and who's going to pick them up, and what's the mechanism? They don't vanish.'

Courage: 'The curriculum needs to be suited to the needs of the children and not the school. The children have to come first, and not the outcomes. Outcomes will follow if you are doing it right. And gaming: gaming is always wrong.'

It seems entirely proper for any professional body to have a code of ethics. But some of the examples that Roberts gives may seem startling to school leaders from places other than England. Why is it necessary to tell headteachers and governors that gaming is always wrong, or that the curriculum must suit the needs of children not the school? What is going on in England's schools that these are the examples that come to Roberts' mind? These are questions of morals as well as ethics.

It is impossible to avoid addressing values and morals in relation to ethics. It may seem at first that these are semantic niceties. The terms ethics and morals are often used interchangeably: both refer to things which are understood to be 'right' and 'wrong' and both concern behaviours – the ways in which we conduct ourselves, relate to others and do our work. Bear with me, if that is your reading. Some clarification about what is meant by values, morals and ethics is key to understanding differences in view about what is right and wrong in schooling in England and beyond.

Both ethics and morals are based on values – the beliefs we have about what's important, what we and other people should and shouldn't do. Values are socially constructed, even if they are individually held, and they are socially enacted. We often talk about people having particular values – they have conservative values, for instance. An example is helpful here. Attitudes to same-sex marriage can be seen as either conservative or liberal. Such attitudes are usually based on specific values: what people believe about individuals' rights and freedoms to choose in relation to sexuality, love and relationships, or beliefs about the paramount importance of religious doctrine. Recent debates about same-sex marriage show us that people do not all have the same values, but also that values can change over time.

The issues raised by Roberts when talking about the ASCL code of ethics are matters in which values play a part. Take the practice of off-rolling, when schools do not formally exclude children who are behaving badly and/or not attending but simply send them home and remove them from the roll (see Chapter 7). Some people may see off-rolling as wrong, while others see it as a lesser wrong than allowing disruptive students to remain in school. Some argue for the value of equality: all children are entitled to the same share of teachers' time. When time-wasting and time-consuming students are off-rolled, less overtly demanding children get a chance. But off-rolling can alternatively be understood as violating the value attached to inclusion. A further possibility is to prioritise the value of self-discipline, and there is thus an imperative to punish those who are undisciplined. The example of off-rolling illustrates that values are not universal and that they can be ranked differently. It currently falls on school leaders to make judgments about which of these values is more important in their school and community. Whether this should be the case is another question (see the discussion about local decision making earlier in this chapter).

Values are animated through a set of (often tacit and implied) rules; these rules are the materialisation of both ethics and morals.

Morals are often understood to refer to an individual's private beliefs about what is right and wrong. People exercise a personal moral code about how they conduct themselves, but this is often extended to cover the behaviour of other people. Private morality is made public. Judgments are made about people's morality – they might be described immoral, amoral or highly moral for instance – and depending on who makes them, judgments might be institutionalised. Rewards or punishments might follow. It is not too difficult to think of examples – for instance, the attribution of the immorality of laziness is often directed to the unemployed or those in poverty. There, the judgment of 'immorality' is translated into media attention – poverty porn – and a raft of government policies which focus on the alleged immorality of lack of effort in finding work. The root economic causes of poverty are ignored.[32]

Importantly, and this is the very practice that economic rationalists sought to eliminate, morals are also often at the heart of social and political change. We can, like neoliberal economist Hayek, think of the toxic moral stance of Nazism (see Chapter 2), but we can also think of the morals that underpinned the struggle against fascism – and still do. We can think of the moral basis of the struggle for universal suffrage, for equality legislation and for current social movements against climate collapse and species extinction. It is, however, more difficult to find a sound moral basis for academisation and for an educational muddle.

By contrast, ethics are not private. They are always social and explicit – they are developed by and for a workplace or an organisation such as a professional association. The codification of a suite of ethical practices is based on a selection and a hierarchy of morals and values. Professions are usually expected to follow a code of ethics – it is highly insulting to someone like a doctor, lawyer or teacher to accuse them of either unprofessional or unethical behaviour. Professional associations may use ethical codes as the basis for sanctioning members who do not abide by them. Researchers are held to strict ethical standards which can result in dismissal if they are not followed. Ethical codes of conduct may be collectively developed and formally adopted, as with the ASCL Ethical Leadership Framework, or historically accepted, like the Hippocratic Oath for doctors. Some professional bodies, such as the Institute for School Business Leadership in England, whose members are largely MAT operational officers, school business managers and bursars, have 'professional standards'[33] which use explicit values and ethics as the basis for a cluster of dispositions that underpin self-assessment of practices in procurement, human resources, marketing, finance and infrastructure.

It might appear from the discussion so far that values, morals and ethics are straightforward and easily separated. This is not so. There is considerable ambiguity and overlap between them as well as difficult and divisive conversations and practices that arise from them. There are three very important ethical complexities which are germane to addressing corruption and its counter-practices. The first is often referred to as the ethics of principled conviction versus the ethics of responsibility, the second is derived from pragmatism and the third is associated with behaviour norms.

Intent versus outcome

The ethic of principled conviction suggests that what matters is having a set of ethical principles which guide decisions about what to do. What you intend is what matters. The ethic of responsibility says that good intentions are not enough, it is the outcomes that matter. You may intend to do no harm, but if harm happens then the principles which underpinned the actions which led to harm do not matter at all.

Public debate often centres on the difference between intention and outcome. Political parties talk about their principled intentions in making a particular policy or pursuing a particular agenda, while critics talk about their responsibility for what is happening as a result of their well-intended policy. An example of this can be seen in debates about the EBacc – Tory government ministers say that the current school performance measure of the EBacc is not intended to devalue the arts (see Chapter 7). Arts advocates point to the drop in arts enrolments and arts teacher numbers and say that it doesn't matter at all if politicians value the arts if their curriculum performance measure has the opposite effect.

Pragmatic behaviours

Pragmatic behaviour is about dealing with events, people and behaviours in what seems to be, at the time, the most sensible and rational way. Pragmatic behaviour may bypass principles of intent and responsibility for long-term outcomes, as the pragmatic action is usually focused on the most immediate consequences.

An example is illustrative here. Evans[34] suggests that most school leaders act pragmatically (see Chapter 7). They may have a personal moral code and adhere to a formal code of professional ethics, but in a highly pressured moment these disappear. Corrupt decisions – to change test results, to charge an airfare to the school, to off-roll a student, to offer a contract to a trustee – may well be the result of a pragmatic decision to deflect sanctions rather than ensure equity or inclusion.[35]

Behavioural norms

Practices are socially constructed and often governed by unwritten cultural norms: this is the way we do things around here.

Wenger argues that 'communities of practice' build identities and practices together.[36] When people are engaged in a common endeavour, they build shared patterned routines and relationships and ways of being. Schools are communities of practice, where shared learning about how to teach and how to lead and manage occurs through both formal and informal processes. School communities of practice – ways of speaking, doing and interacting – may have a basis in a code of ethics, or not.

Unethical or corrupt practices often begin and are maintained through a community of practice. People see what others do and do the same. Some communities of practice may establish a culture in which doing 'things which we can get away with' are not only permitted but expected. People learn from each other and teach each other that this is just how things happen in this school. While individual morals and a professional code of ethics may suggest that a particular practice is wrong, what actually happens in an organisation may stem from its behavioural mores. This is perhaps the case with the widespread practice of pressuring staff to produce good test results (Chapter 7). Darley suggests that some organisational cultures actually promote a 'contagion' of corrupt behaviours.[37]

Each of these three – intent versus outcome, pragmatism and behavioural norms – present challenges for the successful introduction of a formal code of ethics into English schools. Together, they suggest that the road to systemic ethics might be difficult. After all, politicians, civil servants, teachers and educational leaders are already bound by Nolan's seven principles for public life: selflessness, integrity, objectivity, accountability, openness, honesty and leadership.[38] As this book has shown, not all of these are universally enacted. On a positive note, the process of adopting a code of ethics may well go some way to providing both a common language and conversation about values and morals across schools. When combined with a new community of practice – as is the case with ASCL's ethical school leaders action research project, which brings volunteer schools together to show what ethical leadership is and does – then it may effect some change in the system as a whole. The project may, however, become for some a tick-box exercise, which fits neatly into the current public relations, decal-collecting community of practice.

Decades of research suggests that changing organisational culture is crucial for real change.[39] There is a profound difference between individuals following a code of ethics and a culture in which acting with integrity is the norm. Acting with integrity brings together personal morals and ethical codes, and places them within an institutional context (Chapter 1). When organisations act with integrity – doing the right things the right way for the right reasons – they have routine and regular ethical and moral practices based on explicit 'good' values. Their routine and regular integrity-based practices[40] counter and minimise corruption. Organisations in which acting with integrity is important build and sustain trusting relationships internally and with others. An organisation which acts with integrity also takes account of points where its own workings can create macro-ethical problems not amenable to individual actions. The agency of individuals is framed by ethically sound organisational practices.

There is also a case to be made for a school system with a renewed moral commitment to the public that it serves. That is the focus of Chapter 9.

A public good agenda for change

The academy boss who 'totally disagrees with academies'
Times Educational Supplement, 30 March 2018

Headteacher bans 'ridiculous' SATs tests
The Independent, 19 May 2017

Let's go back to the future with co-operative schools – and leave grammars in the past
The Guardian, 15 November 2016

Teacher who won £1m will use windfall to get artists into schools
The Guardian, 26 June 2018

Our schools are beyond breaking point – where is the outrage?
The Guardian, 22 April 2019

In November 2017, a civil service review entitled *Delivering Better Outcomes for Citizens: Practical Steps for Unlocking Value*[1] addressed efficiency in governing, just as many reviews had done before. Led by 'deliverology' expert Sir Michael Barber,[2] the report headlined the importance of public value. Public value is a 'good' defined as public money 'translated into outputs and outcomes which improve people's lives and economic wellbeing'.[3] The key challenge to achieving public value was described as shifting the civil service from focusing on inputs and activities to outputs – again.

Barber's introduction to the report lays out the benefits of a public value productivity approach:

> The United Kingdom spends approximately £800 billion every year, around 40 per cent of GDP. If government were able to maximise the 'good' this sum delivered, if public services were consistently of high quality, if markets were always effectively regulated, if opportunities for innovation were seized, if risks and threats were well-managed, then social mobility would be enhanced, opportunity would be opened up, the country as a whole would be more productive and many, many more people would lead more fulfilling and productive lives. And these gains could be delivered without raising or spending a single extra pound. In short, the potential prize for ordinary people from enhancing government productivity is huge. To maximise the 'good' that government can do in this way demands that government and public services demonstrate their productivity and set out systematically to improve these.[4]

Barber addresses many of the concerns that appear in this book: waste of public funds, the inequities produced through market competition, poor management of risks. These problems are contrasted with a vision of a better, perhaps more equal society – the society imagined is meritocratic, and one where individuals have a responsibility to become more productive.

The report does not examine whether civil service reform can realistically achieve social mobility, equal opportunity and innovation in a globally situated national economy and historically unequal society. The vision is, not surprisingly, in keeping with a highly individualist and economically driven view of the world.

The Barber Review proposes a four-pillar framework for turning public spending into public value: (1) setting clear 3–5 year goals for a set budget including 'potential impact on human capital' (people seen in economic terms); (2) effective management of inputs (procurement, expenditure and so on); (3) engaging users and citizens expressed as 'convincing taxpayers of the value delivered by spending'; and (4) ensuring long-term sustainability of the system through responsible stewardship.[5] The review proposes that effective delivery of the public value framework will be achieved through the use of 'good data', benchmarks derived from 'top performers', 'timely analysis' and 'disruptive innovation' which embeds new practices in civil service departments. There will be no separate public value projects or units. The report describes the public value framework as a 'tool for measuring, tracking and delivering', and a necessary antidote to attention on the quantum of budget allocations and activities.

Questions of value are however neither neutral nor technical. They are inevitably riven with power relationships. But the formulation of public value in the Barber Review bypasses these issues, focusing instead on connecting efficiency to the achievement of redescribed outcomes. The change flagged in the report is in outcomes. Outcomes become complex and harder to measure: the examples given are of hospitals improving population health outcomes and galleries which educate and inspire audiences as well as contribute to their local communities. Proxies such as numbers of hospital appointments, visitors, good financial management and effective procurement processes will not suffice to measure complex outcomes, the review says; what to measure and how is vexed and requires effort. The review establishes the public value problem as one of measurement rather than what is to be valued: the outcomes themselves.

This chapter begins by examining how the Barber Review recommendations might address corruption and corrupted practices in the school system. I consider the scholarly formulation of public value and ask what additional benefits might be gained from a more thorough application of the idea. The chapter then proceeds to an alternative framing of public good: I explore how a moral base might not only afford a better avenue for socially just change but also tackle some longstanding and newer malpractices.

While Chapter 8 argued that changes to audit and regulatory regimes, structural alignments and codes of ethics might offer some potential for change, this concluding chapter argues that while these are necessary they are by no means sufficient. I suggest that without a moral framing for public services such changes will add up to nothing more than 'tinkering with the hot shower tap', as W. Edwards Deming put it.

The public value approach and its possibilities

The Barber Review drew on the work of Harvard public administration academic Mark Moore.[6] Moore proposed that government is not simply a service provider, safety net and regulator, but also a creator of public value. Governments might, he suggested, move away from the neoliberal conception of a minimalist state whose primary function is to stimulate the market. They might instead take a proactive role in shaping the public sphere.

Moore saw public value as a resolution to contradictory perceptions of civil servants – either as neutral agents duty bound to serve their political masters or independent moral actors duty bound to inform their ministers of ethical issues arising from political decisions and to resist if need be. Instead, Moore envisaged a moral and ethical civil servant who not only used due process to assure consistency and fairness in the application of rules, but was also an active aide to government. Moore's moral civil servant did not resist, but brought their doubts and informed and imaginative views to bear on measuring and monitoring the public consequences of policies. Moore calls this 'after the fact' accountability. After the fact accountability supports government to become adaptable and responsive to public needs and changing conditions.

Moore's public value approach creates a warrant for civil servants and those who work in public services, such as education, to engage in policy conversations with policy makers; their role is to provide feedback on policy effects, and to propose new policies or policy changes based on evidence from the current context. Moore notes the risk of reducing democratic accountability if civil servants become the de facto voice of the public. The solution is, he suggests, for civil servants to keep lines of communication open to as many people as is feasible.[7]

Civil servants should, he argues, be in continued contact and communication with the public(s). In this way, he suggested, public interest would be assured.

Moore offers a 'strategic triangle', a new process infrastructure, to align the processes necessary to produce public value. These are: (1) defining public value, (2) authorisation (building a coalition of stakeholders) and (3) operational capacity building. The task of government, Moore says, is to create public value, gain ongoing support from stakeholders and make public value operationally achievable and sustainable by aligning the three processes. Because civil servants have a key role in each of the three arenas, they need a strong mandate from elected politicians in order to do their jobs effectively. Politicians must also recognise and take seriously the value of the feedback and proposals provided.

Critics see Moore as spending insufficient time attending to defining public value itself and more time on operational practices. While supporting the democratisation inherent in his strategic triangle, they say the outcomes that count as public value must be widely debated.

Unlike Moore, the Barber Review does not attend to the potential of providers and civil servants working for the public good. Indeed, the term 'public good' appears only once in the review, values once and ethics not at all. The term public good is contained in a critique of Moore's work as reinstating civil servants encroaching on the rightful territory of elected representatives – not the public or stakeholders – in the name of the public good.[8] The review links value with taxpayer perceptions of effective public services.[9] The notion of public good appears in the review Foreword as an italicised 'the good' in the phrase 'the good that government can do', a quotation from the then Prime Minister Theresa May, and 'the good the sum delivered', referring to the annual national budget.[10] This kind of usage of 'good' continues throughout the book and is, I will argue later, a conflation of moral good with measurable goods.

Moore's work was developed at the height of the neoliberalist agenda in the US, and is largely congruent with the then policy insistence on innovation and effectiveness. However, his public value argument also supported the idea of a public as something more than 'a simple aggregation of individual consumer interests'[11] or the policy agenda of the government of the day. Moore's authorising environment is something more than a market – it is one in which public engagement in policy discussions is crucial. And civil service accountability is not simply to ministers, but also to the public, to the point where:

> There might even on some occasion be a kind of moral legitimacy created by public managers and professionals reminding society and its representatives of important values that are being put at risk by actions that are politically supported ... and would likely work technically, but fail to protect or promote foundational moral values.[12]

Barber is not the only one to engage with Moore's work. Public administration scholars fiercely debate Moore's view of more agentic civil servants and public providers. There are concerns, for instance, about whether his public value approach takes adequate account of social and environmental sustainability. But there is relatively widespread agreement that the framework does support public policy practices that are capable of dealing with complex and 'wicked' problems, with various layers of government and with different services, sectors, producers and users and professional traditions. Public value affords a 'tool' to think horizontally, vertically and diagonally through the processes of policy development, implementation and review, and public management. As Benington and Moore put it, reflecting on the development of the idea of public value, it 'requires a radically different approach to policy development and public management', which is to be achieved 'through radical action on the ground at the front line with communities'.[13]

Ground-level radical action is not a perspective that comes through in the Barber Review. This is not the only significant departure from Moore. Moore sees public value firstly as a moral matter, then a question of effectiveness, with efficiency a key aspect of calculating public value. The Barber Review, on the other hand, claims efficiency as its primary raison d'être. And the Barber Review maintains that the civil service is solely accountable and subservient to government; it just needs to be more efficient and quicker (and thus, presumably, less likely to cause electoral problems).

Nevertheless, the Barber Review approach to public value could support, *inter alia*:

- New structures such as the place-based NHS collaborations (see Chapter 8) which unpick some of the perverse incentives and toxic inefficiencies of the FPP model and the reproductive effects of local markets. Perhaps such structures may also be appropriated in some circumstances to sponsor grassroots co-production of policy.
- A richer notion of outcomes. Rather than simplistic measures such as the narrow test and exam results which currently prevail in education, public value requires a more holistic view of outcomes. In education, current Ofsted moves towards a focus on a broad and balanced curriculum, new regulation to prevent illegal exclusions and renewed interested in 'character' might be indicative of a shift towards public value. Each of these elements *might* in turn be expanded and made much richer by engaging with professionals and school communities to generate more sophisticated understandings of the processes of sorting and selecting by student and school, and develop counter practices – more robust and inclusive curriculum and pedagogies and capacious recognitive notions of social justice.

Moore's framing points strongly to the importance of the local and to democratic participation and accountability. But this requires a more elaborated moral basis to education than currently exists or is advocated in the Barber Review.

A public good(s) framing

Public good is a normative concept. It concerns the social, cultural and economic material well-being of the public. While it is commonplace to refer to society as made up of multiple publics, the notion of public good refers to benefits for society writ large, not a subsection of it. A public good by definition attends to and supports all of the diverse and many publics that exist in a society. Public good is fundamentally about justice and fairness. However, it is most often discussed in economistic and political terms.

Some contemporary dictionaries define public good as the state's distribution of public goods, signalling the active participation and responsibility of the nation state in the production of public good. The nation state is usually taken as the unit of and for 'the public'. The state raises and redistributes taxation income in order to provide services and infrastructure that are of benefit to all citizens, regardless of who or where they are. Citizens hold the state to account through the processes and tiers of democratic election.

Although public good is now rhetorically attached to the state, it wasn't always so. Before the nation state existed, city states, local parishes and other smaller polities addressed the public good, then often called the common good or common weal; commons land councils and town meetings were precursors of the larger and more distant electoral processes of contemporary parliaments and councils. And today the notion of public good also extends to nation states' formal recognition of the laws, practices and citizenship of other polities – Indigenous governing bodies, for instance.

Decisions about what constitutes a public good can be politically contentious. The state must balance various interests and needs. Sometimes, state decisions are not decisive. In the case of equity legislation, for instance, opposition can be ongoing; what one government considers a public good can be seen as wrong by another. This is, for example, the case in moves to shut down abortions in the US and make them legal in Ireland.

While the idea of a public good has its roots in classical philosophy, its definition and operationalisation has largely become the stuff of economics. Smith and Hume are generally signposted as significant figures in the discursive shift from public good to public *goods*.[14] Post-Enlightenment, the public good was no longer taken by governing bodies as an abstract moral concept but as concrete 'stuff' which could be empirically investigated, measured and quantified.[15] Measurement of public goods is not as simple as it sounds, as the Barber Review notes, because while some public goods, such as lighthouses and roads, are easily 'seen', other public goods, such as well-being and education, rely on statistical proxies and indicators. From the 1850s onwards, nation state governments were increasingly preoccupied with not only determining what public goods should be provided, but also with specialist statistical calculations about 'the public' and its economic, physical, social and cultural conditions.[16]

Measurable public goods are commonly defined by what they are not: private goods. Public goods are *non-excludable* (no citizen can be prevented from accessing and using them) and *non-rivalrous* (the use by one citizen does not reduce their use by others). Markets are generally seen as incapable of delivering either non-excludability or non-rivalry by themselves, although there is debate about the degree to which this is the case and under what conditions they might. These two principles – non-excludability and non-rivalry – can be brought into current English political debates about education policy and structural reforms, as well as to policy regimes in other mature capitalist economies such as the US, Australia and the Nordic nations.

As explained in Chapters 2–3, the postwar English welfare state was founded on the premise that a government's role was to provide non-excludable and non-rivalrous services through universally accessible public infrastructure.[17] This postwar policy settlement, as in other welfare states such as Australia and Sweden, has been overtaken by variations of what is popularly called economic rationalism[18] or neoliberalism.[19] Post-welfarism posits a scenario in which the market is harnessed to deliver public goods.[20] The incapacity of the market to deliver equity is mitigated through nation states' contractual and regulatory procedures, while the innovative vigour, client responsiveness and efficiency of the market is directed to public ends. Or so the utopian neoliberalist narrative goes. Political debates in the post-welfare state era often, therefore, focus on the appropriate blend of public and private involvement in the provision of public goods.[21] Governments wanting to involve the private sector in the provision of public goods must deal with several difficulties. Some public services are not particularly profitable and thus unattractive to corporate players, unless sweeteners are offered. Competition can lead to costly duplication and sometimes costly failures. Market failure (Chapter 5) can be electorally disastrous if public good services are involved.

Economists disagree about the role of the state in relation to public goods and what public goods measures to use. For instance, Forster argues that government calculations about public goods are often sequestered from examinations of the impact of budgetary processes and usage patterns,[22] and this is one of the problems that the public value approach is designed to address. It does matter what is included in public goods calculations.

Schooling as public goods

Budgetary decisions and consumer patterns can both undermine non-excludability and non-rivalry, as in the case of school choice and middle-class advantage.[23] And Kallhoff argues that policy decisions about which goods are public and which are private (such as education) generally ignore significant society-wide benefits: 'public goods are particularly suitable for sustaining a well-ordered society. Public goods contribute to social inclusion, they support the generation of the public, and they strengthen a shared sense of citizenship.'[24]

Neal and Neal evidence this point through an examination of the role of the US public school in building social capital.[25] Drawing on a large-scale study of 26 neighbourhoods, the Neals argue that 'quality' public schools positively add to 'community satisfaction'.[26]

Many orthodox economists prefer a relatively generous notion of public goods which includes education:

> education ... benefits the person being educated. To calculate the benefits, we take the income a person earns over a lifetime with education, and subtract that which she would get without an education. But that figure does not tell the whole story. What about the numerous employers the person will have over a lifetime, and the savings realized because

these employers do not have to train her in-house? What about the benefits that literacy brings to all the companies that rely on the written word to advertise? The benefits to those who issue public warnings, put out signs or seek to implement laws? If one were to put a figure on all these benefits, they would dwarf the amount that accrues strictly to the educated person. This difference between the public and the private benefits is called an *externality*. And because of its substantial externalities, education is a public good.[27]

Such externalities are not the stuff of neoliberalist policy which has energetically emphasised the private benefits of education, for example to justify large increases in university fees and abandoning the provision of education maintenance allowances for students in poverty.

It is clear that there is excludability in the English school system. Excludability is most obvious in the case of exclusion and off-rolling, and the practices of selective schools that use school choice based on residence, religion or 'talent' to disadvantage working-class and poor children. Another example lies in the skewing of the curriculum offer via the EBacc, which means that some students are effectively prevented from studying the arts, physical education, computing and other 'non-core' subjects. Distribution of funds for improvement based on narrow calculations such as tests or inspections can also be seen as excludable practices.

There is also rivalrous provision caused by the patchy geographies of new school buildings linked with academisation, the rationalisation of special education provisions in local authorities and MATs and rationed funding for trips and excursions. These economist notions of public goods do highlight some of the inequities currently within the English school system.

Applying the principles of non-excludability and non-rivalry to the current educational muddle in England and elsewhere (see Table 9.1) leads to some interesting questions which might be asked of any new education policy.

Table 9.1: Public goods and schooling

Principle	Some key questions
Non-excludability: no citizen can be prevented from access	Do all students have equal access to the same school offerings?
	Do policies systematically privilege some students over others?
	Are there covert selection practices at work?
Non-rivalry: the use by one does not reduce use by another	Do current school policies leave any students unable to access education?
	Do policies create uneven provision which reduces the participation of some students?

But educators tend not to calculate educational benefits in this way. Rather, they focus on a broader and more moral articulation of outcomes, purposes and benefits.

Public good as a moral virtue

Calculative analyses of processes are not the same as moral and philosophical arguments about what constitutes the public good – not goods – and a good society. Like all questions of value, the notions of public good, common good and a good society are contentious. The Penn State journal, *The Good Society*, nominates 'liberty, democracy, equality and environmental sustainability'[28] as basic 'good' values; but these can still be interpreted in multiple ways.

In order to make interpretations and inclusions/exclusions less ambiguous, discussions about the public good often combine questions of values, strategies and outcomes. Such ethico-political discussions of the public good and a good society are not separated easily from political issues – and inevitably from current party political strategies and critiques of them.

Take the example of Robert Bellah and colleagues' best-selling book, *The good society*.[29] A key plank of their argument is that the value of autonomy has taken precedence over all other possible values. The prioritisation of autonomy, they suggest, led to the diminution of other important virtues such as responsibility and care – values which could only be operationalised at a social level through institutions such as the family, the church and public services. A world where autonomy underpins social life, they say, is one which is largely empty of meaning, comfort and support. Bellah et al propose a revitalised democracy in which social virtues are put first. Using the example of climate collapse, they argue that while individual lifestyle actions are significant, and the 'green' social movement is vital, real and sustainable change can only be effected through institutions. They propose that 'in spite of their complexities and difficulties, large-scale institutions can and indeed must be better understood' and 'made amenable to citizen action and global public opinion'.[30] Institutions, they reason, bring together the moral resources of the community and can thus make decisions which are morally good. To this end it is vital, they write, that we build a language that teaches us how to think about renewing common concern.

But even this argument might have different political interpretations of process, with one side arguing that a good society will be achieved by the state focusing more strongly on questions of equity, and another seeing a call for further market stimulation. Questions of ideology are inevitably at stake in discussions of the public good.

Public good discussions are thus often trenchant in their critique and explicitly politically positioned. Two examples will suffice. In Australia, the Good Society Policy Network (GSPN)[31] says that 'a good society depends on trusting people we know and don't know as well as the institutions that govern us via common resources that foster equity and a sense of community'. 'Excessive use of market models' have damaged the social fabric. The GSPN aims to 'develop social policies that revive the trust and social contract that give our democracy legitimacy'. The GSPN offers a set of guiding principles for social policy – they go to both the intent of policy makers and responsibility for 'measurable' outcomes of inequality and mobility. GSPN principles include:

- We live in a society not an economy.
- We are citizens not consumers.
- We need those who have been responsible for distrusted changes to prove they are listening to voter views, not just lobbyists and powerful elites.

- Governments need to understand that trustworthiness creates social dividends. Voters demonstrate a clear preference for vital, non-market public services rather than privatised options.

The social democratic basis of the GSPN critique is very clear.

A second example from a somewhat different social democratic perspective comes from the journal *Social Europe*.[32] *Social Europe* staged an online 'good society' debate (in cooperation with the journals *Soundings* and *Compass*) to which 90 people contributed. The journal editors identified key themes which, they wrote, were directed towards the current crisis in European democracy.[33] They attributed the crisis to the lack of a coherent and compelling global/European vision, increasing inequality and problems in social and environmental sustainability. They saw an urgent need for reform in finance capitalism and determination of the appropriate role of the state. Many of the contributors in the *Social Europe* debate argued for the importance of reclaiming moral and philosophical foundational ideas, suggesting there was an urgent need to restore a foundation for the development of 'good' public policies. Indeed, decades before this, J. K. Galbraith[34] argued not dissimilarly that conventional economic solutions to problems such as racial equality and personal liberty could only be achieved through the adoption of more ethical ideals.

It is perhaps the quest to reconcile the ethical and political that has led to a revival of interest in Hannah Arendt's work on political responsibility and judgment. Arendt argued that the citizenry needed to recover, ontologically as well as axiologically, a common world as well as a public space in which speaking, acting and deciding together were both possible and desirable. This was not about soliciting public opinion, nor manufacturing a shared set of values, but rather a public engagement of 'disinterest' – setting aside personal private interests in favour of the public world that we share with others – through the practices of 'representative thinking': thinking from the standpoint of everyone else (a moral position). As she wrote, 'to think with an enlarged mentality means that one trains one's imagination to go visiting'.[35]

The disinterested perspective is crucial to any public debate that might occur either about and in the 'authorised sphere' imagined in public value framings or the more open and collaborative processes associated with political philosophies of social democracy.

Public good, efficiency and effectiveness

These ideas of the public good reframe how we might approach questions of effectiveness and efficiency. If the commitment to equity and social justice underpins the public good approach to efficiency and effectiveness, then the vast and growing gap between the most wealthy and the poor becomes simply unacceptable. The gap is wrong, unjust, as well as ineffective and inefficient. The stigmatisation and oppression of people on the basis of their gender, race, sexuality, neurotypicality or able-bodiedness is not only morally reprehensible but also constitutes institutional malpractice.

An equity public good framing would mean that working efficiently and effectively for economic, cultural and political justice demands the redistribution of resources, recognition of differences and representation of all interests.[36] Redistribution, recognition and representation are fundamental moral commitments. Other forms of justice – the right to have diverse knowledges and interpretations equally valued,[37] the right to have the value of one's labour recognised and fairly remunerated[38] and the right to work in an institution where solidarity, love and care are everyday practice[39] – would also be unwavering commitments which inform organisational practice and 'service delivery'. It is important to reiterate that in such articulations of justice, the public becomes both pluralised, publics, in recognition of differences, but is also used in its singular form in order to avoid populist politics which seek to fragment and to create administrative muddles and social anomie.

Because commitments to justice must be more than good intentions, some measurement of practice and outcomes is necessary. Deep engagement with thinking about alternative and justice-oriented approaches to measurement are needed. An example is useful at this point to illustrate that there are alternative approaches to the tasks of measurement other than the application of neoliberalist economistic logics.

A new public accounting?

Henry Mintzberg is critical of scholarship where organisations are seen as rational and amenable to scientific modes of planning.[40] He is concerned about the effects of 'Total Quality Management' and other calculative approaches. A ruthless focus on codifying, elaborating and analysing, Mintzberg suggests, destroys responsiveness and wise anticipation. Strategic planning – specifying outcomes, making plans for achieving them and setting up monitoring systems based on those plans – leads to organisational blindspots and unanticipated difficulties. Organisational planning is always retrospective and based on past experiences, and is often incapable of envisaging different futures. According to Mintzberg, the use of measurement against standards is better suited to stable conditions rather than periods of change. It is difficult to change a rigid organisational infrastructure when wider social and economic conditions alter or fluctuate wildly.

Mintzberg is very concerned about any separation of organisational thinking from doing. He argues that when organisational 'heads' are detached from the everyday reality of their organisation, managers lose the capacity to understand what is actually happening. Reliance on 'hard' data, usually the things most easily measured, gives leaders and managers flawed views of what is happening in their organisation. Rather than attending to 'soft data', they take proxy measurements and costs as complete and authentic representations of organisational reality.

Mintzberg is highly critical of the idea of bringing business approaches, particularly if they centre on formalised business planning, into the public sector. The goal of late 20th-century civil sector reform and beyond was – and is – precisely this. In an interview with *The Guardian* in 1993, Mintzberg was scathing about the conflation of analytical skills with management: 'We've become prisoners of measurement: audits, league tables, targets. It just destroys creativity. Look, I'm not opposed to measuring things that can be measured – I'm opposed to letting those things drive everything else out. It has some destructive effect in business, but in education and healthcare it's absolutely devastating.'[41]

Mintzberg argues for management based on wisdom, not calculation and formalised programming. Wise or 'quiet' management[42] is responsive, uses synthesis and divergent thinking for making sense, and takes a broad and long-term view. Wise management eschews short-term cost-cutting in favour of longer-term investment. Mintzberg sees this as 'engaging management' where, he told *The Guardian*, 'managers are close to the ground and connected with what they do; they don't see their role as being heroic but rather to encourage the heroism of other people'.[43]

Mintzberg's critique of measurement and the evangelical belief in the potential of business models to improve the civil service and public services is supported by evidence provided in previous chapters that competition and particular forms of calculation have warped and tainted the school system in England, as elsewhere. The school system is not spoiled, but it is certainly suffering from the ill effects of the last 30 years of neoliberalist reform. Its moral basis has been corrupted at policy level, as well as in some schools.

Wise management stands in some contrast to the Barber Review discussed at the start of this chapter. Mintzberg's notion of wise management might form the basis for public discussion about how a socially just public good policy agenda and a renewed public sector might be realised.

Rethinking efficiency and effectiveness in education

Acknowledging that schooling cannot change society, a public good approach to education is underpinned by the view that schools can make important differences to the life chances and choices of children and young people. A public good approach would take the diversity of students as a given, together with the goal of generational learning – what we teach now creates a good society now and in the future. A public good approach would see any system which is structured to create winners and losers as morally wrong. All forms of exclusion – from a narrow curriculum to off-rolling – are equally ineffective and morally corrupted.

What follows are indicative examples of a public good approach to education, not a holistic policy agenda. The examples are intended as conversation starters, not a final compilation.

A public good approach to efficiency would hold government to account for waste. Wasting public money is morally wrong. The wise stewardship of resources is a virtuous alternative. This book has identified numerous examples of waste, including: untested models of schooling (studio schools and city colleges); signing up for contracts which compel schools to long-term and onerous payments (PFI); rapidly expanding academisation without due diligence about MAT capacities and regulatory frameworks; and allowing self-regulation in RPTs which permit fraud and cronyism. A public good conception of efficiency would focus on retaining and sustaining teachers and headteachers, rather than scapegoating them for student attainment outcomes resulting from complex policy and social contexts, much of which is out of their control. A public good conception of efficiency would not compel teachers to spend large amounts of time documenting their practice in order to demonstrate that they are performing. A public good conception of efficiency would see that getting goods at the lowest price (the best deal) is not always as beneficial as supporting local businesses and/or using recyclable and reusable materials and equipment.

As outlined in Chapter 8, progress towards a more equitable system must be evaluated: relevant statistics must be collected. However, the toxic effects of calculation can be reduced. The digital data spine from classroom to Westminster can be recalibrated. The use of highly punitive measures as the means of dealing with the minority of underperforming schools can be changed in favour of trust- and improvement-based approaches which value the knowledge of the profession and school communities. The use of place- or network-based collaborative approaches and local accountabilities could be prioritised in public rhetoric and in a restructured governing and regulatory frameworks. Competition between schools could be seen as counterproductive. League tables might be abolished. And so on.

A public good approach demands greater attention to the curriculum, and an explication of what outcomes matter. An examination of the warrants for schooling is helpful to begin with. David Labaree ascribes 'mixed mandates' to schooling, identifying three historical positions, namely:

> democratic equality (schools should focus on preparing citizens), social efficiency (they should focus on training workers), and social mobility (they should prepare individuals to compete for social positions). These goals represent, respectively, the educational perspective of the citizen, the taxpayer, and the consumer. Whereas the first two look on education as a public good, the third sees it as a private good.[44]

Labaree argues that a privatised and individualised social mobility goal is now dominant in the US and elsewhere, and has twisted education to become a 'commodity for the purposes of status attainment', and that this 'has elevated the pursuit of credentials over the acquisition of knowledge'.[45] The same social mobility perspective is taken in England. As argued in previous chapters, social mobility approaches paradoxically prioritise status quo knowledges and promote highly selective practices under the rhetorical guise of merit. Systemic effectiveness is reduced to examining test and exam results and satisfaction.

The elevation of private over public good in education takes different forms in different countries. Since the late 1960s, Australian government policy, for example, has largely focused on funding and the ways in which federal funds are distributed to alleviate/accentuate pre-existing individual class-based positional advantage.[46] Testing is used to gauge the effectiveness of state use of funds. By contrast, debates in England have been largely dominated by structure and selectivity: different types of schooling, school choice and curriculum league tables. Both debates concern the principles of non-excludability and non-rivalry in different ways, as well as depending on similarly marketised imaginaries of a globalised nation state.

It is instructive to see how Labaree's first two mandates of democratic equality and social efficiency frame effectiveness differently. Each has curriculum and governance implications.

According to the democratic equality perspective, education for citizenship suggests that students are not simply future citizens but also citizens now in their communities and schools. They are entitled to a curriculum where learning supports them to make sense of their local and wider world, to understand how the two are connected and to participate in debates about matters of concern.[47] A democratic approach to citizenship eschews a narrow focus on civics, and critiques repressive and discriminatory approaches.[48] It offers an inclusive and cosmopolitan approach which equally values the canon and the popular and holds them both subject to critical appreciative interpretation.[49] Schools are keen to engage parents, teachers and students in governing.[50] A focus on the public good in a curriculum which is not simply captured by the statist notion of citizenship has a greater emphasis on the inclusion of different knowledges, languages and ways of being, knowing, doing and living together.[51]

The social efficiency perspective by contrast emphasises a focus on the vocational in the curriculum, promoting the utility of knowledge and skills, offering workplace oriented programmes and measuring success through employability. Governing bodies include employers and unions.

A social democratic public good view of schooling reframes governing practices. It operationalises the imaginary of Bentham's Public Opinion Tribunal (Chapter 7) and takes further the notion of Moore's public value-authorising sphere to support democratic and open decision making at all levels. Schools would involve staff and students as well as governors and trustees in decision making. Place-based approaches would be used in part to plan and coordinate schooling and other local public services; these will be networked and interlinked with relevant scales of policy making so that decision making is aligned and mutually informing and beneficial. Secrecy would be seen as morally wrong, and transparency valued. Practices of integrity which take up and take on fundamental principles of justice, avoidance of harm and production of benefit, will always be in development, being evaluated and improved.

A public good approach to the civil service that supports schools to do this social work might take up the direction proposed by public values scholars (not the Barber Review) about the moral obligations of civil servants. Both public value and public good approaches support practices of co-production, communication and dialogue, not commissioning, consultation and customer surveys. Rhetoric about lack of expertise, entrepreneurialism and the necessity of business approaches will be minimised. The historical legacy of the cultural correspondence and organisational closeness of mandarins and elected politicians which has remained largely intact since the 19th century will be reconceptualised. The public interest and public good at the core of the civil service would value and operationalise accountability to the public. There will be rather more frank and fearless advice and rather less focus on short-term electoral concerns. The public metaphor for a revitalised public service will be neither a self-interested Sir Humphrey nor a politically driven Malcolm Tucker (Chapter 3), but something yet to be imagined.

But these are of course my interpretations of the public good in education. They require much wider discussion. This of course raises the question of where such public discussions can be held.

Creating public spaces and conversations

Throughout the book there have been references to a lack of transparency, to lies and secrecy and to the privatisation of decision making in quangos and boards. These are forms of corrupted practice. More open, local perusal and participation is important to detect and curb corruption and the corruption of practice.

However, the gradual erosion of local engagement by various publics can be easily seen in changes in the role of local authorities, and the removal of powers from school governing bodies. At the same time, populist politicians claim public mandates and politicised public servants, cast in the role of procurers and commissioners, employ experts to advise on public views and needs. As suggested at the outset of the book, this is often referred to as a democratic deficit[52] or depoliticisation and repoliticisation.[53] It is certainly not easy to see at present where discussions might be convened to debate the public good, reform public services and address corruption and corrupted practices in education.

Janet Newman and John Clarke, in their book *Publics, politics and power*, directly address this difficulty.[54] They suggest that efforts must be directed to both enlarging the existing public sphere and to bring to the surface sedimented forms of commitments to public good, justice and equity within the public services. This is the work they say of 'making things public',[55] a process which works at the 'delicate and elusive intersection between what is political and what is public'.[56] For Newman and Clarke this means three concurrent activities: (1) making new public spaces for discussion, (2) enlarging spaces that are intended to constrain public input and (3) working in resistant public spaces already in social play.

The public services, such as education, have a key role to play here, according to Newman and Clarke, as they produce both publics and a political sense of publicness. Public services such as education are 'worth struggling over' because they 'hold the possibility of de-commodifying goods, services and, above all, relationships … they can enact principles of open access, fairness and equitable treatment … they carry the possibilities of remedying or challenging inequalities … and can offer a sense of belonging, connection and entitlement.'[57]

While achieving this renewed sense of publicness is not an easy task, it is one which *can* be the work of everyday life in schools as well as conversations on social media and in union meetings, parents' committees, school councils and networks of schools. The three areas for enlarging public conversation are within the reach of school communities and professional bodies. Conversations, however, must focus on more than narrowly focused learning and improvement agendas, but on broader questions of the kind of society and future we want for children and young people and what this means across the whole institution of schooling.

Last words: towards reclaiming the public good in education

This book has not offered a comprehensive agenda for change. My intention has been to bring three sources of thinking to the current conversation about schooling policy:

- an organisational perspective that joins the civil service and the schooling sector together, not one that sees them as separate;
- a historical perspective which brings old and new texts together to show continuities as well as changes;
- an interdisciplinary perspective which brings together political and public administration and educational conceptual resources in order to identity arenas and directions for change.

Through these three perspectives, I have explored the development and consequences of economistic rationality and calculative practices operationalised as efficiency and effectiveness practices. My raw material has been media and official government reports primarily from England. I have concluded that there are grounds for saying that the current schooling system is not only a 'muddle' (Chapter 2) but also corrupted in the wider moral sense, as well as marked by numerous examples of more narrowly defined corruption.

It is probably inevitable that the book ends with a plea for extended and extensive conversation about these issues. Many stakeholders in education argue for the same need. As the book began with a dedication to the fourth estate it is fitting to suggest that the media also extend its work beyond much needed investigation and become positively engaged in wider discussions about change. Perhaps it is not too fanciful to propose that in England a public commission on state school education is now warranted – urgently needed, in fact. A commission might bring together all stakeholders at all scales of educational activity and school experience and foster a renewed sense of solidarity and trust in schooling as a good public institution working for the public good.

This last section of the book canvassed some possibilities and directions for reform. Taken together, they amount to the beginnings of an educational agenda which reclaims the public good. I discussed codes of ethics, regulatory changes, structural changes and public value and public good framings. But none of these is sufficient in themselves. They are all necessary.

The book offers some starting points for discussion. Perhaps then it is fitting to end by saying in best teacher style – here are some ideas, discuss and add your own:

- *The public good is the moral foundation for reform.* The public good makes social justice the prime purpose for a democratic approach to governing, an active role for the civil service, a lived ethical code which supports practices of integrity and evaluation and a holistic warrant for schooling. The public good is incompatible with a marketised, punitive competitive education system and practices of exclusion and selection.

An underpinning public good framework supports and shapes change in four key areas:

- *Changes in inspection and audit regimes,* which separate systemic data related to equity and effectiveness from school-based evaluations necessary for diagnostic and improvement work; shift the balance from punishment and competition to support and improvement; and revise the frequency, scale and scope of tests and examinations.
- *Regulatory changes,* which *inter alia* make transparency the norm, ban RPTs, cap excessive salaries and benefits, compel any contracted provider to insure against risk and failure and revise admission codes to prevent schools selecting the students they most desire. Regulations which inhibit networks and cooperative services should be rewritten.
- *Structural changes,* which in the short term manage and reduce the toxic influences of FPP, calculation and competition by (1) reducing expensive contracting out (for example, eliminating costly leasing and outsourcing arrangements and bringing services back in-house); (2) making governing structures including boards of trustees and RSCs open by

bringing teachers, students and parents back into formal decision-making fora; and (3) resourcing local authorities so they can support schools to work together in the interests of local communities. In the longer term the FPP model is replaced by one which brings together local and central goals and processes.

- *Public value approaches*, which support collaborative forms of resourcing and planning, new fora for public discussion and co-production of policy and more generous goals for education, including a rich and inclusive curriculum offer. The role of the civil service shifts away from efficient business planners and commissioners to that of active stewards of public resources, debate, policy development and review.

Notes

Acknowledgements

[1] Niesche, Richard, and Pat Thomson. 2017. 'Freedom to what ends? School autonomy in neoliberal times'. In *The international handbook of educational leadership*, edited by Ira Bogotch and Duncan Waite. New York: Wiley Blackwell; Thomson, Pat. 2019. 'Oh to be in England? The production of an un-public state system'. In *Dismantling public education: Implications for educational leadership, policy and social justice*, edited by Jane Wilkinson, Richard Niesche and Scott Eacott. London: Routledge.

Preface

[1] https://www.gov.uk/government/news/voucher-scheme-launches-for-schools-providing-free-school-meals

[2] See https://www.trusselltrust.org/news-and-blog/latest-stats/end-year-stats/

[3] Sosenko, F., Littlewood, M., Bramley, G., Fitzpatrick, S., Blenkinsopp, J., & Wood, J. (2019). *State of hunger. A study of poverty and food insecurity in the UK.* https://www.stateofhunger.org/wp-content/uploads/2019/11/State-of-Hunger-Report-November2019-Digital.pdf: The Trussell Trust.

[4] https://www.gov.uk/government/news/voucher-scheme-launches-for-schools-providing-free-school-meals

[5] https://schoolsweek.co.uk/revealed-edenred-sued-government-over-tender-free-contract/

[6] https://schoolsweek.co.uk/revealed-edenred-sued-government-over-tender-free-contract/

[7] https://schoolsweek.co.uk/coronavirus-dfes-free-laptops-portal-launch-delayed/

[8] https://schoolsweek.co.uk/coronavirus-williamson-seeks-to-reassure-heads-over-free-laptops-scheme/

[9] https://schoolsweek.co.uk/coronavirus-85m-free-laptops-scheme-falls-short/

[10] https://schoolsweek.co.uk/coronavirus-85m-free-laptops-scheme-falls-short/

[11] See also https://schoolsweek.co.uk/schools-turn-to-philanthropists-for-laptops-as-wait-for-dfe-devices-continues/

12 https://www.theguardian.com/politics/2020/jun/16/boris-johnson-faces-tory-rebellion-over-marcus-rashfords-school-meals-call; https://www.mirror.co.uk/news/politics/free-school-meals-u-turn-22200686

13 https://www.theguardian.com/commentisfree/2020/may/17/the-observer-view-on-how-the-debate-on-schools-has-been-dangerously-mishandled

14 https://www.bbc.com/news/amp/education-52733452

15 https://schoolsweek.co.uk/the-rebel-councils-governments-schools-plan-in-doubt-as-27-town-halls-raise-safety-concerns/

16 https://www.theguardian.com/commentisfree/2020/may/20/british-schools-science-children-education-testing-tracing

17 https://www.thecomet.net/news/when-will-hertfordshire-schools-reopen-after-coronavirus-1-6660009

18 https://www.dailymail.co.uk/debate/article-2298146/I-refuse-surrender-Marxist-teachers-hell-bent-destroying-schools-Education-Secretary-berates-new-enemies-promise-opposing-plans.html

19 https://www.theguardian.com/business/2020/apr/14/how-close-is-the-nhs-to-getting-the-18000-ventilators-it-needs-coronavirus; https://www.theguardian.com/business/2020/may/04/the-inside-story-of-the-uks-nhs-coronavirus-ventilator-challenge

20 https://www.theguardian.com/fashion/2020/apr/16/government-ignores-uk-textiles-firms-desperate-to-make-ppe; https://www.bma.org.uk/news-and-opinion/health-and-manufacturing-unions-join-forces-in-call-for-mass-ppe-manufacturing-effort-1

21 https://www.theguardian.com/world/2020/apr/11/reveal-cost-of-35m-unusable-covid-19-tests-health-chiefs-told

22 https://practicebusiness.co.uk/ppe-ordered-from-turkey-fail-to-meet-safety-standards/

23 https://www.ft.com/content/9680c20f-7b71-4f65-9bec-0e9554a8e0a7; https://www.bbc.co.uk/news/business-52362707; https://www.theguardian.com/world/2020/apr/02/small-laboratories-coronavirus-testing-time-wasted-dunkirk

24 https://www.army.mod.uk/news-and-events/news/2020/04/army-boost-for-testers-at-ikea-wembley-covid-19-testing-facility/

25 https://www.theguardian.com/uk-news/2020/apr/26/uk-military-to-operate-coronavirus-mobile-testing-units-for-frontline-workers

26 https://www.ft.com/content/99b9c49f-9477-45c0-88c2-8151b2f13796

27 https://www.theguardian.com/science/2020/apr/03/why-has-the-uk-lagged-behind-in-testing-for-the-coronavirus

28 https://www.independent.co.uk/news/uk/politics/coronavirus-uk-government-guidance-tests-sage-jeremy-hunt-a9509111.html

29 https://www.thelancet.com/journals/lancet/article/PIIS0140-6736(20)31098-9/fulltext

30 https://www.bmj.com/company/newsroom/time-to-encourage-people-to-wear-face-masks-as-a-precaution-say-experts/

[31] https://consent.yahoo.com/collectConsent?sessionId=3_cc-session_1612910e-959f-4acc-88c0-cad01ddbe0e9&lang=en-GB&inline=false

[32] https://www.theguardian.com/business/2020/may/20/serco-accidentally-shares-contact-tracers-email-addresses-covid-19

[33] https://www.theguardian.com/world/2020/may/05/uk-coronavirus-death-toll-rises-above-32000-to-highest-in-europe

[34] https://www.nytimes.com/2020/05/18/opinion/coronavirus-australia.html

[35] Hal, D., Lister, J., Hobbs, C., & Mercer, H. (2020). *Privatised and unprepared. The NHS supply chain.* https://weownit.org.uk/privatised-and-unprepared-nhs-supply-chain: University of Greenwich.

[36] https://inews.co.uk/news/education/coronavirus-headteachers-drowning-government-school-opening-guidance-2861369

[37] https://bylinetimes.com/2020/04/22/palantir-coronavirus-contract-did-not-go-to-competitive-tender/

[38] https://www.gov.uk/government/news/voucher-scheme-launches-for-schools-providing-free-school-meals

[39] https://www.standard.co.uk/news/uk/david-spiegelhalter-covid19-statistics-coronavirus-government-a4436471.html

[40] https://www.newstatesman.com/politics/education/2019/03/department-education-doublespeak-exposes-how-out-touch-our-schools-it#amp

[41] Corruption during the pandemic is highly likely according to corruption professionals https://www.dlapiper.com/en/ukraine/insights/publications/2020/04/covid19-a-breeding-ground-for-corruption-monitoring-key-risks/, and see https://www.theguardian.com/society/2020/may/01/revealed-nhs-procurement-official-privately-selling-ppe

Chapter 1

[1] Griffiths, Morwenna. 1998. *Educational research for social justice: Getting off the fence.* Buckingham: Open University Press.

[2] Ball, Stephen. 2018. *The education debate.* Third ed. Bristol: Policy Press.

[3] Social Mobility Commission. 2019. *State of the nation 2018–19: Social mobility in Great Britain.* https://assets.publishing.service.gov.uk/government/uploads/system/uploads/attachment_data/file/798404/SMC_State_of_the_Nation_Report_2018–19.pdf: Social Mobility Commission.

[4] Bukodi, Erzsebet, and John H. Goldthorpe. 2018. *Social mobility and education in Britain: Research, politics and policy.* Cambridge: Cambridge University Press.

[5] OECD Publishing. 2019 *Governance as an SDG accelerator.* Paris: OECD. 65.

[6] OECD Publishing. 2015 *Consequences of corruption at the sector level and implications for economic growth and development.* Paris: OECD. 65.

7   OECD 2015. 66.
8   Holmes, Leslie. 2015. *Corruption: A very short introduction*. Oxford: Oxford University Press.
9   Machiavelli, Niccolo. 1532 (2003). *The prince*. London: Penguin.
10 Knights, Mark. 2016. *Old corruption: What British history can tell us about corruption today*. London: Transparency International.
11 Smith, Adam. 1776 (2008). *An inquiry into the nature and causes of the wealth of nations*. Oxford: Oxford Paperbacks.
12 Von Alemann, Ulrich. 2004. 'The unknown depths of political theory: The case for a multidimensional concept of corruption'. *Crime, Law and Social Change* 42 (1): 25–34.
13 Moore, James. 2018. 'Corruption and ethical standards of British public life, national debates and local administration 1880–1914'. In *Anticorruption in history: From antiquity to the modern era*, edited by Ronald Kroeze, Andre Vitoria and G. Geltner, 267–78. Oxford: Oxford University Press.
14 Knights 2016, 14.
15 https://www.transparency.org/what-is-corruption.
16 Kroeze, Ronald, Andre Vitoria, and G. Geltner. 2018. *Anticorruption in history: From antiquity to the modern era*. Oxford: Oxford University Press.
17 In education see for instance Ball, Stephen. 2012. *Global education inc: New policy networks and the neoliberal imaginary*. London: Routledge.
18 Transparency International. 2018. *The cost of secrecy: The role played by companies registered in the UK's overseas territories in money laundering and corruption*. London: Transparency International; 2019. *At your service: Investigating how UK businesses and institutions help corrupt individuals and regimes launder their money and reputations*. London: Transparency International.
19 Transparency International 2019, 8.
20 For example https://www.independent.co.uk/news/education/top-private-schools-unwittingly-accepting-laundered-money-wealthy-foreign-criminals-moldovan-police-a7640811.html; https://qz.com/1392063/money-laundering-in-the-uk-private-schools-in-the-crosshairs/; https://www.ft.com/content/5a2ab2a4-b83b-11e8-b3ef-799c8613f4a1.
21 Rose-Ackerman, Susan. 2018. 'Corruption and purity'. *Daedalus* 147 (3): 98–110.
22 Rose-Ackerman 2018, 102.
23 Rose-Ackerman, Susan. 1999. *Corruption and government: Causes, consequences and reform*. Cambridge: Cambridge University Press.
24 Transparency International UK. 2010. *Corruption in the UK. Part One: National Opinion Survey*. London: Transparency International.
25 Transparency International UK. 2011. *National integrity system assessment: United Kingdom*. London: Transparency International UK.
26 Transparency International UK 2011, 7.
27 Johnston, Michael. 2005. *Syndromes of corruption: Wealth, power and democracy*. Cambridge: Cambridge University Press. 61.

[28] See also Hodge, Margaret. 2016. *Called to account: How corporate bad behaviour and government waste combine to cost us millions.* London: Little. Brown.

[29] Johnston, Michael. 2018. 'Afterword'. In *Anticorruption in history: From antiquity to the modern era,* edited by Ronald Kroeze, Andre Vitoria and Guy Geltner, 305–9. Oxford: Oxford University Press. 308.

[30] Rizvi, Fazal, and Bob Lingard. 2009. *Globalising education policy.* London: Routledge; Ozga, Jenny. 2009. 'Governing education through data in England: from regulation to self evaluation'. *Journal of Education Policy* 24 (2): 149–62; Ball. 2012.

[31] Knights 2016.

[32] Knights 2016, 20.

[33] Rothstein, Bo. 2018. 'Fighting systemic corruption: The indirect strategy'. *Daedalus* 147: 35–49.

[34] Rothstein, Bo, and Aiysha Varraich. 2017. *Making sense of corruption.* Cambridge: Cambridge University Press.

[35] Heywood, Paul. 2018. 'Combatting corruption in the twenty-first century: new approaches'. *Daedalus* 147 (3): 83–97, 85.

[36] Rothstein and Varraich 2017.

[37] Whyte, David. 2015. *How corrupt is Britain?* London: Pluto Press.

[38] Foucault, Michel. 1972. *The archeology of knowledge,* translated by Alan Sheridan. 1995 ed. Routledge: London.

Chapter 2

[1] Webb, Sydney. 1901. *The education muddle and the way out: A constructive criticism of English educational machinery.* London: The Fabian Society. 3.

[2] Webb 1901, 16.

[3] Webb 1901, 16.

[4] Webb 1901, 18.

[5] Brennan, Edward J. T. 1961. 'Sidney Webb and the London Technical Education Board'. *The Vocational Aspect of Secondary and Further Education* 13 (27): 146–71.

[6] Webb, Sidney. 1904. *London education.* London: Longmans, Green and Co., vii.

[7] Webb 1904, viii.

[8] The concern for data as a means of locating and tracking equity has an important history in London, see for instance the pioneering ethnographic 'mapping' of poverty in Mayhew, Henry. 1861. *London Labour and the London poor, Vols 1–4.* 1968 ed. New York: Dover Publications.

[9] Ball, Stephen. 2018. 'The tragedy of state education in England: Reluctance, compromise and a muddle – a system in disarray'. *Journal of the British Academy* 6: 207–38.

[10] Esping-Andersen, Gosta. 1990. *The three worlds of welfare capitalism.* Cambridge: Polity Press.

[11] The five 'giant' social challenges identified in the 1942 Beveridge Report.

[12] Jones, Ken. 1983. *Beyond progressive education*. London: Macmillan; Cunningham, Peter. 1988. *Curriculum change in the primary school since 1945: Dissemination of the progressive ideal*. London: Falmer Press.

[13] Cunningham, 1988.

[14] For instance Young, Michael F. D. 1971. *Knowledge and control*. London: Collier Macmillan; Bernstein, Basil. 1971. *Class, codes and control, Vol. 1: Theoretical studies towards a sociology of language*. London: Routledge & Kegan Paul.

[15] See the journal *Critical Story* 1969, Vol. 4; often called The Black Papers.

[16] Jones, Ken. 1983. *Beyond progressive education*. London: Macmillan.

[17] Tomlinson, Sally. 2001. *Education in post-welfare society*. Buckingham: Open University Press.

[18] Whitty, Geoff, and Tony Edwards. 1998. 'School choice policies in England and the United States: an exploration of their origins and significance'. *Comparative Education* 34 (2): 211–27.

[19] Thomson, Pat. 2008. 'Answering back to policy? Headteachers' stress and the logic of the sympathetic interview'. *Journal of Education Policy* 23 (6): 649–68.

[20] Rivzi, Fazal, and Bob Lingard. 2009. *Globalising education policy*. London: Routledge.

[21] Steger, Manfred B., and Ravi K. Roy. 2010. *Neoliberalism: A very short introduction*. Oxford: Oxford University Press.

[22] Brown, Wendy. 2015. *Undoing the demos: Neoliberalism's stealth revolution*. New York: Zone Books.

[23] Springer, Simon, Kean Birch and Julie MacLeavy. 2016. 'An introduction to neoliberalism'. In *The handbook of neoliberalism*, edited by Simon Springer, Kean Birch and Julie Macleavy, 1–13. London: Routledge, 3.

[24] Cahill, Damien, Lindy Edwards and Frank Stilwell. Eds. 2012. *Neoliberalism. Beyond the free market*. Cheltenham: Edward Elgar Publishing; Berry, Craig. 2011. *Globalisation and ideology in Britain: neoliberalism, free trade and the global economy*. Manchester: Manchester University Press.

[25] Harvey, David. 2005. *A brief history of neoliberalism*. Oxford: Oxford University Press.

[26] Davies, William. 2017. *The limits of neoliberalism: Authority, sovereignty and the logics of competition*. Los Angeles: Sage.

[27] Cutler, Tony, and Barbara Waine. 1997. 'The politics of quasi-markets'. *Critical Social Policy* 17 (2): 3–26.

[28] Chitty, Clyde. 1997. 'Privatisation and marketisation'. *Oxford Review of Education* 23 (1): 45–61.

[29] Jayasuriya, Kanishka. 2002. 'The new contractualism: neoliberal or democratic?' *The Political Quarterly* 73 (3): 309–20.

[30] Newman, Janet, and John Clarke. 2009. *Publics, politics and power: Remaking the public in public services*. London: Sage, 7.

[31] Stedman-Jones, Daniel. 2012. *Masters of the universe: Hayek, Friedman and the birth of neoliberal politics*. Princeton, NJ: Princeton University Press.

[32] Friedman, Milton. 2002. *Capitalism and freedom*. Chicago: University of Chicago Press.

[33] Hayek, Friedrich A. 2001. *The road to serfdom*. New York: Routledge.

[34] Eagleton-Pierce, Matthew. 2016. *Neoliberalism: Key concepts*. London: Routledge.

[35] England, Kim, and Kevin Ward. 2016. 'Theorizing neoliberalization'. In *The handbook of neoliberalism*, edited by Simon Springer, Kean Birch and Julie Macleavy. London: Routledge, 57.

[36] Sakellariou, Dikaios, and Elena S. Rotarou. 2017. 'The effects of neoliberal policies on access to healthcare for people with disabilities'. *Journal of Equity in Health* 16 (1): 199–208; Rizq, Rosemary. 2014. 'Perversion, neoliberalism and therapy: the audit culture in mental health services'. *Psychoanalysis, Culture and Society* 19 (2): 209–18.

[37] Bambra, Clare. Ed. 2019. *Health in hard times*. Bristol: Policy Press.

[38] Newman, Janet. 2001. *Modernising governance: New Labour, policy and society*. London: Sage.

[39] Hood, Christopher. 1998. *The art of the state: Culture, rhetoric and public management*. Oxford: Clarendon Press; Pollitt, Christopher. 2011. *Public management reform: A comparative analysis. New Public Management, governance and the neo-Weberian state*. Third ed. Oxford: Oxford University Press.

[40] Pilcher, Jane, and Stephen Wagg. Eds. 1996. *Thatcher's children? Politics, childhood and society in the 1980s and 1990s*. London: Falmer Press.

[41] Edgerton, David. 2019. *The rise and fall of the British nation: A twentieth century history*. London: Penguin; Harvey, David. 2005. *A brief history of neoliberalism*. Oxford: Oxford University Press.

[42] Whitty, Geoff, Sally Power and David Halpin. 1998. *Devolution and choice in education: The school, the state and the market*. Buckingham: Open University Press.

[43] Maclure, Stuart. 1988. *Education re-formed: Guide to the Education Act 1988*. London: Hodder Arnold.

[44] Jones, Ken. 2003. *Education in Britain: 1944 to the present*. Oxford: Polity Press; Ball, Stephen. 2018. *The education debate*. Third ed. Bristol: Policy Press; Gewirtz, Sharon. 2002. *The managerial school: Post-welfarism and social justice in education*. London: Routledge.

[45] Giddens, Anthony. 1998. *The third way*. Cambridge and Oxford: Polity Press.

[46] Bowe, Richard, Stephen Ball and Anne Gold. 1992. *Reforming education and changing schools: Case studies in policy sociology*. London: Routledge.

[47] Gunter, Helen, and Gillian Forrester. 2008. 'New Labour and school leadership 1997–2007'. *British Journal of Educational Studies* 56 (2): 144–62.

[48] Jones, Ken, and Pat Thomson. 2008. 'Policy rhetoric and the renovation of English schooling: the case of Creative Partnerships'. *Journal of Education Policy* 23 (6): 715–28.

[49] Francis, Becky. 2017. The role of academies in English education policy. Paper presented at the Eleventh Whitehall Lecture, 22 June.

50 West, Anne, and Elizabeth Bailey. 2014. 'The development of the academies programme: "privatising" school-based education in England 1986–2013'. *British Journal of Educational Studies* 61 (2): 137–59.

51 West and Bailey 2014.

52 Francis 2017.

53 https://assets.publishing.service.gov.uk/government/uploads/system/uploads/attachment_data/file/719226/Schools_Pupils_and_their_Characteristics_2018_Main_Text.pdf.

54 https://www.nao.org.uk/press-release/converting-maintained-schools-to-academies/.

55 *Open academies and academy projects in development*. https://www.gov.uk/government/publications/open-academies-and-academy-projects-in-development.

56 *Free schools: open schools and successful applications*. https://www.gov.uk/government/publications/free-schools-open-schools-and-successful-applications.

57 Roberts, Nerys. 2017. *FAQs: Academies and free schools*. House of Commons Briefing Paper. Westminster: House of Commons Library.,3.

58 Roberts 2017.

59 Phillips, Robert. 1996. 'History teaching, cultural restorationism and national identity in England and Wales'. *Curriculum Studies* 4 (3): 385–99.

60 Apple, Michael. 2001. *Educating the 'right' way: Markets, standards, God and inequality*. New York and London: Routledge.

61 Kulz, Christy. 2017. *Factories for learning: Making race, class and inequality in the neoliberal academy*. Manchester: Manchester University Press.

62 Gorard, Stephen. 2014. 'The link between academies in England, pupil outcomes and local patterns of socio-economic segregation between schools'. *Research Papers in Education* 29 (3): 268–84.

63 Caldwell, Brian, and Jim Spinks. 1988. *The self managing school*. London: Falmer Press.

64 https://www.tes.com/news/school-news/breaking-news/academies-boss-maintained-school-headteachers-have-more-freedom-those.

65 https://www.gov.uk/government/news/10-facts-you-need-to-know-about-academies.

66 Wilkins, Andrew. 2017. 'Rescaling the local: multi-academy trusts, private monopoly and statecraft in England'. *Journal of Educational Administration and History* 49(2): 171–85.

67 Hattie, John. 2011. *Visible learning for teachers: Maximising impact on leaders*. London: Routledge.

68 https://www.gov.uk/types-of-school/overview.

69 Courtney, Steve. 2016. 'Mapping school types in England'. *Oxford Review of Education* 41 (6): 799–818.

70 Courtney 2016, 814.

71 https://schoolsweek.co.uk/johnson-re-announces-latest-free-schools-application-round/.

72 Commons Select Committee. 2017. 'Government must show new grammars close attainment gap'. In https://www.parliament.uk/business/committees/committees-a-z/commons-select/education-committee/news-parliament-2015/evidence-check-grammar-schools-report-published-16-17/: UK Government.

73 See https://www.thetimes.co.uk/article/tories-pledge-new-grammar-school-places-gzg0250f2; and https://www.bbc.co.uk/news/education-44727857.

74 https://www.tes.com/news/academisation-its-time-final-stage-reform. This call to total academisation is repeated, see the most recent https://www.tes.com/news/call-all-schools-be-academy-trusts-2030.

75 Bernadelli, Danielle, Simon Rutt, Toby Greany and Rob Higham. 2018. *Multi-academy trusts: Do they make a difference to pupil outcomes?* London: UCL Institute of Education Press.

76 https://assets.publishing.service.gov.uk/government/uploads/system/uploads/attachment_data/file/756328/Opening_and_Closing_maintained_schools_Guidance.pdf, 4.

77 https://epi.org.uk/publications-and-research/free-schools-2019-report/; also see the House of Commons report on special needs where it suggests that local authorities must be able to open new schools and not rely on free schools as the means to carry out their statutory responsibilities, https://houseofcommons.shorthandstories.com/SEND/index.html?utm_source=twitter&utm_medium=tweet&utm_campaign=education-special-needs&utm_content=organic.

Chapter 3

1 The British call the organisation that makes government possible a civil service. The term civil derives from the Latin *civilis*, civic order benefitting a citizen, and the term is thus associated with the workings of the state. Indeed, the old French term 'civil' relates to the internal affairs of state, as opposed to an ecclesiastical or military organisation. Civil is also used to describe the courtesy and respect required to sustain public debates. The term 'public' by contrast comes from the Latin *poplicus* – of the people. In the 15th century, public in the English language also came to be associated with 'being open to all in the community'. Ironically, in the UK, public schools once run by churches or local bodies intended to be for the people have morphed into selective schools for those who can afford to pay for them. In Australia fee-paying schools are most often called 'private'.

In England, the civil service refers only to the national organisation centred in Westminster. It does not refer to local authority staff, or service staff in schools, health or transport. While these people are engaged in a public service role, they are not called either public servants or civil servants. While these differences may seem a fine semantic point, thinking about serving a local authority, serving a particular system, serving the state or serving the people are not the same thing. The differences between who or what counts as the public are important to the organisational analysis offered in this book.

2   O'Toole, Brian. 2006. *The ideal of public service*. London: Routledge. 5.

3   Northcote, Stafford F., and C. E. Trevelyan. 1853. *Report of the organisation of the permanent civil service*. London: Her Majesty's Stationery Office.

4   Weller, Patrick, and Catherine Haddon. 2016. 'Westminster traditions: continuity and change'. *Governance: An International Journal of Policy, Administration and Institutions* 29 (4): 483–98.

5   Committee of Inquiry, House of Commons. 1854. 'On the organisation of the permanent civil service'. London: Her Majesty's Stationery Office. 2.

6   See for example https://www.civilservant.org.uk/csr_detail-note1.html.

7   Lynn, Laurence E. 2006. *Public management old and new*. New York: Routledge; Smith, Kevin B., and Michael J. Licari. 2006. *Public administrations: Power and politics in the fourth branch of government*. New York: Open University Press; Fry, G. 1995. *Policy and management in the British civil service*. Hemel Hempstead: Prentice Hall.

8   Weber, Max, Peter Baehr and Gordon C. Wells. 2002. *The Protestant ethic and the spirit of capitalism and other writings*. New York: Penguin.

9   Du Gay, Paul. 2000. *In praise of bureaucracy. Weber, organisation, ethics*. Thousand Oaks: Sage.

10 Pilkington, Colin. 1999. *The civil service in Britain today*. Manchester: Manchester University Press.

11 Parris, H. 1969. *Constitutional bureaucracy*. London: Allen and Unwin.

12 Coolican, Michael. 2018. *No tradesmen and no women: The origins of the British civil service*. London: Biteback Publishing.

13 Du Gay, Paul. 2009. 'In defence of Mandarins: recovering the "core business" of public management'. *Management & Organizational History* 4 (4): 359–84, 370.

14 Du Gay 2009, 371.

15 O'Toole 2006, 3.

16 Plato. 2007. *The republic*, translated by H. D. P. Lee and Desmond Lee. New York: Penguin.

17 Fraser, Derek. 2017. *The evolution of the British welfare estate*. Fifth ed. London: Palgrave.

18 Clarke, John, and Janet E. Newman. 2009. *The managerial state: Power, politics and ideology in the remaking of social welfare*. London: Sage; Pierre, Jon. 1995. *Bureaucracy in the modern state: An introduction to comparative public administration*. Cheltenham: Edward Elgar.

19 Pollitt, Christopher. 2011. *Public management reform: A comparative analysis. New Public Management, governance and the neo-Weberian state*. 3rd ed. Oxford: Oxford University Press.

20 Committee on the Civil Service, J. Fulton and B. Fulton. 1968. *The civil service: Report of the committee, 1966–68*. London: HM Stationery Office.

21 Lynn. 2006; Clarke and Newman. 2009.

22 Chapman, Richard A. 1968. 'The Fulton Report: a summary'. *Public Administration* 46 (4): 443–52, 448.

23 See http://www.yes-minister.com/ymseas1b.htm#YM%201.6.

24 Stanley, Martin. 2016. *How to be a civil servant.* London: Biteback Pubishing.

25 Osborne, D., and T. Gaebler. 1993. *Reinventing government: How the entrepreneurial spirit is transforming the public sector.* New York: Plume, Penguin, xvii.

26 See for instance a discussion of the history of NPM in development contexts in the 2015 special issue of *Public Administration and Development* 35: 94.

27 Stoker, Gerry. 1998. 'Governance as theory: Five propositions'. *International Social Science Journal* 50 (1): 17–28.

28 Rhodes, R. A. W. 1994. 'The hollowing out of the state: the changing nature of the public service in Britain'. *The Political Quarterly* 65 (2): 138–51.

29 Newman, Janet. 2001. *Modernising governance: New Labour, policy and society.* London: Sage.

30 Hood, Christopher. 1995. 'The "New Public Management" in the 1980s: variations on a theme'. *Accounting, Organisations and Society* 20 (2/3): 93–109.

31 Hood 1995, 94.

32 Gunter, Helen, Emiliano Grimaldi, David Hall and Roberto Serpieri. Eds. 2016. *New Public Management and the reform of education: European lessons for policy and practice.* London: Routledge.

33 Dunleavy, Patrick. 2014. *The state is a multi-system: Understanding the oneness and diversity of government.* Manchester: UK Political Studies Association. LSE Research online. http://eprints.lse.ac.uk/56492/.

34 Hirschman, E. 1970. *Exit, voice and loyalty: Responses to decline in firms, organizations and states.* Boston: Harvard University Press.

35 Donnelly, Kevin. 2007. *Dumbing down: Outcomes-based and politically correct – the impact of the culture wars on our schools.* Sydney: Hardie Grant Books.

36 Lockhart, Johanna M. 2016. *Maximise your school marketing.* London: Rowman & Littlefield.

37 Stoker, Gerry. 1998; Pierre, Jon, and B. Guy Peters. 2000. *Governance, politics and the state.* New York: St Martin's Press.

38 Pollitt, Christopher, and Geert Bouckaert. 2011. *Public management reform: A comparative analysis. New Public Management, governance and the neo-Weberian state.* Fourth ed. Oxford: Oxford University Press, 6.

39 Panchamia, Nehal, and Peter Thomas. 2015. *Civil service reform in the real world.* https://www.instituteforgovernment.org.uk/sites/default/files/publications/260314%20CSRW%20-%20final.pdf: Institute for Government; Hood, Christopher. 1998. *The art of the state: Culture, rhetoric and public management.* Oxford: Clarendon Press; Pollitt, Christopher. 2011. *Public management reform: A comparative analysis. New Public Management, governance and the neo-Weberian state.* Third ed. Oxford: Oxford University Press.

40 See https://publications.parliament.uk/pa/ld199798/ldselect/ldpubsrv/055/psrep07.htm.

41 For instance in education, New Labour funded locality-based equity programmes and early intervention through Every Child Matters, Children's Centres and the 'Extended School' agenda.

42 O'Toole 2006, 152.

43 Gunter, Helen. 2015. 'Consultants, consultancy and consultocracy in education policymaking in England'. *Journal of Education Policy* 30 (4): 518–39.

44 Olmedo, Antonio, and Eduardo Santa Cruz Grau. 2013. 'Neoliberalism, policy advocacy networks and think tanks in the Spanish education arena'. *Education Inquiry* 4 (3): 473–96; Plehwe, Dieter, Moritz Neujeffski and Werner Kramer. 2018. 'Saving the dangerous idea: austerity think tank networks in the European Union'. *Policy and Society* 37 (2): 188–205.

45 Keshavjee, Salmaan. 2014. *Blind spot. How neoliberalism infiltrated global health.* Los Angeles: University of California Press; Aldred, Rachel. 2008. 'NHS LIFT and the new shape of neoliberal welfare'. *Capital and class* 32 (2): 31–57.

46 Paton, Calum. 2008. 'The NHS after 10 years of New Labour'. In *Modernising the welfare state: The Blair legacy*, edited by Martin Powell, 17–34. Bristol: Policy Press; Hunter, David J. 2016. *The health debate*. Second ed. Bristol: Policy Press.

47 Davies, W. 2017. *The limits of neoliberalism: Authority, sovereignty and the logics of competition.* Los Angeles: Sage.

48 Dean, Mitchell. 2014. 'Rethinking neoliberalism'. *Journal of Sociology* 50 (2): 150–63.

49 Panchamia and Thomas 2015.

50 Margetts, Helen, and Patrick Dunleavy. 2013. 'The second wave of digital-era governance: a quasi-paradigm for government on the web'. *Philosophical Transactions of the Royal Society A*, https://doi.org/10.1098/rsta.2012.0382; Dunleavy, Patrick, Helen Margetts, Simon Bastow and Jane Tinkler. 2006. 'New Public Management is dead – long live digital era governance'. *Journal of Public Administration Research and Theory* 16 (3): 467–94.

51 Horton, Sylvia. 2006. 'The public service ethos in the British civil service: an historical institutional analysis'. *Public Policy and Administration* 21 (1): 32–48.

52 Veronesi, Gianluca, Ian Kirkpatrick and Ali Atlantar. 2019. 'Are public sector managers a "bureaucratic burden"? The case of English public hospitals'. *Journal of Public Administration Research and Theory*, doi:10.1093/jopart/muy072.

53 See also Bach, Tobias, and Sylvia Veit. 2018. 'The determinants of promotion to high public office in Germany: partisan loyalty, political craft, or managerial competencies?' *Journal of Public Administration Research and Theory* 28 (2): 254–69.

54 Du Gay 2009, 278; see also Stanley 2016.

55 Russell, Meg, and Philip Cowley. 2016. 'The policy power of the Westminster Parliament: the "parliamentary state" and the empirical

evidence'. *Governance: An International Journal of Policy, Administration and Institutions* 29 (1): 121–37.

[56] Baekgaard, Martin, Peter B. Mortensen and Heenrik Bech Seeberg. 2018. 'The bureaucracy and the policy agenda'. *Journal of Public Administration Research and Theory* 28 (2): 239–53.

[57] Richards, David, and Martin J. Smith. 2016. 'The Westminster model and the "indivisibility of the political and administrative elite": a convenient myth whose time is up?' *Governance: An International Journal of Policy, Administration and Institutions* 29 (4): 499–516.

[58] Knight, John, and Bob Lingard. 1996. 'Ministerialisation and politicisation: changing practices of educational policy production'. In *A national approach to schooling in Australia? Essays on the development of national policies in schools education*, edited by Bob Lingard and Paige Porter. Canberra, Australia: Australian College of Education.

[59] O'Toole 2006.

[60] Maravic, Patrick, and Christoph Reichard. 2003. 'New Public Management and corruption IPNM dialogue and analysis'. *International Public Management Review* 4 (1): 84–129.

[61] Asthana, Anand N. 2012. 'Decentralisation and corruption revisited: evidence from a natural experiment'. *Public Administration and Development* 32 (1): 27–37.

[62] Levacic, Rosalind, Peter Downes, Brian Caldwell, David Gurr, Jim Spinks, Jan Herczunski, Maria Beatriz Luce and Nalu Farenzena. 2012. *Formula funding of schools: Decentralisaton and corruption. A comparative analysis*. Paris: UNESCO.

[63] Levacic et al 2012, 143.

[64] Segal, Lydia G. 2004. *Battling corruption in America's public schools*. Boston: Northeastern University Press.

[65] Hanna, Rema, Sarah Bishop, Sara Nadel, Gabe Scheffer and Katherine Durlacher. 2011. *The effectiveness of anti-corruption policy: What has worked, what hasn't, and what we don't know*. EPPI Centre Report 1909. London: EPPI Centre, Instituted of Education, University of London.

[66] Flinders, Matt, and Matt Wood. Eds. 2015. *Tracing the political: Depoliticisation, governance and the state*. Bristol: Bristol University Press.

[67] Norris, Pippa. 2011. *Democratic deficit: Critical citizens revisited*. Cambridge: Cambridge University Press.

[68] Clarke and Newman 2009.

Chapter 4

[1] Bates, Richard. 1987. 'Corporate culture, schooling, and educational administration'. *Educational Administration Quarterly* 23 (4): 79–115; Bates, Richard, 1993. 'On knowing: cultural and critical approaches to educational administration'. *Educational Management and Administration* 21 (3): 171–6; Davis, Charles R. 1985. 'A critique of the ideology of efficiency'. *Humboldt Journal of Social Relations* 12 (2): 73–86.

2   Spicer, Andre, Mats Alvesson and Dan Kärreman. 2009. 'Critical performativity: the unfinished business of critical management studies'. *Human Relations* 62 (4): 537–6; Clegg, Stewart, Eduardo Ibarra-Colada and Luis Bueno-Rodriquez. Eds. 1999. *Global management: Universal theories and local realities.* London: Sage.

3   Taylor, F. W. 1919. *The principles of scientific management.* New York: Harper & Brothers.

4   Taylor 1919, 36.

5   Businesses were already involved in specialist schools and the area based intervention Education Action Zones.

6   Mahony, Pat, Ian Hextall, and Malcolm Richardson. 2011. '"Building schools for the future": reflections on a new social architecture'. *Journal of Education Policy.* 26(3): 341–60.

7   https://publications.parliament.uk/pa/cm200405/cmselect/cmeduski/86/8605.htm, point 22.

8   http://news.bbc.co.uk/1/hi/education/4952004.stm.

9   National Audit Office (NAO). 2007. *The academies programme.* London: House of Commons. https://www.nao.org.uk/wp-content/uploads/2007/02/0607254es.pdf.

10 http://news.bbc.co.uk/1/hi/education/4952004.stm.

11 https://www.theguardian.com/education/2009/dec/01/academies-sponsors-government-funding.

12 https://www.theguardian.com/education/2009/nov/05/united-learning-trust-academy-schools.

13 https://www.theguardian.com/education/2009/dec/01/academies-sponsors-government-funding.

14 See also Beckett, Francis. 2007. *The great city academy fraud.* London: Continuum.

15 https://assets.publishing.service.gov.uk/government/uploads/system/uploads/attachment_data/file/206382/Academies_Annual_Report_2011–12.pdf.

16 https://www.gov.uk/.../Copy_of_Post_Opening_Ready_Reckoner_v1_8__3_.xlsx *(page no longer available).*

17 http://www.bbc.co.uk/news/mobile/education-12712079.

18 https://www.theguardian.com/education/2012/jun/04/academy-status-incentive-cuts.

19 https://www.ft.com/content/d4af866a-15f1–11e1-a691–00144feabdc0.

20 House of Commons Public Accounts Committee. 2018. *Converting schools to academies.* HC 697. https://publications.parliament.uk/pa/cm201719/cmselect/cmpubacc/697/697.pdf: House of Commons.

21 House of Commons Public Accounts Committee 2018, 12.

22 https://schoolsweek.co.uk/wp-content/uploads/2018/09/SW-150-digi.pdf, 6.

23 https://www.theguardian.com/education/2016/mar/08/turn-schools-into-academies-cuts-teacher-shortages.

Notes

[24] https://assets.publishing.service.gov.uk/government/uploads/system/uploads/attachment_data/file/692787/School_balances_on_conversion_submission.pdf, 5.

[25] https://schoolsweek.co.uk/trusts-seeks-legal-advice-after-council-claims-parents-are-fearful-of-tough-love-approach/.

[26] https://consult.education.gov.uk/local-authorities-and-funding-policy-team/school-loan-schemes-implementation-of-changes-1/supporting_documents/Government%20consultation%20%20implementation%20of%20the%20changes%20to%20the%20criteria%20....pdf, 3.

[27] https://www.tes.com/news/schools-ordered-become-academies-set-close-because-no-one-will-sponsor-them

[28] https://www.theguardian.com/education/2018/jan/22/rose-hill-primary-oxford-an-orphan-school-at-the-sharp-end-of-academisation

[29] https://www.bbc.co.uk/news/uk-england-33136997.

[30] National Audit Office (NAO). 2018a. *Converting maintained schools to academies*. London: House of Commons. https://www.nao.org.uk/wp-content/uploads/2018/02/Converting-maintained-schools-to-academies.pdf, 13.

[31] NAO 2018a, 9.

[32] https://www.nao.org.uk/press-release/converting-maintained-schools-to-academies/.

[33] https://assets.publishing.service.gov.uk/government/uploads/system/uploads/attachment_data/file/726556/Academy_Transfers_and_Funding_2017_to_2018_Text.pdf.

[34] https://www.gov.uk/government/statistics/academy-transfers-and-funding-england-financial-year-2017-to-2018#history.

[35] http://schoolsweek.co.uk/booming-academy-transfer-market-pushes-costs-to-potential-30m/.

[36] https://www.theguardian.com/education/2018/jan/22/rose-hill-primary-oxford-an-orphan-school-at-the-sharp-end-of-academisation.

[37] https://www.theguardian.com/education/2018/jul/22/academy-schools-scandal-failing-trusts.

[38] https://schoolsweek.co.uk/investigation-dfe-hid-damaging-lord-nash-academy-cost-emails/

[39] https://www.localschoolsnetwork.org.uk/2017/07/119m-in-grants-for-academy-trusts-converting-or-rebrokering-last-year-dfe-accounts-reveal.

[40] https://www.gov.uk/government/uploads/system/uploads/attachment_data/file/630523/DfE_Consolidated_annual_report_and_accounts_2016–17_WEB.pdf.

[41] https://schoolsweek.co.uk/dfe-wont-answer-on-massaged-transfer-figures/.

[42] https://schoolsweek.co.uk/academy-transfer-market-costs-hit-30m-as-300-more-schools-rebrokered-this-year/.

[43] https://www.theguardian.com/education/2017/feb/07/failing-schools-academy-sponsor-ofsted.

[44] https://www.tes.com/news/exclusive-failure-find-sponsors-raises-serious-questions-over-academisation-law.

45 https://schoolsweek.co.uk/academys-new-start-delayed-by-deficit-discussions/.

46 For example, Sweet, Rod. 2017. 'Haemorrhaging cash: assessing the long-term costs of PFI'. *Construction Research and Innovation* 8 (4): 113–16; Asenova, Darinka, and Matthias Beck. 2010. 'Crucial silences: when accountability met PFI and finance capital'. *Critical Perspectives on Accounting* 21 (1): 1–13.

47 https://publications.parliament.uk/pa/cm201012/cmselect/cmtreasy/1146/114602.htm.

48 https://publications.parliament.uk/pa/cm201012/cmselect/cmtreasy/1146/114608.htm.

49 https://www.nao.org.uk/wp-content/uploads/2018/01/PFI-and-PF2.pdf.

50 National Audit Office (NAO). 2018b. *PFI and PF2*. London: House of Commons. https://www.nao.org.uk/wp-content/uploads/2018/01/PFI-and-PF2.pdf, 4.

51 https://www.scotsman.com/news/politics/revealed-scottish-schools-built-under-pfi-costing-millions-more-than-originally-estimated-1-5024056/amp?__twitter_impression=true.

52 https://www.ons.gov.uk/economy/inflationandpriceindices/articles/shortcomingsoftheretailpricesindexasameasureofinflation/2018-03-08)

53 NAO 2018b, 5.

54 https://www.telegraph.co.uk/education/educationnews/12186124/Ghost-school-that-costs-12k-a-day-to-keep-closed.html.

55 https://www.tes.com/news/exclusive-ps8k-blind-ps2k-tap-true-cost-pfi.

56 http://www.edinburgh.gov.uk/info/20074/schools/1423/independent_inquiry_into_school_closures_published; https://www.edinburgh.gov.uk/download/meetings/id/53239/report_of_the_independent_inquiry_into_the_construction_of_edinburgh_schools.

57 https://www.publicfinance.co.uk/news/2017/02/pfi-not-blame-edinburgh-school-wall-collapse-report-finds.

58 NAO 2018b, 5.

59 https://schoolfinance101.wordpress.com/2015/07/21/we-bought-it-twice-but-we-no-longer-own-it-is-co-location-the-better-option/.

60 https://dianeravitch.net/2018/06/22/andre-agassi-tennis-legend-now-profits-from-privatizing-public-education/.

61 Saltman, Kenneth. 2019. *The swindle of innovative educational finance*. Minneapolis: University of Minnesota Press.

62 https://www.theguardian.com/society/2019/may/29/bringing-services-back-in-house-is-good-councils?fbclid=IwAR2_UwSwuhgZRI9ZxezKMRC1Q37iSB8brRv54OTOlTZGce8xJC8ECoBwn3c.

63 See https://common-wealth.co.uk/Public-common-partnerships.html.

64 https://assets.publishing.service.gov.uk/government/uploads/system/uploads/attachment_data/file/180876/DFE-00073–2011.pdf, see 2.25.

65 https://assets.publishing.service.gov.uk/government/uploads/system/uploads/attachment_data/file/728074/DfE_annual_reports_and_accounts_17_to_18_-_WEB.pdf, 96.

66 https://www.consultancy.uk/news/18534/uk-education-consulting-spend-rises-196-in-14-years.

67 Kirkpatrick, Ian, Andrew Sturdy, Andrew J. Alvarado, Nuria Reguera, Antonio Blanco-Oliver and Gianluca Veronesi. 2019. 'The impact of management consultants on public service efficiency'. *Policy & Politics* 47 (1): 77–96.

68 Kirkpatrick et al 2019, 77.

69 Gunter, Helen, and Colin Mills. 2017. *Consultants and consultancy: the case of education*. New York: Springer.

70 https://bylinetimes.com/2019/06/03/the-extraordinary-cost-of-chris-grayling-part-i-2010–2015/?preview=true&_thumbnail_id=13957.

71 https://schoolsweek.co.uk/dfe-to-spend-2–3m-on-new-army-of-cost-cutting-consultants/.

72 https://schoolsweek.co.uk/schools-handed-repairs-cash-expected-to-follow-dfe-cost-cutting-advice/.

73 https://schoolsweek.co.uk/schools-handed-repairs-cash-expected-to-follow-dfe-cost-cutting-advice/.

74 https://www.tes.com/news/lord-agnew-man-who-wants-chair-every-mat-england.

75 https://www.tes.com/news/minister-bets-champagne-schools-are-wasting-money.

Chapter 5

1 See an example in Thomson, Pat, Belinda Harris, Kerry Vincent and Richard Toalster. 2005. *Evaluation of the Mansfield Alternatives to Exclusion (MATE) programme*. Nottingham: Centre for Research in Equity and Diversity in Education, School of Education, University of Nottingham.

2 This kind of collective procurement did happen prior to system-wide academisation. My colleague Chris Day and I documented some of this collective practice for the National College of School Leadership; the report, however, remains unpublished.

3 https://schoolsweek.co.uk/new-academies-minister-mat-sweet-spot-is-12-to-20-schools/.

4 West, Anne, and David Wolfe. 2018. *Academies, the school system in England and a vision for the future*. London: London School of Economics, Matrix.

5 See https://schoolsweek.co.uk/the-broken-promise-of-autonomy-for-heads-in-multi-academy-trusts/ and https://www.tes.com/news/academies-have-less-freedom.

6 https://schoolsweek.co.uk/not-all-multi-academy-trusts-reduce-autonomy/.

7 See MAT policy https://www.e-act.org.uk/e-act-policies/.

8 https://schoolsweek.co.uk/top-slice-how-much-do-you-pay/.

9 https://assets.publishing.service.gov.uk/government/uploads/system/uploads/attachment_data/file/576240/Multi-academy_trusts_good_practice_guidance_and_expectations_for_growth.pdf.

10 See for instance legal opposition to the 2010 Academies Bill https://www.theguardian.com/education/2010/jun/06/academies-bill-gove-teachers-authorities; academic evidence in the special issue of *Forum* journal, 61 (2); concerns in the media https://www.theguardian.com/commentisfree/2019/jan/30/britain-schools-conversion-academies-eu.

11 https://schoolsweek.co.uk/what-is-the-role-of-local-governing-bodies-in-mats/.

12 See also https://www.bbc.co.uk/news/education-35347602.

13 Putnam, Robert. 1993. *Making democracy work: Civic traditions in modern Italy*. Princeton: Princeton University Press.

14 https://www.theguardian.com/education/2019/jun/28/academies-without-parents-on-boards-risk-community-rejection.

15 https://www.theyworkforyou.com/lords/?id=2019–02–14b.1941.3.

16 https://publications.parliament.uk/pa/cm201719/cmselect/cmpubacc/760/760.pdf, 6.

17 School workforce census 2016–17. https://assets.publishing.service.gov.uk/government/uploads/system/uploads/attachment_data/file/719772/SWFC_MainText.pdf.

18 The total number of pupils divided by the total number of teachers.

19 Davies, Peter, Colin Diamond and Thomas Perry (2020) 'Implications of autonomy and networks for costs and inclusion: Comparing patterns of spending under different governance systems'. *Educational Management Administration and Leadership*, https://doi.org/10.1177/1741143219888738.

20 https://schoolsweek.co.uk/named-the-92-academy-trusts-with-multiple-staff-on-100k/.

21 https://schoolsweek.co.uk/no-pay-rise-for-highest-paid-academy-chief-for-the-first-time-in-six-years/.

22 https://schoolsweek.co.uk/investigation-the-highs-and-occasional-lows-of-academy-ceo-pay/.

23 https://www.independent.co.uk/news/education/education-news/academy-ceo-pay-headteacher-salaries-dan-moynihan-harris-federation-a9205101.html.

24 https://www.thescottishsun.co.uk/news/4936534/four-school-headteachers-are-earning-more-than-200000-a-year-shock-figures-show/.

25 https://schoolsweek.co.uk/investigation-the-highs-and-occasional-lows-of-academy-ceo-pay/.

26 https://www.theguardian.com/education/2019/may/10/department-for-education-academy-chains-cut-executive-pay.

27 https://assets.publishing.service.gov.uk/government/uploads/system/uploads/attachment_data/file/800948/ESFA_letter_to_newly_identified_academy_trusts_about_high_pay_May_2019.pdf.

28 https://schoolsweek.co.uk/over-30-trusts-fail-to-justify-pay-but-dfe-admits-its-powerless-to-act/.

29 https://getintoteaching.education.gov.uk/teachers-salary-and-teaching-benefits/teacher-salaries.

30 https://www.tes.com/news/exclusive-dramatic-increase-pay-gap-between-heads-and-classroom-teachers.

31 The FPP model is now fully functional in England.

32 https://schoolleaders.thekeysupport.com/administration-and-management/la-funds/core-funding/how-academies-funded/.

33 https://www.gov.uk/government/publications/the-7-principles-of-public-life/the-7-principles-of-public-life--2.

34 https://schoolsweek.co.uk/lord-agnew-resigns-from-inspiration-trust/.

35 https://www.tes.com/news/exclusive-dfe-may-let-agnew-take-decisions-his-former-mat.

36 https://www.tes.com/news/secrecy-over-agnew-conflicts-interest.

37 https://www.tes.com/news/dfe-threatens-terminate-inspiration-trust-academys-funding-agreement.

38 https://www.gov.uk/government/collections/academy-trust-accounting-officer-letters-from-efa.

39 https://www.gov.uk/government/collections/academies-financial-notices-to-improve#history.

40 https://www.edp24.co.uk/news/education/lord-agnew-academies-minister-certain-of-system-transparency-1–5951316.

41 See West and Wolfe 2018.

42 https://assets.publishing.service.gov.uk/government/uploads/system/uploads/attachment_data/file/811261/Academies_Financial_Handbook_2019.pdf.

43 https://schoolsweek.co.uk/financial-self-assessment-check-for-academies-to-become-mandatory/amp/?__twitter_impression=true.

44 https://assets.publishing.service.gov.uk/government/uploads/system/uploads/attachment_data/file/579378/DfE_Consolidated_annual_report_and_accounts_2015–16Web.pdf.

45 https://www.gov.uk/government/publications/dfe-consolidated-annual-report-and-accounts-2017-to-2018.

46 https://www.gov.uk/government/publications/school-land-decisions-about-disposals/decisions-on-the-disposal-of-school-land#list-of-approved-applications.

47 https://www.teachers.org.uk/campaigns/academies.

48 https://www.tes.com/news/exclusive-councils-sell-hundreds-acres-school-playing-field-land.

49 Moore, James. 2018. 'Corruption and ethical standards of British public life: national debates and local administration 1880–1914'. In *Anticorruption in history: From antiquity to the modern era*, edited by Ronald Kroeze, Andre Vitoria and G. Geltner, 267–78. Oxford: Oxford University Press.

50 Roberts, Nerys. 2017. *FAQs: Academies and free schools*. House of Commons Briefing Paper. Westminster: House of Commons Library, 8.

51 https://schoolsweek.co.uk/revealed-the-23-trusts-that-broke-rules-over-4m-related-party-transactions/.

52 House of Commons Committee of Public Accounts. 2018. *Academy schools' finances: Thirtieth report of session 2017–19*. https://publications.parliament.

uk/pa/cm201719/cmselect/cmpubacc/760/760.pdf: House of Commons, 5.

53 House of Commons Committee of Public Accounts 2018, 5.

54 https://publications.parliament.uk/pa/cm201719/cmselect/cmpubacc/1597/159703.htm.

55 https://publications.parliament.uk/pa/cm201719/cmselect/cmpubacc/1597/159703.htm.

56 https://schoolsweek.co.uk/dfe-troubleshooter-hugely-embarrassed-by-bright-tribe-scandal/.

57 https://schoolsweek.co.uk/bright-tribe-investigation-referred-to-fraud-police/.

58 https://schoolsweek.co.uk/bright-tribe-and-alat-could-face-1–8m-bill-for-improper-use-of-historic-grants/.

59 https://schoolsweek.co.uk/academy-rapped-over-consultancy-payments-to-chair-of-trustees/.

60 https://schoolsweek.co.uk/former-free-schools-chair-broke-the-law-over-500k-payments-to-own-company-report-finds/.

61 https://www.tombennetttraining.co.uk.

62 https://www.tes.com/news/exclusive-how-our-behaviour-crackdown-will-work.

63 https://www.publicfinance.co.uk/news/2018/11/academies-record-ps61bn-deficit.

64 https://www.standard.co.uk/news/education/serious-failings-and-financial-mismanagement-at-michael-goves-flagship-free-schools-8905944.html; https://www.unison.org.uk/news/2018/09/mismanagement-academy-trust-leaves-vulnerable-students-staff-facing-huge-cuts/.

65 https://www.tes.com/news/exclusive-auditors-failed-spot-problems-academy-trusts.

66 https://schoolsweek.co.uk/accounts-reveal-shocking-financial-mismanagement-at-defunct-academy-trust/; https://www.independent.co.uk/news/education/education-news/revealed-police-investigate-lost-162000-at-academy-school-9134753.html.

67 See for instance https://www.dailymail.co.uk/news/article-3312890/Arrogant-200–000-year-headteacher-bought-spa-pool-DVD-players-condoms-school-credit-card-series-internet-shopping-sprees.html; https://www.cambridge-news.co.uk/news/cambridge-news/live-headteacher-sawtry-stewart-court-13724890; and https://www.portsmouth.co.uk/news/crime/school-business-manager-took-31–000-from-fareham-school-including-cash-for-pupils-trips-1–8776179.

68 https://schoolsweek.co.uk/dfe-writes-off-failed-schools-company-trusts-3m-debt/.

69 https://www.theguardian.com/education/2017/dec/06/wakefield-city-academies-trust-west-yorkshire-police.

70 https://www.tes.com/news/school-news/breaking-news/academy-chain-spends-ps440000-deals-firms-run-ceo-and-his-daughter.

71 https://www.theguardian.com/education/2019/nov/18/yorkshire-schools-will-not-get-back-millions-lost-in-trusts-collapse.

72 https://www.smh.com.au/business/failed-abc-learning-wound-up-20100602-wzrs.html.

73 https://www.smh.com.au/national/what-comes-after-abc-20120519–1yxf2.html.

74 https://www.smh.com.au/national/cradle-snatcher-20060311.

75 https://www.nurseryworld.co.uk/nursery-world/analysis/1094017/analysis-australia-childcare-reformed-wake-abc-collapse.

76 https://www.building.co.uk/focus/carillion-one-year-on-how-the-contractors-collapse-unfolded/5097348.article.

77 https://www.independent.co.uk/news/business/comment/interserve-government-contractors-outsourcing-carillion-school-dinners-hospital-cleaning-lenders-a8676016.html.

78 https://schoolsweek.co.uk/fact-check-how-many-free-schools-have-actually-closed/.

79 https://schoolsweek.co.uk/dfe-spent-more-than-23m-on-failed-studio-schools/.

80 https://www.theguardian.com/education/2018/jun/19/academy-schools-collapse-executive-pay-assets.

81 https://schoolsweek.co.uk/absolutely-devastated-free-school-stuck-in-temporary-premises-closed-by-dfe/.

82 https://schoolsweek.co.uk/dfe-spent-115m-on-doomed-free-schools-utcs-and-studio-schools/.

83 https://www.independent.co.uk/news/education/education-news/university-technical-colleges-utc-vocational-education-students-schools-dfe-a8578156.html.

84 https://www.theguardian.com/education/2019/jul/13/vanity-project-debts-pile-up-for-english-free-schools-scheme

85 https://epi.org.uk/publications-and-research/utcs/.

86 https://www.theguardian.com/education/2017/oct/21/collapsing-wakefield-city-academies-trust-asset-stripped-schools-millions-say-furious-parents.

87 https://schoolsweek.co.uk/academy-trust-top-sliced-376k-from-school-with-1m-deficit/.

88 https://schoolsweek.co.uk/hefty-bills-for-the-government-as-more-academy-trusts-close/.

89 https://schoolsweek.co.uk/trustees-of-closed-herefordshire-academy-publish-blistering-report-into-dfe-treatment/.

90 https://www.forbes.com/sites/petergreene/2019/03/29/report-the-department-of-education-has-spent-1-billion-on-charter-school-waste-and-fraud/#5d3a323a27b6.

91 http://networkforpubliceducation.org/asleepatthewheel/.

Chapter 6

[1] Chubb, J. E., and T. E. Moe. 1990. *Politics, markets, and America's schools.* Washington, DC: The Brookings Institute.

[2] See for instance the review symposium in *British Journal of Sociology of Education*, 12 (3) and the review by Glass and Matthews at http://www.gvglass.info/papers/chubbrev.html.

[3] https://en.oxforddictionaries.com/definition/effectiveness.

[4] See https://www.bbc.co.uk/news/education-41580550.

[5] Rutter, Michael, Peter Mortimore and Barbara Maugham. 1979. *Fifteen thousand hours: Secondary schools and their effects.* Boston: Harvard University Press; Karabel, Jerome, and A.H. Halsey. 1977. *Power and ideology in education.* Oxford: Oxford University Press.

[6] Teddlie, Charles, and David Reynolds. Eds. 2000. *The international handbook of school effectiveness.* London: Falmer Press; Macbeath, John, and Peter Mortimore. Eds. 2001. *Improving school effectiveness.* London: Routledge; Stoll, Louise, and Dean Fink. 1996. *Changing our schools: Linking school effectiveness and school improvement.* Buckingham: Open University Press.

[7] Sylva, Kathy, Edward Melhuish, Pam Sammons, Iram Siraj-Blatchford and Brenda Taggart. 2004. *The effective provision of pre-school education (EPPE) project.* https://dera.ioe.ac.uk/18189/2/SSU-SF-2004-01.pdf: Sure Start.

[8] Gorard, Stephen. 2018. *Education policy, equity and effectiveness: Evidence of equity and effectiveness.* Bristol: Policy Press; Savage, Mike. 2015. *Social class in the 21st century.* London: Pelican; Reay, Diane. 2017. *Miseducation: Inequality, education and the working classes.* Bristol: Policy Press.

[9] Young, Michael. 1994. *The rise of the meritocracy.* Brunswick, NJ: Transaction Publishers.

[10] Bourdieu, Pierre, and Jean Claude Passeron. 1977. *Reproduction in society, education and culture.* London: Sage; Bourdieu, Pierre and Jean-Claude Passeron. 1979. *The inheritors, French students and their relation to culture.* Chicago: University of Chicago Press.

[11] Gorard, Stephen, Chris Taylor and John Fitz. 2003. *Schools, markets and choice policies.* London: Routledge.

[12] Gibson, Alex, and Sheena Asthana. 2013. 'Schools, pupils and examination results: contextualising school "performance".' *British Educational Research Journal* 24 (3): 269–82; Thomson, Pat. 2000. 'Like schools, educational disadvantage and "thisness".' *Australian Educational Researcher* 27 (3): 151–66; Lupton, Ruth. 2004. *Schools in disadvantaged areas: Recognising context and raising performance.* CASE paper 76. London: Centre for Analysis of Social Exclusion, London School of Economics; Thrupp, Martin, and Ruth Lupton. 2011. *The impact of school context: What headteachers say.* London: Centre for Analysis of Social Exclusion, London School of Economics.

[13] For example, Abrams, Samuel E. 2016. *Education and the commercial mindset.* Boston: Harvard University Press.

[14] Goldstein, Harvey, and George Leckie. 2018. *Should we adjust for pupil background in school value-added measures?* https://www.bristol.ac.uk/media-

library/sites/education/documents/FINAL.pdf: University of Bristol, School of Education.

[15] Goldstein and Leckie 2018, 24.

[16] Ainscow, Mel, and Mel West. Eds. 2006. *Improving urban schools: Leadership and collaboration*. Buckingham: Open University Press; Macbeath and Mortimore 2001; Earl, Lorna, and Steven Katz. 2006. *Leading schools in a data-rich world: Harnessing data for school improvement*. Thousand Oaks: Corwin Press.

[17] https://ffteducationdatalab.org.uk/2019/10/how-do-headteachers-in-england-use-test-data-and-does-this-differ-to-other-countries/.

[18] https://www.tes.com/news/try-sats-reading-paper-left-pupils-tears.

[19] https://www.tes.com/news/sats-reading-tests-too-middle-class-and-would-have-no-relevance-inner-city-children-teachers.

[20] https://www.tes.com/news/less-middle-class-bias-sats-reading-paper-year.

[21] Ainscow, Mel, Alan Dyson, Sue Goldrick, and Mel West. 2012. 'Making schools effective for all: rethinking the risk.' *School Leadership & Management* 32 (3): 197–213; Watkins, Amanda, and Serge Ebershold. 2016. 'Efficiency, effectiveness and equity within inclusive education systems.' In *Implementing inclusive education: Issues in bridging the policy-practice gap*, edited by Amanda Watkins and Cor Meijer. New York: Emerald.

[22] https://www.chronicle.com/blogs/letters/standardized-tests-favor-students-from-high-income-families/.

[23] Chubb and Moe 1990.

[24] Gorard, Stephen, and John Fitz. 2000. 'Markets and stratification: a view from England and Wales.' *Educational Policy* 14 (3): 405–28; Gorard, Stephen, Chris Taylor, and John Fitz. 2003. *Schools, markets and choice policies*. London: Routledge.

[25] Benn, Melissa. 2011. *School wars: The battle for Britain's education*. London: Verso; Johnson, Alan. 2016. *The long and winding road*. London: Bantam Press.

[26] Adonis, Andrew. 2012. *Education, education, education: Reforming England's schools*. London: Biteback Publishing.

[27] https://assets.publishing.service.gov.uk/government/uploads/system/uploads/attachment_data/file/807796/2019_Release_AppsOffers_Text.pdf.

[28] Burgess, Simon, Ellen Greaves and Anna Vignoles. 2019. 'School choice in England: evidence from national administrative data.' *Oxford Review of Education*, doi.org/10.1080/03054985.2019.1604332.

[29] http://www.bristol.ac.uk/news/2019/may/school-choice-system.html.

[30] Bergman, Peter, and Isaac McFarlin. 2018. *Education for all? A nationwide audit study of schools of choice*. NBER Working Paper No 25396. Cambridge, MA: National Bureau of Economic Research.

[31] E.g. https://schoolsweek.co.uk/church-schools-accused-of-discriminatory-admissions/.

[32] Allen, Rebecca, and Anna Vignoles. 2010. *Can school competition improve standards? The case of faith schools in England*. DoQSS Working Paper No 9-04. London: Institute of Education.

[33] For a summary of Gorard's argument, see https://publications.parliament. uk/pa/cm200304/cmselect/cmeduski/58/58we08.htm.

[34] https://ffteducationdatalab.org.uk/2018/03/how-much-does-private-tutoring-matter-for-grammar-school-admissions/; Jerrim, John, and Sam Sims. 2018. *Why do so few low and middle-income children attend a grammar school? New evidence from the Millennium Cohort Study.* https://johnjerrim. files.wordpress.com/2018/03/working_paper_nuffield_version_clean.pdf: Institute of Education.

[35] Higham, Rob. 2014. 'Free schools in the Big Society: the motivations, aims and demography of free school proposers'. *Journal of Education Policy* 29 (1): 122–39.

[36] https://www.tes.com/news/exclusive-radical-change-needed-school-admissions.

[37] Brill, Frances, Hilary Grayson, Lisa Kuhn and Sharon O'Donnell. 2018. *What impact does accountability have on curriculum, standards and engagement in education?* Slough National Foundation for Educational Research (NFER), ii.

[38] Andrews, Jon, and Natalie Perera. 2017. *The impact of academies on educational outcomes.* London: Education Policy Institute.

[39] https://fullfact.org/education/academies-and-maintained-schools-what-do-we-know/.

[40] Worth, Jack. 2016. *Analysis of academy school performance in 2015.* Slough: NFER. https://www.nfer.ac.uk/media/1943/lggg01.pdf.

[41] Hatton, Adam, Rebekah Hampson, and Rob Drake. 2019. *An analysis of the performance of sponsored academies.* London: Department for Education. https://assets.publishing.service.gov.uk/government/uploads/system/ uploads/attachment_data/file/772088/Sponsored_Academy_Research_ Report.pdf.

[42] Hutchings, Merryn, and Becky Francis. 2018. *Chain effects 2018: The impact of academy chains on low-income pupils.* London: The Sutton Trust.

[43] Hutchings and Francis 2018.

[44] https://www.culandsoc.com/wp-content/uploads/2018/09/Final-Copy-Becky-Francis-lecture_LR.pdf, 24.

[45] https://www.culandsoc.com/wp-content/uploads/2018/09/Final-Copy-Becky-Francis-lecture_LR.pdf, 25.

[46] https://www.culandsoc.com/wp-content/uploads/2018/09/Final-Copy-Becky-Francis-lecture_LR.pdf, 26.

[47] https://epi.org.uk/publications-and-research/free-schools-2019-report/.

[48] Lubienski, Christopher A., and Sarah Theule Lubienski. 2014. *The public school advantage: Why public schools outperform private schools.* Chicago: University of Chicago Press; Ravitch, Diane. 2014. *Reign of error: The hoax of the privatization movement and the danger to America's public schools.* New York: Vintage Books.

[49] Jason, Zachary. 2017. 'The battle over charter schools'. *Harvard Education Magazine*, Summer. https://www.gse.harvard.edu/news/ed/17/05/battle-over-charter-schools.

50 Lyotard, Jean-François. 1984. *The postmodern condition: A report on knowledge.* 1993 ed. *Theory and history of literature, Vol. 10.* Minneapolis: University of Minnesota Press.

51 Ball, Stephen. 2003. "The teacher's soul and the terrors of performativity'. *Journal of Education Policy* 18 (2): 215–28.

52 See Hayes, Deborah, Robert Hattam, Barbara Comber, Lyn Kerkham, Ruth Lupton and Pat Thomson. 2018. *Literacy, leading and learning: Beyond pedagogies of poverty.* London: Routledge, for detailed observations and analysis of the ways in which different teachers in differently positioned schools adjust to testing regimes.

53 Mertier, Craig A. 2014. *The data-driven classroom: How do I use student data to improve my instruction?* Washington, MD: ASCD.

54 Earl and Katz 2006.

55 Thomson, Pat, and Christine Hall. 2011. 'Sense-making as a lens on everyday change leadership practice: the case of Holly Tree Primary'. *International Journal of Leadership in Education* 14 (4): 385–403.

56 Gillborn, David, and Deborah Youdell. 2000. *Rationing education: Policy, practice, reform and equity.* Buckingham and Philadelphia: Open University Press.

57 Thomson, Pat, Christine Hall and Ken Jones. 2010. 'Maggie's day: a small scale analysis of English education policy'. *Journal of Education Policy* 25 (5): 639–56.

58 Levin, Benjamin. 2001. *Reforming education: From origins to outcomes.* London: Falmer Press.

59 Hirsch, E. D. 2006. *The knowledge deficit: Closing the shocking education gap for American children.* New York: Houghton Mifflin.

60 See https://culturallearningalliance.org.uk/further-decline-in-arts-gcse-and-a-level-entries/; https://www.theguardian.com/education/2018/oct/10/music-disappearing-school-curriculum-england-survey-gcse-a-level.

61 https://www.artsprofessional.co.uk/news/dcms-minister-ebacc-partly-blame-decline-music-gcse.

62 https://www.telegraph.co.uk/education/6156861/School-uniforms-a-uniform-approach-to-improving-exam-results.html.

63 https://schoolsweek.co.uk/dfe-tsar-tom-bennett-to-oversee-10m-behaviour-network-of-500-schools/.

64 https://www.theguardian.com/education/2018/oct/22/secondary-school-bans-talking-in-the-corridors-to-keep-children-calm.

65 https://www.bbc.co.uk/news/education-46044394.

66 https://www.theguardian.com/education/2019/mar/16/outwood-grange-academy-trust-accused-assemblies-intimidate-students-discipline.

67 https://schoolsweek.co.uk/silent-corridors-whats-all-the-fuss-about/.

68 See for example commentary from the US http://theconversation.com/does-wearing-a-school-uniform-improve-student-behavior-51553; and Kulz, Christy. 2017. *Factories for learning: Making race, class and inequality in the neoliberal academy.* Manchester: Manchester University Press.

69 Brooks, J. E. 2006. 'Strengthening resilience in children and youths: maximizing opportunities through the schools'. *Children & Schools* 28 (2): 69–76.

70 See https://www.jubileecentre.ac.uk/432/character-education.

71 Dweck, Carol. 2012. *Mindset: How you can fulfil your potential.* New York: Ballantine Books.

72 https://www.theguardian.com/news/2017/may/04/grammar-schools-secondary-modern-11-plus-theresa-may.

73 Gorard, Stephen, and Nadia Siddiqui. 2018. 'Grammar schools in England: a new analysis of social segregation and academic outcomes'. *British Journal of Sociology of Education* 39 (7): 909–24, p 909.

Chapter 7

1 Semple, Janet. 1993. *Bentham's prison: A study of the Panopticon penitentiary.* Oxford: Clarendon Press.

2 Foucault, Michel. 1977. *Discipline and punish: The birth of the prison,* translated by Alan Sheridan. 1991 ed. London: Penguin.

3 Bogard, William. 1996. *The simulation of surveillance: Hypercontrol in telematic societies.* Cambridge: Cambridge University Press; Lupton, Deborah. 2016. *The quantified self.* Cambridge: Polity Press.

4 Schofield, Philip. 1996. 'Bentham on the identification of interests'. *Utilitas* 8 (2): 223–34.

5 Cutler, Fred. 1999. 'Jeremy Bentham and the public opinion tribunal'. *The Public Opinion Quarterly* 63 (3): 321–46.

6 Shafe, James. 2014. 'Challenges for a revised view of Bentham on public reasoning'. *Revue d'études benthamiennes* 13 (Droit International). http://journals.openedition.org/etudes-benthamiennes/761.

7 Pateman, Carol. 1970. *Participation and democratic theory.* Cambridge: Cambridge University Press; Schofield, Philip. 2006. *Utility and democracy: The political thought of Jeremy Bentham.* Oxford: Oxford University Press.

8 Llewellyn, Sue, and Stephen Brookes. Eds. 2018. *Trust and confidence in government and public services.* London: Routledge.

9 Orwell, George. 1949. *1984.* Harmondsworth: Penguin.

10 Thomson, Pat. 2009. *School leadership: Heads on the block?* London: Routledge.

11 https://www.theguardian.com/uk-news/2019/may/26/birmingham-anderton-park-primary-muslim-protests-lgbt-teaching-rights.

12 This figure recorded on 20 November 2019.

13 https://ico.org.uk/media/for-organisations/documents/1156/minutes andagendas.pdf.

14 See https://icosearch.ico.org.uk/s/search.html?query=DfE&collection =ico-meta&profile=_default for decisions on DfE-related appeals and https://ico.org.uk/media/action-weve-taken/decision-notices/2017/2013863/fs50641799.pdf for a sample letter sent to subjects of appeal.

15 https://ico.org.uk/action-weve-taken/.

16 https://www.lauramcinerney.com/2012/11/05/free-school-foi-turned-down-too-many-risks/.

17 https://www.lauramcinerney.com/2012/11/08/request-for-internal-review-of-foi-request-for-free-school-applications-decision-letters/.

18 https://www.lauramcinerney.com/2013/12/17/massive-yawn-dfe-have-appealed-my-free-school-foi-judgement/.

19 https://www.lauramcinerney.com/2014/07/16/how-i-lost-a-court-case-but-got-a-new-job/.

20 https://www.independent.co.uk/news/world/close-keating-ally-resigns-in-grants-scandal-1426241.html.

21 Nye, Joseph. 1997. *Why people don't trust government*. Boston: Harvard University Press.

22 https://www.smh.com.au/national/the-boat-that-changed-it-all-20110819–1j2o2.html.

23 https://www.independent.co.uk/voices/trump-iran-sanctions-us-drone-shot-down-attack-twitter-supreme-leader-khamenei-a8972766.html.

24 https://schoolsweek.co.uk/damian-hinds-censured-by-stats-watchdog-over-school-funding-claims/.

25 https://www.statisticsauthority.gov.uk/correspondence/department-for-education-funding-statistics-2/.

26 https://www.statisticsauthority.gov.uk/wp-content/uploads/2018/10/Education-statistics-Ed-Humpherson-to-Neil-McIvor-20181008.pdf.

27 https://www.statisticsauthority.gov.uk/correspondence/department-for-education-funding-statistics/.

28 https://schoolsweek.co.uk/dfe-publish-school-spending-figures-watchdog/.

29 https://schoolsweek.co.uk/ministers-still-relying-on-misleading-record-funding-claims/.

30 See the whole survey results on https://www.surveymonkey.com/results/SM-Y8QQ7C62V/.

31 https://schoolsweek.co.uk/four-out-of-five-heads-personally-funding-school-coffers/.

32 https://www.bbc.co.uk/news/education-47964154.

33 https://www.denverpost.com/2019/06/03/colorado-school-performance-test/.

34 https://www.eastbaytimes.com/2017/03/17/editorial-new-state-education-portal-hides-school-disparities/.

35 https://brighterworld.mcmaster.ca/articles/why-wont-canada-collect-data-on-race-and-student-success/.

36 https://schoolsweek.co.uk/well-build-trust-in-our-school-funding-stats-says-dfe-chief/

37 https://www.tes.com/news/we-need-transparency-say-heads-campaigning-scrutinise-academies-system.

38 https://www.tes.com/news/exclusive-academy-secrets-dfe-wanted-hide-part-2.

39 https://schoolsweek.co.uk/more-than-80-academy-trusts-named-for-submitting-spending-data-late/.

40 For example Spillane, James. 2006. *Distributed leadership*. San Francisco: Jossey Bass; Hargreaves, Andy, and Pasi Sahlberg. 2012. *Finnish lessons: What can the world learn from educational change in Finland?* London: Routledge.

41 Hirschman, E. 1970. *Exit, voice and loyalty: Responses to decline in firms, organizations and states*. Boston: Harvard University Press.

42 Chubb, J. E., and T. E. Moe. (1990). *Politics, markets, and America's schools*. Washington, DC: The Brookings Institute.

43 https://ffteducationdatalab.org.uk/2018/10/how-did-life-turn-out-for-pupils-who-took-gnvqs/.

44 Ingram, Jenni, Victoria Elliott, Caroline Morin, Ashmita Randhawa and Carol Brown. 2018. 'Playing the system: incentives to "game" and educational ethics in school examination entry policies in England'. *Oxford Review of Education* 44 (5): 545–62.

45 Meadows, Michelle, and Beth Black. 2018. 'Teachers' experience of and attitudes toward activities to maximise qualification results in England'. *Oxford Review of Education* 44 (5): 563–80.

46 Meadows and Black 2018, 578.

47 https://www.independent.co.uk/news/education/private-schools-gcse-results-secondary-cheat-rig-answers-a8703996.html.

48 https://www.theguardian.com/education/2018/dec/29/exam-reforms-boost-private-pupils-in-race-for-universities?CMP=share_btn_tw.

49 https://www.theguardian.com/education/2018/dec/30/labour-demands-inquiry-into-private-schools-evading-gcse-reform?CMP=Share_AndroidApp_WhatsApp.

50 https://www.thetimes.co.uk/article/should-schools-offer-gcses-or-igcses-k8d7gh7pf.

51 https://www.independent.co.uk/news/education/education-news/schools-lie-vulnerable-children-parents-league-table-pressures-report-a8201196.html.

52 https://www.dailymail.co.uk/news/article-5978259/Britains-best-school-SATs-results-ruled-null-void-cheating-storm.html; https://www.sthelensreporter.co.uk/news/pictured-the-st-helens-headteacher-banned-for-life-from-the-classroom-1-8011316.

53 https://www.bbc.co.uk/news/uk-england-london-39194587.

54 https://schoolsimprovement.net/primary-school-head-banned-from-classroom-for-life-after-fiddling-sats-results/.

55 https://www.telegraph.co.uk/education/educationnews/9590680/Flagship-academy-cheated-in-GCSEs-claim-pupils.html.

56 https://schoolsweek.co.uk/harris-schools-swamp-esol-exam-with-native-english-speakers/.

57 https://guce.huffingtonpost.co.uk/copyConsent?sessionId=3_cc-session_49952102–19cd-40f9–887d-1ce3ebcbe9f8&inline=false&lang=en-gb.

58 https://schoolsweek.co.uk/governors-go-as-eight-staff-suspended-in-exam-enquiry/.

59 https://www.dailymail.co.uk/news/article-3595876/Headteacher-doctored-SATs-tests-moment-madness-protect-school-ahead-Ofsted-inspection-banned-classroom.html.

60 https://www.mirror.co.uk/news/uk-news/investigation-exam-fixing-claims-tory-4721163.

61 https://www.theguardian.com/education/2015/jun/15/cheating-rife-in-uk-education-system-dispatches-investigation-shows.

62 https://schoolsweek.co.uk/ofsted-letter-to-inspectors-clamp-down-on-gaming/.

63 https://www.theguardian.com/education/2018/feb/11/thousands-of-teachers-caught-cheating-to-boost-exam-results.

64 https://schoolsweek.co.uk/trust-boss-demands-crackdown-on-sats-cheating/.

65 https://www.gov.uk/government/news/report-cheating-malpractice-or-wrongdoing-ofqual-urges.

66 Evidence for Barton's statement here: https://www.gov.uk/government/publications/ofqual-2018-summer-exam-series-report.

67 https://www.tes.com/news/level-leaks-and-our-monstrous-exam-system.

68 https://schoolsweek.co.uk/isolation-rooms-how-schools-are-removing-pupils-from-classrooms/.

69 https://www.theguardian.com/education/2018/dec/11/pupil-brings-legal-action-against-schools-isolation-booths-outwood-grange-academies-trust.

70 https://assets.publishing.service.gov.uk/government/uploads/system/uploads/attachment_data/file/726741/text_exc1617.pdf.

71 https://www.gov.uk/government/publications/exploring-moving-to-home-education-in-secondary-schools/exploring-moving-to-home-education-in-secondary-schools-research-summary.

72 https://educationinspection.blog.gov.uk/2019/05/10/what-is-off-rolling-and-how-does-ofsted-look-at-it-on-inspection/.

73 https://assets.publishing.service.gov.uk/government/uploads/system/uploads/attachment_data/file/800582/Ofsted_offrolling_report_YouGov_090519.pdf.

74 Osler, Audrey, and Kerry Vincent. 2003. *Girls and exclusion.* London: Routledge; Wright, Cecile, Penny Standen, Gus John, Gerry German and Tina Patel. 2005. *School exclusion and transition into adulthood in African-Caribbean communities.* York: Joseph Rowntree Foundation; Smyth, John, and Robert Hattam. 2004. *Dropping out, drifting off, being excluded: Becoming somebody without school.* New York: Peter Lang.

75 https://www.tes.com/news/rolling-unethical-inappropriate-and-beyond-repugnant-consequences-are-devastating.

76 https://educationinspection.blog.gov.uk/2018/06/26/off-rolling-using-data-to-see-a-fuller-picture/; https://schoolsweek.co.uk/ofsted-refuses-to-name-300-off-rolling-schools/.

77 http://blog.ukdataservice.ac.uk/whos-left-off-rolling/.

78 https://ffteducationdatalab.org.uk/2018/06/whos-left-2018-part-one-the-main-findings/.

79 Thomson, Pat, and Jodie Pennacchia. 2014. *What's the alternative? Effective support for young people disengaging from mainstream education*. http://www.princes-trust.org.uk/pdf/whats-the-alternative-effective-support-for-young-people.pdf: The Princes Trust; Institute of Education (University of London) and the National Foundation for Educational Research (NFER). 2014. *School exclusion trial evaluation*. London: Department for Education.

80 Long, Robert, and Danechi Shadi. 2019. *Off-rolling in English schools*. Briefing Paper 08444. London: House of Commons Library.

81 Evans, Rodney. 1999. *The pedagogic principal*. Edmonton, Alberta: Qual Institute Press.

82 Soltes, Eugene. 2016. *Why they do it: Inside the mind of the white-collar criminal*. Philadelphia: Public Affairs Books; Green, Stuart P. 2006. *Lying, cheating, and stealing: A moral theory of white-collar crime*. Oxford: Oxford University Press; Payne, Brian K. 2016. *White-collar crime: The essentials*. Thousand Oaks: Sage.

83 Bauman, Zygmunt. 1993. *Postmodern ethics*. Oxford: Blackwell Publishers.

84 Wexler, Philip, Warren Crichlow, Julie Kern and Rebecca Martusewicz. 1992. *Becoming somebody: Toward a social psychology of school*. London: Falmer Press.

85 Auge, Marc. 1995. *Non-places: Introduction to an anthropology of supermodernity*. Translated by John Howe. London and New York: Verso.

86 Greany, Toby, and Rob Higham. 2018. *Hierarchy, markets and networks: Analysing the 'self-improving school-led system' agenda in England and the implications for schools*. London: UCL Institute of Education Press.

87 Thomson, Pat. 2017. *Educational leadership and Pierre Bourdieu*. London: Routledge; Lumby, Jacky, and Fenwick English. 2010. *Leadership as lunacy and other metaphors for educational leadership*. Thousand Oaks: Corwin.

88 Gunter, Helen. 2012. *Leadership and the reform of education*. Bristol: Policy Press; Eacott, Scott. 2011. 'Preparing "educational" leaders in managerialist times: an Australian story'. *Journal of Educational Administration and History* 43 (1): 43–59; Anderson, Gary. 2001. 'Disciplining leaders: a critical discourse analysis of the ISLLC National Examination and Performance Standards in educational administration'. *International Journal of Leadership in Education* 4 (3): 199–216.

89 Erickson, Anthony, Ben Shaw, Jane Murray and Sara Branch. 2005. 'Destructive leadership: causes, consequences and countermeasures'. *Organizational Dynamics* 20 (5): 266–72.

90 Samier, Eugenie, and Peter Milley. Eds. 2018. *International perspectives on maladministration in education*. London: Routledge; Normore, Anthony H., and Jeffrey S Brooks. 2016. *The dark side of leadership: Identifying and overcoming unethical practice in organisations*. New York: Emerald; English, Fenwick. 2013. *Educational leadership in the age of greed*. Michigan: National Council of Professors of Educational Administration.

91 Schyns, Birgit, and Jan Schilling. 2013. 'How bad are the effects of bad leaders? A meta-analysis of destructive leadership and its outcomes'. *The Leadership Quarterly* 24: 138–58.

92 Milley, Peter. 2018. 'Strategies of discursive closure maladministrators use to "manage" their misdeeds'. In *International perspectives on maladministration in education*, edited by Eugenie Samier and Peter Milley, 169–83. London: Routledge, 175.

93 Milley 2018, 175–8.

94 Troman, Geoff. 2000. 'Teacher stress in the low-trust society'. *British Journal of Sociology of Education* 21 (3): 331–53; Conley, Sharon, and Sherry A. Woosley. 2000. 'Teacher role stress, higher order needs and work outcomes'. *Journal of Educational Administration* 38 (2): 179–201; Cosgrove, John. 2000. *Breakdown: The facts about stress in teaching*. London: Routledge.

95 Bottery, Mike. 2003. 'The leadership of learning communities in a culture of unhappiness'. *School Leadership and Management* 23 (2): 187–207; Willis, Mario, and Lynn Varner. 2010. 'Factors that affect teachers' morale'. *Academic Leadership: The Online Journal* 8 (4): https://scholars.fhsu.edu/alj/vol8/iss4/24; Rubin, Daniel Ian. 2011. 'The disheartened teacher: living in the age of standardisataion, high-stakes assessment and No Child Left Behind (NCLB)'. *Changing English* 18 (4): 407–16.

96 Geiger, Tray, and Margarita Pivarova. 2018. 'The effects of working conditions on teacher retention'. *Teachers and Teaching: Theory and Practice* 24 (6): 604–25; Day, Christopher, Gordon Stobart, Pam Sammons, Alison Kington, Qing Gu, Rebecca Smees and Tamjid Mujtaba. 2006. *Variations in teachers' work, lives and effectiveness*. Research Report 743. London: Department for Education and Skills (DfES).

97 https://www.theguardian.com/education/2018/oct/04/teacher-crisis-hits-london-as-nearly-half-quit-within-five-years.

98 https://neu.org.uk/press-releases/neu-survey-shows-workload-causing-80-teachers-consider-leaving-profession.

99 Perryman, Jane, and Graham Calvert. 2019. 'What motivates people to teach, and why do they leave? Accountability, performativity and teacher retention'. *British Journal of Educational Studies*. https://doi.org/10.1080/00071005.2019.1589417; Keichtermans, Geert. 2017. '"Should I stay or should I go?": unpacking teacher attrition/retention as an educational issue'. *Teachers and Teaching: Theory and Practice* 23 (8): 961–77.

100 Galton, Maurice, and John Macbeath. 2008. *Teachers under pressure*. London: National Union of Teachers/SAGE; Bricheno, Pat, and Mary Thornton. 2016. *Crying in cupboards: What happens when teachers are bullied?* Leicestershire: Matador; Hayward, Vanessa, and Pat Thomson. 2012. 'Performing health: an ethnographic investigation of emotional health and wellbeing (EHWB) in a high-performance school'. In *Performativity in UK education: Ethnographic cases of its effects, agency and reconstitutions*, edited by Bob Jeffrey and Geoff Troman, 109–26. Gloucestershire: E & E Publishing.

101 https://www.theguardian.com/teacher-network/2018/mar/17/secret-teacher-workplace-bullying-headteacher.

[102] Bricheno and Thornton 2016.

[103] Bricheno and Thornton 2016, 204.

[104] https://www.telegraph.co.uk/education/educationnews/12064102/Head-and-26-teachers-quit-school-after-allegations-of-bullying.html.

[105] Thomson 2009.

[106] For example https://www.expressandstar.com/news/education/2019/02/11/wolverhampton-headteacher-suspended/; https://www.telegraph.co.uk/education/2018/03/27/headteacher-suspended-parent-backlash-schools-controversial/; and https://www.liverpoolecho.co.uk/news/liverpool-news/parents-still-dark-over-suspended-15242262.

[107] https://www.tes.com/news/day-my-husband-was-suspended-headship; https://www.theguardian.com/education/2017/oct/24/sacked-school-headteacher-alevel-results.

[108] https://www.theguardian.com/education/2017/oct/24/disappeared-headteacher-sacked-academy-dismissal.

[109] https://schoolsweek.co.uk/former-ceo-taking-legal-action-against-trust-that-forced-his-resignation/.

[110] https://www.manchestereveningnews.co.uk/news/greater-manchester-news/reason-educating-greater-manchester-headteacher-14915819.

[111] https://www.mirror.co.uk/tv/tv-news/headteacher-who-starred-channel-4-11718149.

[112] Woodley, Helen, and Ross Morrison McGill. 2018. *Toxic schools: How to avoid them and leave them.* Melton: John Catt.

Chapter 8

[1] http://www.oecd.org/education/skills-beyond-school/48631428.pdf.

[2] http://www.oecd.org/education/skills-beyond-school/48631428.pdf, figure D5.2.

[3] https://www.bbc.co.uk/news/education-49785130.

[4] Sahlberg, Pasi. 2007. 'Education policies for raising student learning: the Finnish approach'. *Journal of Education Policy* 22 (2): 147–71, 147.

[5] Sahlberg 2007, 155.

[6] https://publications.parliament.uk/pa/cm201719/cmselect/cmpubacc/2370/237004.htm#_idTextAnchor004.

[7] https://publications.parliament.uk/pa/cm201719/cmselect/cmwomeq/1720/172002.htm.

[8] Segal, Lydia G. 2004. *Battling corruption in America's public schools.* Boston: Northeastern University Press.

[9] Bellah, Robert, Richard Madsen, William M. Sullivan, Ann Swidler and Steven M Tipton. 1992. *The good society.* New York: Vintage Books.

[10] https://www.independent.co.uk/news/education/education-news/councils-academy-chains-schools-local-authorities-gcse-epi-david-laws-a8406266.html.

[11] https://schoolsweek.co.uk/councils-to-get-sweeping-powers-over-academies-under-labour-reforms/.

12 https://www.local.gov.uk/sites/default/files/documents/15.36%20 Education_v08WEB_0.pdf.

13 https://www.theguardian.com/commentisfree/2018/aug/09/schools-broken-radical-action-education.

14 https://www.tes.com/news/academisation-its-time-final-stage-reform.

15 https://www.telegraph.co.uk/education/2019/03/21/first-new-grammar-schools-could-open-theresa-may-expansion-plan/.

16 https://www.tes.com/news/free-school-programme-needs-rebooting-says-gibb.

17 https://comprehensivefuture.org.uk/school-choice-isnt-working/.

18 https://www.bbc.co.uk/news/education-35351763.

19 https://schoolsweek.co.uk/the-hoodinerney-model-or-how-to-fix-the-school-system/.

20 Coverage of several issues: https://schoolsweek.co.uk/the-hoodinerney-model-or-how-to-fix-the-school-system/; https://schoolsweek.co.uk/return-oversight-of-schools-to-local-people-says-sir-michael-wilshaw/; https://schoolsweek.co.uk/labour-wont-return-to-the-past-on-school-accountability/; https://www.bbc.co.uk/news/uk-politics-45620778.

21 Newman, Janet, and John Clarke. 2009. *Publics, politics and power: Remaking the public and public services.* London: Sage, 7.

22 Greany, Toby, and Rob Higham. 2018. *Hierarchy, markets and networks: Analysing the 'self-improving school'-led system' agenda in England and the implications for schools.* London: UCL Institute of Education Press, 17.

23 Abdelnoor, Adam. 2007. *Managed moves: A complete guide to managed moves as an alternative to permanent exclusion.* London: Gulbenkian Foundation; Vincent, Kerry, Belinda Harris, Pat Thomson and Richard Toalster. 2007. 'Managed moves: schools collaborating for collective gain'. *Emotional and Behavioural Difficulties* 121 (4): 283–98.

24 See for instance this guidance for GPs on https://www.guidelinesinpractice. co.uk/non-clinical-best-practice/commissioning-in-england-past-and-present/454017.article.

25 https://nhsproviders.org/stp-governor-briefing.

26 Charles, Anna, Lillie Wenzel, Matthew Kershaw, Chris Ham and Nicola Walsh. 2018. *A year of integrated care systems: Reviewing the journey so far.* London: The King's Fund.

27 https://www.kingsfund.org.uk/blog/2018/05/what-has-stp-ics-done, my emphasis.

28 Power, Sally, Gareth Rees and Chris Taylor. 2005. 'New Labour and educational disadvantage: the limits of area based initiatives'. *London Review of Education* 3 (2): 101–16; Rees, Gareth, Sally Power and Chris Taylor. 2007. 'The governance of educational inequalities: the limits of area-based initiatives'. *International Journal of Comparative Policy Analysis* 9 (3): 261–74.

29 ASCL. 2018. *Report of the Ethical Leadership Commission to the Association of School and College Leaders' Annual Conference 2018.* https://www.ascl.org. uk/download.F477E8AB-270E-4BBF-8406607491E70DE7.html: ASCL.

30 ASCL 2018, 2.

31 https://www.tes.com/news/exclusive-end-exam-tricks-and-willy-nilly-rolling-heads-told.

32 Tyler, Imogen. 2013. *Revolting subjects: Social abjection and resistance in neoliberal Britain*. London: Zed Books.

33 https://www.ascl.org.uk/utilities/document-summary.html?id=F477E8AB-270E-4BBF-8406607491E70DE7.

34 Evans, Rodney. 1999. *The pedagogic principal*. Edmonton, Alberta: Qual Institute Press.

35 Rusch, Jonathan. 2016. 'The social psychology of corruption'. *OECD Integrity Forum*. Paris: OECD.

36 Wenger, Etienne. 1998. *Communities of practice: Learning, meaning and identity*. Cambridge: Cambridge University Press; 2000. 'Communities of practice and social learning systems'. *Organization: Speaking Out* 7 (2): 225–46.

37 Darley, John. 2005. 'The cognitive and social psychology of contagious organizational corruption'. *Brooklyn Law Review* 70 (4): 1177–94.

38 https://www.gov.uk/government/publications/the-7-principles-of-public-life/the-7-principles-of-public-life--2.

39 See Thomson, Pat. 2011. *Whole school change: A reading of the literatures*. Second ed. London: Creative Partnerships, Arts Council England.

40 Schatzki, Theodore, Karin Knorr Cetina and Eike Von Savigny. Eds. 2001. *The practice turn in contemporary theory*. London: Routledge.

Chapter 9

1 Barber, Michael. 2017. *Delivering better outcomes for citizens: Practical steps for unlocking public value*. https://assets.publishing.service.gov.uk/government/uploads/system/uploads/attachment_data/file/660408: HM Treasury.

2 Barber, Michael, Andy Moffit and Paul Kihn. 2010. *Deliverology 101: A field guide for educational leaders*. Thousand Oaks: Corwin.

3 Barber 2017, 62.

4 Barber 2017, 3.

5 Barber 2017, 6–7.

6 Moore, Mark. 1997. *Creating public value: Strategic management in government*. Boston: Harvard University Press.

7 Moore 1997, 295–303.

8 Barber 2017, 30.

9 Barber 2017, 24.

10 Barber 2017, 3.

11 Benington, John, and Mark Moore. 2011. 'Public value in complex and changing times'. In *Public value: Theory and practice*, edited by John Benington and Mark Moore, 1–30. New York: Palgrave Macmillan, 10.

12 Benington and Moore 2011, 11.

13 Benington and Moore 2011, 15.

14 Neubauer, Deane. 2008. 'The historical transformation of public good'. *Journal of Asian Public Policy* 1 (2): 127–38.

[15] MacIntyre, Alasdair. 1984. *After virtue: A study in moral theory*. Second ed. Notre Dame: University of Notre Dame Press.

[16] Hacking, Ian. 1999. *The social construction of what?* Cambridge, MA: Harvard University Press.

[17] Fraser, Derek. 2009. *The evolution of the British welfare state: A history of social policy since the industrial revolution*. London: Palgrave Macmillan.

[18] Pusey, Michael. 1991. *Economic rationalism in Canberra: A nation building state changes its mind*. Cambridge: Cambridge University Press.

[19] Harvey, David. 2005. *A brief history of neoliberalism*. Oxford: Oxford University Press.

[20] For example, Osborne, D., and Ted Gaebler. 1993. *Reinventing government: How the entrepreneurial spirit is transforming the public sector*. New York: Plume, Penguin.

[21] Clarke, John, and Janet E. Newman. 2009. *The managerial state: Power, politics and ideology in the remaking of social welfare*. London: Sage.

[22] Forster, John. 2006. 'The creation, maintenance and governance of public goods and free goods'. *Public Management: An International Journal of Research and Theory* 1 (3): 313–27.

[23] Power, Sally, Tim Edwards, Geoff Whitty and Valerie Wigfall. 2002. *Education and the middle class*. Buckingham: Open University Press.

[24] Kallhoff, Angela. 2014. 'Why societies need public goods'. *Critical Review of International Social and Political Philosophy* 17 (6): 635–51, 635.

[25] Neal, Zachary P., and Jennifer Watling Neal. 2016. 'The public school as a public good: direct pathways to community satisfaction'. *Journal of Urban Affairs* 34 (5): 469–86.

[26] Compare with the study of Italian provincial governments and their role supporting the integrated growth of economic and social capital in Putnam, Robert. 1993. *Making democracy work: civic traditions in modern Italy*. Princeton: Princeton University Press.

[27] Kaul, Inge, Isabelle Grunberg and Marc A. Stern. 1999. 'Defining global public goods'. In *Global public goods: International cooperation in the 21st century*, edited by Inge Kaul, Isabelle Grunberg and Marc A. Stern, xix–xxviii. New York: Oxford University Press, xx.

[28] http://www.psupress.org/Journals/jnls_GS.html.

[29] Bellah, Robert, Richard Madsen, William M. Sullivan, Ann Swidler and Steven M. Tipton. 1992. *The good society*. New York: Vintage Books.

[30] Bellah et al 1992, 15.

[31] https://www.thegoodsociety.net.au.

[32] https://www.fes-london.org/big-issues/the-good-society/.

[33] Meyer, Henning, and Karl-Heinz Spiegel. 2013. 'What next for European social democracy?' *Social Europe*, https://www.fes-london.org/fileadmin/user_upload/publications/files/What_next_for_European_social_democracy.pdf.

[34] Galbraith, J. K. 1996. *The good society*. Boston: Houghton Mifflin.

[35] Arendt, Hannah. 1982. *Lectures on Kant's political philosophy*. Chicago: University of Chicago Press, 43.

36 Fraser, Nancy. 1997. *Justice interruptus: Critical reflections on the 'postsocialist' condition*. London: Routledge; 2007. 'Identity, exclusion, and critique: a response to four critics'. *European Journal of Political Theory* 6 (3): 305–58.

37 Fricker, Miranda. 2007. *Epistemic injustice: Power and the ethics of knowing*. Oxford: Oxford University Press.

38 Gomberg, Paul. 2007. *How to make opportunity equal: Race and contributive justice*. Oxford: Blackwell Publishing.

39 Lynch, Kathleen, John Baker, Maureen Lyons, Maggie Feeley, Niall Hanlon, Maeve O'Brian, Judy Walsh and Sara Cantillon. 2009. *Affective equality: Love, care and injustice*. London: Palgrave Macmillan; Held, Virginia. Ed. 1995. *Justice and care: Essential readings in feminist ethics*. Boulder, CO: Westview Press.

40 Mintzberg, Henry. 1994. *The rise and fall of strategic planning*. New York: Prentice Hall.

41 https://www.theguardian.com/business/2003/jan/26/theobserver.observerbusiness11.

42 Mintzberg, Henry. 1999. 'Managing quietly'. *Leader to Leader* 12 (Spring): 24–30.

43 https://www.theguardian.com/business/2003/jan/26/theobserver.observerbusiness11.

44 Labaree, David. 1997. 'Public goods, private goods: the American struggle over educational goals'. *American Educational Research Journal* 34 (1): 39–81, 39.

45 Labaree 1997, 39.

46 Gerrard, Jessica, Glenn Clifton Savage and Kate O'Connor. 2017. 'Searching for the public: school funding and shifting meanings of "the public" in Australian education'. *Journal of Education Policy* 32 (4): 503–19.

47 Turner, Bryan S. 2007. 'Citizenship studies: a general theory'. *Citizenship Studies* 1 (1): 5–18.

48 Merry, Michael S. 2018. 'Can schools teach citizenship?' *Discourse*, DOI: 10.1080/01596306.2018.1488242.

49 Stevenson, Nick. 2003. 'Cultural citizenship in the "cultural society": a cosmopolitan approach'. *Citizenship Studies* 7 (3): 331–48; 2010. 'Cultural citizenship, education and democracy: redefining the good society'. *Citizenship Studies* 14 (3): 275–91.

50 Pring, Richard. 2016. 'Preparing for citizenship: bring back John Dewey'. *Citizenship, Social Economics and Education* 15 (1): 6–14.

51 Delors, Jacques. 1996. *Learning: The treasure within*. Paris: UNESCO; Kymlicka, Will. 1997. *Education for citizenship*. Vienna: Institute for Advanced Studies.

52 Norris, Pippa. 2011. *Democratic deficit: Critical citizens revisited*. Cambridge: Cambridge University Press.

53 Flinders, Matt, and Matt Wood. Eds. 2015. *Tracing the political: Depoliticisation, governance and the state*. Bristol: Bristol University Press.

54 Newman, Janet, and John Clarke. 2009. *Publics, politics and power: Remaking the public and public services*. London: Sage.

55   Newman and Clarke 2009, 184.
56   Newman and Clarke 2009, 184.
57   Newman and Clarke 2009, 184–5.

Bibliography

Abdelnoor, Adam. 2007. *Managed moves: A complete guide to managed moves as an alternative to permanent exclusion.* London: Gulbenkian Foundation.

Abrams, Samuel E. 2016. *Education and the commercial mindset.* Boston: Harvard University Press.

Adonis, Andrew. 2012. *Education, education, education: Reforming England's schools.* London: Biteback Publishing.

Aguayo, Rafael. 1990. *Dr Deming: The American who taught the Japanese about quality.* New York: Simon & Schuster.

Ainscow, Mel. 2015. *Towards self-improving school systems: Lessons from a city challenge.* London: Routledge.

Ainscow, Mel, and Mel West. Eds. 2006. *Improving urban schools: Leadership and collaboration.* Buckingham: Open University Press.

Ainscow, Mel, Alan Dyson, Sue Goldrick and Mel West. 2012. 'Making schools effective for all: rethinking the risk'. *School Leadership & Management* 32 (3): 197–213.

Aldred, Rachel. 2008. 'NHS LIFT and the new shape of neoliberal welfare'. *Capital and Class* 32 (2): 31–57.

Allen, Rebecca, and Anna Vignoles. 2010. *Can school competition improve standards? The case of faith schools in England.* DoQSS Working Paper No -9–04. London: Institute of Education.

Anderson, Gary. 2001. 'Disciplining leaders: a critical discourse analysis of the ISLLC National Examination and Performance Standards in educational administration'. *International Journal of Leadership in Education* 4 (3): 199–216.

Andrews, Jon, and Natalie Perera. 2017. *The impact of academies on educational outcomes.* London: Education Policy Institute.

Apple, Michael. 2001. *Educating the 'right' way: Markets, standards, God and inequality.* New York & London: Routledge.

Arendt, Hannah. 1982. *Lectures on Kant's political philosophy.* Chicago: University of Chicago Press.

ASCL. 2018. *Report of the Ethical Leadership Commission to the Association of School and College Leaders' Annual Conference 2018*. https://www.ascl.org.uk/download.F477E8AB-270E-4BBF-8406607491E70DE7.html: ASCL.

Asenova, Darinka, and Matthias Beck. 2010. 'Crucial silences: when accountability met PFI and finance capital'. *Critical Perspectives on Accounting* 21 (1): 1–13.

Asthana, Anand N. 2012. 'Decentralisation and corruption revisited: evidence from a natural experiment'. *Public Administration and Development* 32 (1): 27–37.

Auge, Marc. 1995. *Non-places: Introduction to an anthropology of supermodernity*, translated by John Howe. New York: Verso.

Bach, Tobias, and Sylvia Veit. 2018. 'The determinants of promotion to high public office in Germany: partisan loyalty, political craft, or managerial competencies?' *Journal of Public Administration Research and Theory* 28 (2): 254–69.

Baekgaard, Martin, Peter B. Mortensen and Heenrik Bech Seeberg. 2018. 'The bureaucracy and the policy agenda'. *Journal of Public Administration Research and Theory* 28 (2): 239–53.

Ball, Stephen. 2003. 'The teacher's soul and the terrors of performativity'. *Journal of Education Policy* 18 (2): 215–28.

———. 2012. *Global education inc: New policy networks and the neoliberal imaginary*. London: Routledge.

———. 2018a. *The education debate*. Third ed. Bristol: Policy Press.

———. 2018b. 'The tragedy of state education in England: reluctance, compromise and a muddle – a system in disarray'. *Journal of the British Academy* 6 (207–38).

Bambra, Clare. Ed. 2019. *Health in hard times*. Bristol: Policy Press.

Barber, Michael. 2017. *Delivering better outcomes for citizens: Practical steps for unlocking public value*. https://assets.publishing.service.gov.uk/government/uploads/system/uploads/attachment_data/file/660408: HM Treasury.

Barber, Michael, Andy Moffit and Paul Kihn. 2010. *Deliverology 101: A field guide for educational leaders*. Thousand Oaks: Corwin.

Bates, Richard. 1987. 'Corporate culture, schooling, and educational administration'. *Educational Administration Quarterly* 23 (4): 79–115.

————. 1993. 'On knowing: cultural and critical approaches to educational administration'. *Educational Management and Administration* 21 (3): 171–6.

Bauman, Zygmunt. 1993. *Postmodern ethics*. Oxford: Blackwell Publishers.

Beckett, Francis. 2007. *The great city academy fraud*. London: Continuum.

Bellah, Robert, Richard Madsen, William M. Sullivan, Ann Swidler and Steven M. Tipton. 1992. *The good society*. New York: Vintage Books.

Benington, John, and Mark Moore. 2011. 'Public value in complex and changing times'. In *Public value: Theory and practice*, edited by John Benington and Mark Moore, 1–30. New York: Palgrave Macmillan.

Benn, Melissa. 2011. *School wars: The battle for Britain's education*. London: Verso.

Bergman, Peter, and Isaac McFarlin. 2018. *Education for all? A nationwide audit study of schools of choice*. NBER Working Paper No 25396. Cambridge, MA: National Bureau of Economic Research.

Bernadelli, Danielle, Simon Rutt, Toby Greany and Rob Higham. 2018. *Multi-academy Trusts: Do they make a difference to pupil outcomes?* London: UCL Institute of Education Press.

Bernstein, Basil. 1971. *Class, codes and control: Vol. 1. Theoretical studies towards a sociology of language*. London: Routledge & Kegan Paul.

Berry, Craig. 2011. *Globalisation and ideology in Britain: neoliberalism, free trade and the global economy*. Manchester: Manchester University Press.

Bogard, William. 1996. *The simulation of surveillance: Hypercontrol in telematic societies*. Cambridge: Cambridge University Press.

Bottery, Mike. 2003. 'The leadership of learning communities in a culture of unhappiness'. *School Leadership and Management* 23 (2): 187–207.

Bourdieu, Pierre, and Jean Claude Passeron. 1977. *Reproduction in society, education and culture*. London: Sage.

————. 1979. *The inheritors, French students and their relation to culture*. Chicago: University of Chicago Press.

Bowe, Richard, Stephen Ball and Anne Gold. 1992. *Reforming education and changing schools: Case studies in policy sociology.* London: Routledge.

Brennan, Edward J. T. 1961. 'Sidney Webb and the London Technical Education Board'. *The Vocational Aspect of Secondary and Further Education* 13 (27): 146–71.

Bricheno, Pat, and Mary Thornton. 2016. *Crying in cupboards: What happens when teachers are bullied?* Leicestershire: Matador.

Brill, Frances, Hilary Grayson, Lisa Kuhn and Sharon O'Donnell. 2018. *What impact does accountability have on curriculum, standards and engagement in education?* Slough: National Foundation for Educational Research (NFER).

Brooks, Jean E. 2006. 'Strengthening resilience in children and youths: maximizing opportunities through the schools'. *Children & Schools* 28 (2): 69–76.

Brown, Wendy. 2015. *Undoing the demos: Neoliberalism's stealth revolution.* New York: Zone Books.

Bukodi, Erzsebet, and John H. Goldthorpe. 2018. *Social mobility and education in Britain: Research, politics and policy.* Cambridge: Cambridge University Press.

Burgess, Simon, Ellen Greaves and Anna Vignoles. 2019. 'School choice in England: evidence from national administrative data'. *Oxford Review of Education*, doi.org/10.1080/03054985.2019.1604332.

Cahill, Damien, Lindy Edwards and Frank Stilwell. Eds. 2012. *Neoliberalism: Beyond the free market.* Cheltenham: Edward Elgar Publishing.

Caldwell, Brian, and Jim Spinks. 1988. *The self managing school.* London: Falmer Press.

Chapman, Richard A. 1968. 'The Fulton Report: a summary'. *Public Administration* 46 (4): 443–52.

Charles, Anna, Lillie Wenzel, Matthew Kershaw, Chris Ham and Nicola Walsh. 2018. *A year of integrated care systems: Reviewing the journey so far.* London: The King's Fund.

Chitty, Clyde. 1997. 'Privatisation and marketisation'. *Oxford Review of Education* 23 (1): 45–61.

Chubb, J. E., and T. E. Moe. 1990. *Politics, markets, and America's schools.* Washington, DC: The Brookings Institute.

Clarke, John, and Janet E. Newman. 2009. *The managerial state: Power, politics and ideology in the remaking of social welfare*. London: Sage.

Clegg, Stewart, Eduardo Ibarra-Colada and Luis Bueno-Rodriquez. Eds. 1999. *Global management. Universal theories and local realities*. London: Sage.

Committee of Inquiry, House of Commons. 1854. 'On the organisation of the permanent civil service'. London: Her Majesty's Stationery Office.

Committee on the Civil Service, J. Fulton and B. Fulton. 1968. *Committee on the civil service*. London: HM Stationery Office.

Commons Select Committee. 2017. 'Government must show new grammars close attainment gap'. https://www.parliament.uk/business/committees/committees-a-z/commons-select/education-committee/news-parliament-2015/evidence-check-grammar-schools-report-published-16-17/: UK Government.

Conley, Sharon, and Sherry A. Woosley. 2000. 'Teacher role stress, higher order needs and work outcomes'. *Journal of Educational Administration* 38 (2): 179–201.

Coolican, Michael. 2018. *No tradesmen and no women: The origins of the British civil service*. London: Biteback Publishing.

Cosgrove, John. 2000. *Breakdown: The facts about stress in teaching*. London: Routledge.

Courtney, Steve. 2016. 'Mapping school types in England'. *Oxford Review of Education* 41 (6): 799–818.

Cunningham, Peter. 1988. *Curriculum change in the primary school since 1945: Dissemination of the progressive ideal*. London: Falmer Press.

Cutler, Fred. 1999. 'Jeremy Bentham and the public opinion tribunal'. *The Public Opinion Quarterly* 63 (3): 321–46.

Cutler, Tony, and Barbara Waine. 1997. 'The politics of quasi-markets'. *Critical Social Policy* 17 (2): 3–26.

Darley, John. 2005. 'The cognitive and social psychology of contagious organizational corruption'. *Brooklyn Law Review* 70 (4): 1177–94.

Davies, Peter, Colin Diamond and Thomas Perry (2020) 'Implications of autonomy and networks for costs and inclusion: Comparing patterns of spending under different governance systems'. *Educational Management Administration and Leadership*, https://doi.org/10.1177/1741143219888738.

Davies, William. 2017. *The limits of neoliberalism: Authority, sovereignty and the logics of competition*. Los Angeles: Sage.

Davis, Charles R. 1985. 'A critique of the ideology of efficiency'. *Humboldt Journal of Social Relations* 12 (2): 73–86.

Day, Christopher, Gordon Stobart, Pam Sammons, Alison Kington, Qing Gu, Rebecca Smees and Tamjid Mujtaba. 2006. *Variations in teachers' work, lives and effectiveness*. Research report 743. London: Department for Education and Skills (DfES).

Dean, Mitchell. 2014. 'Rethinking neoliberalism'. *Journal of Sociology* 50 (2): 150–63.

Delors, Jacques. 1996. *Learning: The treasure within*. Paris: UNESCO.

Deming, W. Edwards. 1992. *The Deming Management Method*. Cambridge, MA: MIT Press.

———. 2000. *The new economics for industry, government and education*. Cambridge, MA: MIT Press.

Donnelly, Kevin. 2007. *Dumbing down: Outcomes-based and politically correct – the impact of the culture wars on our schools*. Sydney: Hardie Grant Books.

Du Gay, Paul. 2000. *In praise of bureaucracy: Weber, organisation, ethics*. Thousand Oaks: Sage.

———. 2009. 'In defence of Mandarins: recovering the "core business" of public management'. *Management & Organizational History* 4 (4): 359–84.

Dunleavy, Patrick. 2014. *The state is a multi-system: Understanding the oneness and diversity of government*. Manchester: UK Political Studies Association. LSE Research online. http://eprints.lse.ac.uk/56492/.

Dunleavy, Patrick and Helen Margetts. 2010. 'The second wave of digital-era governance'. American Political Science Association Conference, Washington, DC. http://eprints.lse.ac.uk/27684/1/The_second_wave_of_digital_era_governance_(LSERO).pdf.

Dunleavy, Patrick, Helen Margetts, Simon Bastow and Jane Tinkler. 2006. 'New Public Management is dead – long live digital era governance'. *Journal of Public Administration Research and Theory* 16 (3): 467–94.

Dweck, Carol. 2012. *Mindset: How you can fulfil your potential*. New York: Ballantine Books.

Eacott, Scott. 2011. 'Preparing "educational" leaders in managerialist times: an Australian story'. *Journal of Educational Administration and History* 43 (1): 43–59.

Eagleton-Pierce, Matthew. 2016. *Neoliberalism: Key concepts.* London: Routledge.

Earl, Lorna, and Steven Katz. 2006. *Leading schools in a data-rich world: Harnessing data for school improvement.* Thousand Oaks: Corwin Press.

Edgerton, David. 2019. *The rise and fall of the British nation: A twentieth century history.* London: Penguin.

England, Kim, and Kevin Ward. 2016. 'Theorizing neoliberalization'. In *The handbook of neoliberalism*, edited by Simon Springer, Kean Birch and Julie Macleavy. London: Routledge.

English, Fenwick. 2013. *Educational leadership in the age of greed.* Michigan: National Council of Professors of Educational Administration.

Erickson, Anthony, Ben Shaw, Jane Murray and Sara Branch. 2005. 'Destructive leadership: causes, consequences and countermeasures'. *Organizational Dynamics* 20 (5): 266–72.

Esping-Andersen, Gosta. 1990. *The three worlds of welfare capitalism.* Cambridge: Polity Press.

Evans, Rodney. 1999. *The pedagogic principal.* Edmonton, Alberta: Qual Institute Press.

Flinders, Matt, and Matt Wood. Eds. 2015. *Tracing the political: Depoliticisation, governance and the state.* Bristol: Bristol University Press.

Forster, John. 2006. 'The creation, maintenance and governance of public goods and free goods'. *Public Management: An International Journal of Research and Theory* 1 (3): 313–27.

Foucault, Michel. 1972. *The archeology of knowledge*, translated by Alan Sheridan. 1995 ed. Routledge: London.

———. 1977. *Discipline and punish: The birth of the prison*, translated by Alan Sheridan. 1991 ed. London: Penguin.

Francis, Becky. 2017. The role of academies in English education policy. Paper presented at the Eleventh Whitehall Lecture, 22 June.

Fraser, Derek. 2009. *The evolution of the British welfare state: A history of social policy since the Industrial Revolution.* London: Palgrave Macmillan.

————. 2017. *The evolution of the British welfare estate*. Fifth ed. London: Palgrave.

Fraser, Nancy. 1997. *Justice interruptus. Critical reflections on the 'postsocialist' condition*. London: Routledge.

————. 2007. 'Identity, exclusion, and critique: a response to four critics'. *European Journal of Political Theory* 6 (3): 305–58.

Fricker, Miranda. 2007. *Epistemic injustice: Power and the ethics of knowing*. Oxford: Oxford University Press.

Friedman, Milton. 2002. *Capitalism and freedom*. Chicago: University of Chicago Press.

Fry, G. 1995. *Policy and management in the British civil service*. Hemel Hempstead: Prentice Hall.

Galbraith, J. K. 1996. *The good society*. Boston: Houghton Mifflin.

Galton, Maurice, and John Macbeath. 2008. *Teachers under pressure*. London: National Union of Teachers/SAGE.

Geiger, Tray, and Margarita Pivarova. 2018. 'The effects of working conditions on teacher retention'. *Teachers and Teaching: Theory and Practice* 24 (6): 604–25.

Gerrard, Jessica, Glenn Clifton Savage and Kate O'Connor. 2017. 'Searching for the public: school funding and shifting meanings of "the public" in Australian education'. *Journal of Education Policy* 32 (4): 503–19.

Gewirtz, Sharon. 2002. *The managerial school: Post-welfarism and social justice in education*. London: Routledge.

Gibson, Alex, and Sheena Asthana. 2013. 'Schools, pupils and examination results: contextualising school "performance"'. *British Educational Research Journal* 24 (3): 269–82.

Giddens, Anthony. 1998. *The third way*. Cambridge and Oxford: Polity Press.

Gillborn, David, and Deborah Youdell. 2000. *Rationing education: Policy, practice, reform and equity*. Buckingham and Philadelphia: Open University Press.

Goldstein, Harvey, and George Leckie. 2018. *Should we adjust for pupil background in school value-added measures?* https://www.bristol.ac.uk/media-library/sites/education/documents/FINAL.pdf: University of Bristol, School of Education.

Gomberg, Paul. 2007. *How to make opportunity equal: Race and contributive justice*. Oxford: Blackwell Publishing.

Gorard, Stephen. 2014. 'The link between academies in England, pupil outcomes and local patterns of socio-economic segregation between schools'. *Research Papers in Education* 29 (3): 268–84.

———. 2018. *Education policy, equity and effectiveness: Evidence of equity and effectiveness.* Bristol: Policy Press.

Gorard, Stephen, and John Fitz. 2000. 'Markets and stratification: a view from England and Wales'. *Educational Policy* 14 (3): 405–28.

Gorard, Stephen, and Nadia Siddiqui. 2018. 'Grammar schools in England: a new analysis of social segregation and academic outcomes'. *British Journal of Sociology of Education* 39 (7): 909–24.

Gorard, Stephen, Chris Taylor and John Fitz. 2003. *Schools, markets and choice policies.* London: Routledge.

Greany, Toby, and Rob Higham. 2018. *Hierarchy, markets and networks: Analysing the 'self-improving school-led system' agenda in England and the implications for schools.* London: UCL Institute of Education Press.

Green, Stuart P. 2006. *Lying, cheating, and stealing: A moral theory of white-collar crime.* Oxford: Oxford University Press.

Griffiths, Morwenna. 1998. *Educational research for social justice: Getting off the fence.* Buckingham: Open University Press.

Gunter, Helen. 2012. *Leadership and the reform of education.* Bristol: Policy Press.

———. 2015. 'Consultants, consultancy and consultocracy in education policymaking in England'. *Journal of Education Policy* 30 (4): 518–39.

Gunter, Helen, and Gillian Forrester. 2008. 'New Labour and school leadership 1997–2007'. *British Journal of Educational Studies* 56 (2): 144–62.

Gunter, Helen, and Colin Mills. 2017. *Consultants and consultancy: The case of education.* New York: Springer.

Gunter, Helen, Emiliano Grimaldi, David Hall and Roberto Serpieri. Eds. 2016. *New Public Management and the reform of education: European lessons for policy and practice.* London: Routledge.

Hacking, Ian. 1999. *The social construction of what?* Cambridge, MA: Harvard University Press.

Hal, D., Lister, J., Hobbs, C. and Mercer, H. (2020). *Privatised and unprepared. The NHS supply chain.* https://weownit.org.uk/privatised-and-unprepared-nhs-supply-chain: University of Greenwich.

Hanna, Rema, Sarah Bishop, Sara Nadel, Gabe Scheffer and Katherine Durlacher. 2011. *The effectiveness of anti-corruption policy: What has worked, what hasn't, and what we don't know.* EPPI Centre Report 1909. London: EPPI Centre, Instituted of Education, University of London.

Hargreaves, Andy, and Pasi Sahlberg. 2012. *Finnish lessons: What can the world learn from educational change in Finland?* London: Routledge.

Harvey, David. 2005. *A brief history of neoliberalism.* Oxford: Oxford University Press.

Hattie, John. 2011. *Visible learning for teachers: Maximising impact on leaders.* London: Routledge.

Hatton, Adam, Rebekah Hampson and Rob Drake. 2019. *An analysis of the performance of sponsored academies.* London: Department for Education.

Hayek, Friedrich. A. 2001. *The road to serfdom.* New York: Routledge.

Hayes, Deborah, Robert Hattam, Barbara Comber, Lyn Kerkham, Ruth Lupton and Pat Thomson. 2018. *Literacy, leading and learning: Beyond pedagogies of poverty.* London: Routledge.

Hayward, Vanessa, and Pat Thomson. 2012. 'Performing health: an ethnographic investigation of emotional health and wellbeing (EHWB) in a high-performance school'. In *Performativity in UK education: Ethnographic cases of its effects, agency and reconstitutions*, edited by Bob Jeffrey and Geoff Troman, 109–26. Gloucestershire: E & E Publishing.

Held, Virginia. Ed. 1995. *Justice and care: Essential readings in feminist ethics.* Boulder, CO: Westview Press.

Heywood, Paul. 2018. 'Combatting corruption in the twenty-first century: new approaches'. *Daedalus* 147 (3): 83–97.

Higham, Rob. 2014. 'Free schools in the Big Society: the motivations, aims and demography of free school proposers'. *Journal of Education Policy* 29 (1): 122–39.

Hirsch, E. D. 2006. *The knowledge deficit: Closing the shocking education gap for American children.* New York: Houghton Mifflin.

Hirschman, E. 1970. *Exit, voice and loyalty: Responses to decline in firms, organizations and states.* Boston: Harvard University Press.

Hodge, Margaret. 2016. *Called to account: How corporate bad behaviour and government waste combine to cost us millions.* London: Little. Brown.

Holmes, Leslie. 2015. *Corruption: A very short introduction.* Oxford: Oxford University Press.

Hood, Christopher. 1995. 'The "New Public Management" in the 1980s: variations on a theme'. *Accounting, Organisations and Society* 20 (2/3): 93–109.

———. 1998. *The art of the state: Culture, rhetoric and public management.* Oxford: Clarendon Press.

Horton, Sylvia. 2006. 'The public service ethos in the British civil service: an historical institutional analysis'. *Public Policy and Administration* 21 (1): 32–48.

House of Commons Committee of Public Accounts. 2018. *Academy schools' finances: Thirtieth report of session 2017–19.* https://publications.parliament.uk/pa/cm201719/cmselect/cmpubacc/760/760.pdf: House of Commons, 5.

Hunter, David J. 2016. *The health debate.* Second ed. Bristol: Policy Press.

Hutchings, Merryn, and Becky Francis. 2018. *Chain effects 2018: The impact of academy chains on low-income pupils.* London: The Sutton Trust.

Ingram, Jenni, Victoria Elliott, Caroline Morin, Ashmita Randhawa and Carol Brown. 2018. 'Playing the system: incentives to "game" and educational ethics in school examination entry policies in England'. *Oxford Review of Education* 44 (5): 545–62.

Institute of Education (University of London) and the National Foundation for Educational Research (NFER). 2014. *School exclusion trial evaluation.* London: Department for Education.

Jason, Zachary. 2017. 'The battle over charter schools'. *Harvard Education Magazine*, Summer. https://www.gse.harvard.edu/news/ed/17/05/battle-over-charter-schools.

Jayasuriya, Kanishka. 2002. 'The new contractualism: neoliberal or democratic?' *The Political Quarterly* 73 (3): 309–20.

Jerrim, John, and Sam Sims. 2018. *Why do so few low and middle-income children attend a grammar school? New evidence from the Millennium Cohort Study*. https://johnjerrim.files.wordpress.com/2018/03/working_paper_nuffield_version_clean.pdf. London: Institute of Education.

Johnson, Alan. 2016. *The long and winding road*. London: Bantam Press.

Johnston, Michael. 2005. *Syndromes of corruption: Wealth, power and democracy*. Cambridge: Cambridge University Press.

———. 2018. 'Afterword'. In *Anticorruption in history: From antiquity to the modern era*, edited by Ronald Kroeze, Andre Vitoria and G. Geltner, 305–9. Oxford: Oxford University Press.

Jones, Ken. 1983. *Beyond progressive education*. London: Macmillan.

———. 2003. *Education in Britain: 1944 to the present*. Oxford: Polity Press.

Jones, Ken, and Pat Thomson. 2008. 'Policy rhetoric and the renovation of English schooling: the case of Creative Partnerships'. *Journal of Education Policy* 23 (6): 715–28.

Kalihoff, Angela. 2014. 'Why societies need public goods'. *Critical Review of International Social and Political Philosophy* 17 (6): 635–51.

Karabel, Jerome, and A.H. Halsey. 1977. *Power and ideology in education*. Oxford: Oxford University Press.

Kaul, Inge, Isabelle Grunberg and Marc A. Stern. 1999. 'Defining global public goods'. In *Global public goods: International cooperation in the 21st century*, edited by Inge Kaul, Isabelle Grunberg and Marc A. Stern, xix–xxviii. New York: Oxford University Press.

Keichtermans, Geert. 2017. '"Should I stay or should I go?": unpacking teacher attrition/retention as an educational issue'. *Teachers and Teaching: Theory and Practice* 23 (8): 961–77.

Keshavjee, Salmaan. 2014. *Blind spot: How neoliberalism infiltrated global health*. Los Angeles: University of California Press.

Kirkpatrick, Ian, Andrew Sturdy, Andrew J. Alvarado, Nuria Reguera, Antonio Blanco-Oliver and Gianluca Veronesi. 2019. 'The impact of management consultants on public service efficiency'. *Policy & Politics* 47 (1): 77–96.

Knight, John, and Bob Lingard. 1996. 'Ministerialisation and politicisation: changing practices of educational policy production'. In *A national approach to schooling in Australia? Essays on the development of national policies in schools education*, edited by Bob Lingard and Page Porter. Canberra: Australian College of Education.

Knights, Mark. 2016. *Old corruption: What British history can tell us about corruption today*. London: Transparency International.

Kroeze, Ronald, Andre Vitoria and Guy Geltner. 2018. *Anticorruption in history: From antiquity to the modern era*. Oxford: Oxford University Press.

Kulz, Christy. 2017. *Factories for learning: Making race, class and inequality in the neoliberal academy*. Manchester: Manchester University Press.

Kymlicka, Will. 1997. *Education for citizenship*. Vienna: Institute for Advanced Studies.

Labaree, David. 1997. 'Public goods, private goods: the American struggle over educational goals'. *American Educational Research Journal* 34 (1): 39–81.

Levacic, Rosalind, Peter Downes, Brian Caldwell, David Gurr, Jim Spinks, Jan Herczunski, Maria Beatriz Luce and Nalu Farenzena. 2012. *Formula funding of schools: Decentralisaton and corruption. A comparative analysis*. Paris: UNESCO.

Levin, Benjamin. 2001. *Reforming education: From origins to outcomes*. London: Falmer Press.

Llewellyn, Sue, and Stephen Brookes. Eds. 2018. *Trust and confidence in government and public services*. London: Routledge.

Lockhart, Johanna M. 2016. *Maximise your school marketing*. London: Rowman & Littlefield.

Long, Robert, and Danechi Shadi. 2019. *Off-rolling in English schools*. Briefing Paper 08444. London: House of Commons Library.

Lubienski, Christopher A., and Sarah Theule Lubienski. 2014. *The public school advantage: Why public schools outperform private schools*. Chicago: University of Chicago Press.

Lumby, Jacky, and Fenwick English. 2010. *Leadership as lunacy and other metaphors for educational leadership*. Thousand Oaks: Corwin.

Lupton, Deborah. 2016. *The quantified self*. Cambridge: Polity Press.

Lupton, Ruth. 2004. *Schools in disadvantaged areas: Recognising context and raising performance.* CASE paper 76. London: Centre for Analysis of Social Exclusion, London School of Economics.

Lynch, Kathleen, John Baker, Maureen Lyons, Maggie Feeley, Niall Hanlon, Maeve O'Brian, Judy Walsh and Sara Cantillon. 2009. *Affective equality: Love, care and injustice.* London: Palgrave Macmillan.

Lynn, Laurence E. 2006. *Public management old and new.* New York: Routledge.

Lyotard, Jean-François. 1984. *The postmodern condition: A report on knowledge.* 1993 ed. *Theory and history of literature, Vol. 10.* Minneapolis: University of Minnesota Press.

Macbeath, John, and Peter Mortimore. Eds. 2001. *Improving school effectiveness.* London: Routledge.

Macdougall, Alex, and Ruth Lupton. 2015. *The 'London effect': Literature review.* Manchester: Joseph Rowntree Foundation.

Machiavelli, Niccolo. 1532 (2003). *The prince.* London: Penguin.

MacIntyre, Alasdair. 1984. *After virtue: A study in moral theory.* Second ed. Notre Dame: University of Notre Dame Press.

Maclure, Stuart. 1988. *Education re-formed: Guide to the Education Act 1988.* London: Hodder Arnold.

Mahony, Pat, Ian Hextall and Malcolm Richardson. 2011. '"Building Schools for the Future": reflections on a new social architecture'. *Journal of Education Policy* 26 (3): 341–60.

Maravic, Patrick, and Christoph Reichard. 2003. 'New Public Management and corruption IPNM dialogue and analysis'. *International Public Management Review* 4 (1): 84–129.

Margetts, Helen, and Patrick Dunleavy. 2013. 'The second wave of digital-era governance: a quasi-paradigm for government on the web'. *Philosophical Transactions of the Royal Society A*, https://doi.org/10.1098/rsta.2012.0382.

Mayhew, Henry. 1861. *London Labour and the London poor, Vols 1–4.* 1968 ed. New York: Dover Publications.

Meadows, Michelle, and Beth Black. 2018. 'Teachers' experience of and attitudes toward activities to maximise qualification results in England'. *Oxford Review of Education* 44 (5): 563–80.

Merry, Michael S. 2018. 'Can schools teach citizenship?' *Discourse*, DOI: 10.1080/01596306.2018.1488242.

Mertier, Craig A. 2014. *The data-driven classroom: How do I use student data to improve my instruction?* Washington, MD: ASCD.

Meyer, Henning, and Karl-Heinz Spiegel. 2013. 'What next for European social democracy?' *Social Europe*, https://www.fes-london.org/fileadmin/user_upload/publications/files/What_next_for_European_social_democracy.pdf.

Milley, Peter. 2018. 'Strategies of discursive closure maladministrators use to "manage" their misdeeds'. In *International perspectives on maladministration in education*, edited by Eugenie Samier and Peter Milley, 169–83. London: Routledge.

Mintzberg, Henry. 1994. *The rise and fall of strategic planning.* New York: Prentice Hall.

———. 1999. 'Managing quietly'. *Leader to Leader* 12 (Spring): 24–30.

Moore, James. 2018. 'Corruption and ethical standards of British public life, national debates and local administration 1880–1914'. In *Anticorruption in history: From antiquity to the modern era*, edited by Ronald Kroeze, Andre Vitoria and G. Geltner, 267–78. Oxford: Oxford University Press.

Moore, Mark. 1997. *Creating public value: Strategic management in government.* Boston: Harvard University Press.

National Audit Office (NAO). 2007. *The academies programme.* London: House of Commons. https://www.nao.org.uk/wp-content/uploads/2007/02/0607254es.pdf.

———. 2018a. *Converting maintained schools to academies.* London: House of Commons. https://www.nao.org.uk/wp-content/uploads/2018/02/Converting-maintained-schools-to-academies.pdf.

———. 2018b. *PFI and PF2.* London: House of Commons. https://www.nao.org.uk/wp-content/uploads/2018/01/PFI-and-PF2.pdf.

Neal, Zachary P., and Jennifer Watling Neal. 2016. 'The public school as a public good: direct pathways to community satisfaction'. *Journal of Urban Affairs* 34 (5): 469–86.

Neubauer, Deane. 2008. 'The historical transformation of public good'. *Journal of Asian Public Policy* 1 (2): 127–38.

Newman, Janet. 2001. *Modernising governance: New Labour, policy and society.* London: Sage.

Newman, Janet, and John Clarke. 2009. *Publics, politics and power: Remaking the public and public services*. London: Sage.

Niesche, Richard, and Pat Thomson. 2017. 'Freedom to what ends? School autonomy in neoliberal times'. In *The international handbook of educational leadership*, edited by Ira Bogotch and Duncan Waite. New York: Wiley Blackwell.

Normore, Anthony H., and Jeffrey S. Brooks. 2016. *The dark side of leadership: Identifying and overcoming unethical practice in organisations*. New York: Emerald.

Norris, Pippa. 2011. *Democratic deficit: Critical citizens revisited*. Cambridge: Cambridge University Press.

Northcote, Stafford F., and C. E. Trevelyan. 1853. *Report of the organisation of the permanent civil service*. London: Her Majesty's Stationery Office.

Nye, Joseph. 1997. *Why people don't trust government*. Boston: Harvard University Press.

O'Toole, Brian. 2006. *The ideal of public service*. London: Routledge.

OECD Publishing. 2015. *Consequences of corruption at the sector level and implications for economic growth and development*. Paris: OECD.

———. 2019. *Governance as an SDG accelerator*. Paris: OECD.

Olmedo, Antonio, and Eduardo Santa Cruz Grau. 2013. 'Neoliberalism, poilicy advocacy networks and think tanks in the Spanish education arena'. *Education Inquiry* 4 (3): 473–96.

Orwell, George. 1949. *1984*. Harmondsworth: Penguin.

Osborne, D., and T. Gaebler. 1993. *Reinventing government: How the entrepreneurial spirit is transforming the public sector*. New York: Plume, Penguin.

Osler, Audrey, and Kerry Vincent. 2003. *Girls and exclusion*. London: Routledge.

Ozga, Jenny. 2009. 'Governing education through data in England: from regulation to self evaluation'. *Journal of Education Policy* 24 (2): 149–62.

Panchamia, Nehal, and Peter Thomas. 2015. *Civil service reform in the real world*. https://www.instituteforgovernment.org.uk/sites/default/files/publications/260314%20CSRW%20-%20final.pdf: Institute for Government.

Parris, Henry. 1969. *Constitutional bureaucracy*. London: Allen and Unwin.

Pateman, Carol. 1970. *Participation and democratic theory*. Cambridge: Cambridge University Press.

Paton, Calum. 2008. 'The NHS after 10 years of New Labour'. In *Modernising the welfare state: The Blair legacy*, edited by Martin Powell, 17–34. Bristol: Policy Press.

Payne, Brian K. 2016. *White-collar crime: The essentials*. Thousand Oaks: Sage.

Perryman, Jane, and Graham Calvert. 2019. 'What motivates people to teach, and why do they leave? Accountability, performativity and teacher retention'. *British Journal of Educational Studies* https://doi.org/10.1080/00071005.2019.1589417.

Phillips, Robert. 1996. 'History teaching, cultural restorationism and national identity in England and Wales'. *Curriculum Studies* 4 (3): 385–99.

Pierre, Jon. Ed. 1995. *Bureaucracy in the modern state: An introduction to comparative public administration*. Cheltenham: Edward Elgar.

Pierre, Jon, and B. Guy Peters. 2000. *Governance, politics and the state*. New York: St Martins Press.

Pilcher, Jane, and Stephen Wagg. Eds. 1996. *Thatcher's children? Politics, childhood and society in the 1980s and 1990s*. London: Falmer Press.

Pilkington, Colin. 1999. *The civil service in Britain today*. Manchester: Manchester University Press.

Plato. 2007. *The republic*, translated by H. D. P. Lee and Desmond Lee. New York: Penguin.

Plehwe, Dieter, Moritz Neujeffski and Werner Kramer. 2018. 'Saving the dangerous idea: austerity think tank networks in the European Union'. *Policy and Society* 37 (2): 188–205.

Pollitt, Christopher. 2011. *Public management reform: A comparative analysis. New Public Management, governance and the neo-Weberian state*. Third ed. Oxford: Oxford University Press.

Pollitt, Christopher, and Geert Bouckaert. 2011. *Public management reform: A comparative analysis. New Public Management, governance and the neo-Weberian state*. Fourth ed. Oxford: Oxford University Press.

Power, Sally, Gareth Rees and Chris Taylor. 2005. 'New Labour and educational disadvantage: the limits of area based initiatives'. *London Review of Education* 3 (2): 101–16.

Power, Sally, Tim Edwards, Geoff Whitty and Valerie Wigfall. 2002. *Education and the middle class.* Buckingham: Open University Press.

Pring, Richard. 2016. 'Preparing for citizenship: bring back John Dewey'. *Citizenship, Social Economics and Education* 15 (1): 6–14.

Pusey, Michael. 1991. *Economic rationalism in Canberra: A nation building state changes its mind.* Cambridge: Cambridge University Press.

Putnam, Robert. 1993. *Making democracy work: Civic traditions in modern Italy.* Princeton: Princeton University Press.

Ravitch, Diane. 2014. *Reign of error: The hoax of the privatization movement and the danger to America's public schools.* New York: Vintage Books.

Reay, Diane. 2017. *Miseducation: Inequality, education and the working classes.* Bristol: Policy Press.

Rees, Gareth, Sally Power and Chris Taylor. 2007. 'The governance of educational inequalities: the limits of area-based initiatives'. *International Journal of Comparative Policy Analysis* 9 (3): 261–74.

Rhodes, R. A. W. 1994. 'The hollowing out of the state: the changing nature of the public service in Britain'. *The Political Quarterly* 65 (2): 138–51.

Richards, David, and Martin J. Smith. 2016. 'The Westminster model and the "indivisibility of the political and administrative elite": a convenient myth whose time is up?' *Governance: An International Journal of Policy, Administration and Institutions* 29 (4): 499–516.

Rivzi, Fazal, and Bob Lingard. 2009. *Globalising education policy.* London: Routledge.

Rizq, Rosemary. 2014. 'Perversion, neoliberalism and therapy: the audit culture in mental health services'. *Psychoanalysis, culture and society* 19 (2): 209–18.

Roberts, Nerys. 2017. *FAQs: Academies and free schools.* House of Commons Briefing Paper. London: House of Commons Library.

Rose-Ackerman, Susan. 1999. *Corruption and government: Causes, consequences and reform*. Cambridge: Cambridge University Press.

————. 2018. 'Corruption and purity'. *Daedalus* 147 (3): 98–110.

Rothstein, Bo. 2018. 'Fighting systemic corruption: the indirect strategy'. *Daedalus* 147 (35–49).

Rothstein, Bo, and Aiysha Varraich. 2017. *Making sense of corruption*. Cambridge: Cambridge University Press.

Rubin, Daniel Ian. 2011. 'The disheartened teacher: living in the age of standardisataion, high-stakes assessment and No Child Left Behind (NCLB)'. *Changing English* 18 (4): 407–16.

Rusch, Jonathan. 2016. 'The social psychology of corruption'. In *OECD Integrity Forum*. Paris: OECD.

Russell, Meg, and Philip Cowley. 2016. 'The policy power of the Westminster Parliament: the "parliamentary state" and the empirical evidence'. *Governance: An International Journal of Policy, Administration and Institutions* 29 (1): 121–37.

Rutter, Michael, Peter Mortimore and Barbara Maugham. 1979. *Fifteen thousand hours: Secondary schools and their effects*. Boston: Harvard University Press.

Sahlberg, Pasi. 2007. 'Education policies for raising student learning: the Finnish approach'. *Journal of Education Policy* 22 (2): 147–71.

Sakellariou, Dikaios, and Elena S. Rotarou. 2017. 'The effects of neoliberal policies on access to healthcare for people with disabilities'. *Journal of Equity in Health* 16 (1): 199–208.

Saltman, Kenneth. 2019. *The swindle of innovative educational finance*. Minneapolis: University of Minnesota Press.

Samier, Eugenie, and Peter Milley. Eds. 2018. *International perspectives on maladministration in education*. London: Routledge.

Savage, Mike. 2015. *Social class in the 21st century*. London: Pelican.

Schatzki, Theodore, Karin Knorr Cetina and Eike Von Savigny. Eds. 2001. *The practice turn in contemporary theory*. London: Routledge.

Schofield, Philip. 1996. 'Bentham on the identification of interests'. *Utilitas* 8 (2): 223–34.

————. 2006. *Utility and democracy: The political thought of Jeremy Bentham*. Oxford: Oxford University Press.

Schyns, Birgit, and Jan Schilling. 2013. 'How bad are the effects of bad leaders? A meta-analysis of destructive leadership and its outcomes'. *The Leadership Quarterly* 24: 138–58.

Segal, Lydia G. 2004. *Battling corruption in America's public schools*. Boston: Northeastern University Press.

Semple, Janet. 1993. *Bentham's prison: A study of the Panopticon penitentiary*. Oxford: Clarendon Press.

Shafe, James. 2014. 'Challenges for a revised view of Bentham on public reasoning'. *Revue d'études benthamiennes* 13 (Droit international). http://journals.openedition.org/etudes-benthamiennes/761.

Smith, Adam. 1776 (2008). *An inquiry into the nature and causes of the wealth of nations*. Oxford: Oxford Paperbacks.

Smith, Kevin B., and Michael J. Licari. 2006. *Public administrations: Power and politics in the fourth branch of government*. New York: Open University Press.

Smyth, John, and Robert Hattam. 2004. *Dropping out, drifting off, being excluded: Becoming somebody without school*. New York: Peter Lang.

Social Mobility Commission. 2019. *State of the nation 2018–19: Social mobility in Great Britain*. https://assets.publishing.service.gov.uk/government/uploads/system/uploads/attachment_data/file/798404/SMC_State_of_the_Nation_Report_2018–19.pdf: Social Mobility Commission.

Soltes, Eugene. 2016. *Why they do it: Inside the mind of the white-collar criminal*. Public Affairs Books: Philadelphia Books.

Sosenko, F., Littlewood, M., Bramley, G., Fitzpatrick, S., Blenkinsopp, J. and Wood, J. (2019). *State of hunger. A study of poverty and food insecurity in the UK*. https://www.stateofhunger.org/wp-content/uploads/2019/11/State-of-Hunger-Report-November2019-Digital.pdf: The Trussell Trust.

Spicer, Andre, Mats Alvesson and Dan Kärreman. 2009. 'Critical performativity: the unfinished business of critical management studies'. *Human Relations* 62 (4): 537–60.

Spillane, James. 2006. *Distributed leadership*. San Francisco: Jossey Bass.

Springer, Simon, Kean Birch and Julie MacLeavy. 2016. 'An introduction to neoliberalism'. In *The handbook of neoliberalism*, edited by Simon Springer, Kean Birch and Julie Macleavy, 1–13. London: Routledge.

Stanley, Martin. 2016. *How to be a civil servant*. London: Biteback Publishing.

Stedman-Jones, Daniel. 2012. *Masters of the universe: Hayek, Friedman and the birth of neoliberal politics*. Princeton, NJ: Princeton University Press.

Steger, Manfred B., and Ravi K. Roy. 2010. *Neoliberalism: A very short introduction*. Oxford: Oxford University Press.

Stevenson, Nick. 2003. 'Cultural citizenship in the "cultural society": a cosmopolitan approach'. *Citizenship Studies* 7 (3): 331–48.

———. 2010. 'Cultural citizenship, education and democracy: redefining the good society'. *Citizenship Studies* 14 (3): 275–91.

Stoker, Gerry. 1998. 'Governance as theory: five propositions'. *International Social Science Journal* 50 (1): 17–28.

Stoll, Louise, and Dean Fink. 1996. *Changing our schools: Linking school effectiveness and school improvement*. Buckingham: Open University Press.

Sweet, Rod. 2017. 'Haemorrhaging cash: assessing the long-term costs of PFI'. *Construction Research and Innovation* 8 (4): 113–16.

Sylva, Kathy, Edward Melhuish, Pam Sammons, Iram Siraj-Blatchford and Brenda Taggart. 2004. *The effective provision of pre-school education (EPPE) project*. https://dera.ioe. ac.uk/18189/2/SSU-SF-2004–01.pdf: Sure Start.

Taylor, F. W. 1919. *The principles of scientific management*. New York: Harper & Brothers.

Teddlie, Charles, and David Reynolds. Eds. 2000. *The international handbook of school effectiveness*. London: Falmer Press.

Thomson, Pat. 2000. 'Like schools, educational disadvantage and "thisness"'. *Australian Educational Researcher* 27 (3): 151–66.

———. 2008. 'Answering back to policy? Headteachers' stress and the logic of the sympathetic interview'. *Journal of Education Policy* 23 (6): 649–68.

———. 2009. *School leadership: Heads on the block?* London: Routledge.

————. 2011. *Whole school change: A reading of the literatures.* Second ed. London: Creative Partnerships, Arts Council England.

————. 2017. *Educational leadership and Pierre Bourdieu.* London: Routledge.

————. 2019. 'Oh to be in England? The production of an un-public state system'. In *Dismantling public education: Implications for educational leadership, policy and social justice*, edited by Jane Wilkinson, Richard Niesche and Scott Eacott. London: Routledge.

Thomson, Pat, and Christine Hall. 2011. 'Sense-making as a lens on everyday change leadership practice: the case of Holly Tree Primary'. *International Journal of Leadership in Education* 14 (4): 385–403.

Thomson, Pat, Christine Hall and Ken Jones. 2010. 'Maggie's day: a small scale analysis of English education policy'. *Journal of Education Policy* 25 (5): 639–56.

Thomson, Pat, and Jodie Pennacchia. 2014. *What's the alternative? Effective support for young people disengaging from mainstream education.* http://www.princes-trust.org.uk/pdf/whats-the-alternative-effective-support-for-young-people.pdf: The Princes Trust.

Thomson, Pat, Belinda Harris, Kerry Vincent and Richard Toalster. 2005. *Evaluation of the Mansfield Alternatives to Exclusion (MATE) programme.* Nottingham: Centre for Research in Equity and Diversity in Education, School of Education, University of Nottingham.

Thrupp, Martin, and Ruth Lupton. 2011. *The impact of school context: What headteachers say.* London: Centre for Analysis of Social Exclusion, London School of Economics.

Tomlinson, Sally. 2001. *Education in post-welfare society.* Buckingham: Open University Press.

Transparency International. 2010. *Corruption in the UK: Part One. National Opinion Survey.* London: Transparency International.

————. 2011. *National integrity system assessment: United Kingdom.* London: Transparency International UK.

————. 2018. *The cost of secrecy: The role played by companies registered in the UK's overseas territories in money laundering and corruption.* London: Transparency International.

———. 2019. *At your service: Investigating how UK businesses and institutions help corrupt individuals and regimes launder their money and reputations*. London: Transparency International.

Troman, Geoff. 2000. 'Teacher stress in the low-trust society'. *British Journal of Sociology of Education* 21 (3): 331–53.

Turner, Bryan S. 2007. 'Citizenship studies: a general theory'. *Citizenship Studies* 1 (1): 5–18.

Tyler, Imogen. 2013. *Revolting subjects: Social abjection and resistance in neoliberal Britain*. London: Zed Books.

Veronesi, Gianluca, Ian Kirkpatrick and Ali Atlantar. 2019. 'Are public sector managers a "bureaucratic burden"? The case of English public hospitals'. *Journal of Public Administration Research and Theory*, doi: 10.1093/jopart/muy072.

Vincent, Kerry, Belinda Harris, Pat Thomson and Richard Toalster. 2007. 'Managed moves: schools collaborating for collective gain'. *Emotional and Behavioural Difficulties* 121 (4): 283–98.

Von Alemann, Ulrich. 2004. 'The unknown depths of political theory: the case for a multidimensional concept of corruption'. *Crime, Law and Social Change* 42 (1): 25–34.

Watkins, Amanda, and Serge Ebershold. 2016. 'Efficiency, effectiveness and equity within inclusive education systems'. In *Implementing inclusive education: Issues in bridging the policy-practice gap*, edited by Amanda Watkins and Cor Meijer. New York: Emerald.

Webb, Sydney. 1901. *The education muddle and the way out: A constructive criticism of English educational machinery*. London: The Fabian Society.

———. 1904. *London education*. London: Longmans, Green and Co.

Weber, Max, Peter Baehr and Gordon C. Wells. 2002. *The Protestant ethic and the spirit of capitalism and other writings*. New York: Penguin.

Weller, Patrick, and Catherine Haddon. 2016. 'Westminster traditions: continuity and change'. *Governance: An International Journal of Policy, Administration and Institutions* 29 (4): 483–98.

Wenger, Etienne. 1998. *Communities of practice: Learning, meaning and identity*. Cambridge: Cambridge University Press.

————. 2000. 'Communities of practice and social learning systems'. *Organization: Speaking Out* 7 (2): 225–46.

West, Anne, and Elizabeth Bailey. 2014. 'The development of the academies programme: "privatising" school-based education in England 1986–2013'. *British Journal of Educational Studies* 61 (2): 137–59.

West, Anne, and David Wolfe. 2018. *Academies, the school system in England and a vision for the future.* London: London School of Economics, Matrix.

Wexler, Philip, Warren Crichlow, Julie Kern and Rebecca Martusewicz. 1992. *Becoming somebody: Toward a social psychology of school.* London: Falmer Press.

Whitty, Geoff, and Tony Edwards. 1998. 'School choice policies in England and the United States: an exploration of their origins and significance'. *Comparative Education* 34 (2): 211–27.

Whitty, Geoff, Sally Power and David Halpin. 1998. *Devolution and choice in education: The school, the state and the market.* Buckingham: Open University Press.

Whyte, David. 2015. *How corrupt is Britain?* London: Pluto Press.

Willis, Mario, and Lynn Varner. 2010. 'Factors that affect teachers' morale'. *Academic Leadership: The Online Journal* 8 (4): https://scholars.fhsu.edu/alj/vol8/iss4/24.

Wilkins, Andrew. 2017. 'Rescaling the local: multi-academy trusts, private monopoly and statecraft in England'. *Journal of Educational Administration and History.* http://dx.doi.org/10.1080/00220620.2017.1284769.

Woodley, Helen, and Ross Morrison McGill. 2018. *Toxic schools: How to avoid them and leave them.* Melton: John Catt.

Worth, Jack. 2016. *Analysis of academy school performance in 2015.* Slough: NFER.

Wright, Cecile, Penny Standen, Gus John, Gerry German and Tina Patel. 2005. *School exclusion and transition into adulthood in African-Caribbean communities.* York: Joseph Rowntree Foundation.

Young, Michael. 1994. *The rise of the meritocracy.* Brunswick, NJ: Transaction Publishers.

Young, Michael F. D. 1971. *Knowledge and control.* London: Collier-Macmillan.

Index

Printed in Great Britain
by Amazon